Strategy, HRM, and Performance

Strategy, HRM, and Performance

A Contextual Approach

Second Edition

Jaap Paauwe

Elaine Farndale

OXFORD
UNIVERSITY PRESS

OXFORD
UNIVERSITY PRESS

Great Clarendon Street, Oxford, OX2 6DP,
United Kingdom

Oxford University Press is a department of the University of Oxford.
It furthers the University's objective of excellence in research, scholarship,
and education by publishing worldwide. Oxford is a registered trade mark of
Oxford University Press in the UK and in certain other countries

First Edition published in 2004
Second Edition published in 2017

Impression: 8

Published in the United States of America by Oxford University Press
198 Madison Avenue, New York, NY 10016, United States of America

British Library Cataloguing in Publication Data

Data available

Library of Congress Control Number: 2017941626

ISBN 978-0-19-880859-6 (hbk.)
      978-0-19-880860-2 (pbk.)

Printed and bound by
CPI Group (UK) Ltd, Croydon, CR0 4YY

■ COPYRIGHT ACKNOWLEDGEMENTS

Figure 11.5 Reprinted from European Management Journal, 19/7: 510-25, J. Peppard and A. Rylander, Using an intellectual capital perspective to design and implement a growth strategy: the case of ApiON, Copyright 2001, with permission from Elsevier.

Tables

Table 2.3 from Volberda, H. W., Crisis in strategy: fragmentation, integration or synthesis, *European Management Review*, 1/1: 35-42. Copyright © 2004 by John Wiley Sons, Inc. Reprinted by permission of John Wiley & Sons, Inc.

Table 2.4 Strategy: Process, content, context. An international perspective, Wit, B. de, & Meyer, R., © 2010 Cengage Learning EMEA. Reproduced by permission of Cengage Learning EMEA Ltd.

Table 2.5 Republished with permission of Academy of Management, from Linking competitive strategies with human resource management practices, R. Schuler and S. Jackson, Academy of Management Executive, 1/3: 207-19, 1987; permission conveyed through Copyright Clearance Center, Inc.

Table A2.1 Reprinted by permission of Harvard Business Review. (Exhibit). From "'A players' or 'A positions'?" by Huselid, M. A., Beatty, R. W., & Becker, B. E., 2005. Copyright © 2005 by Harvard Business Publishing; all rights reserved.

Table 3.1 from: Strategy: Process, content, context. An international perspective, Wit, B. de, & Meyer, R., © 2004 Cengage Learning EMEA. Reproduced by permission of Cengage Learning EMEA Ltd.

Table 4.1 from C. Oliver (1991) 'Strategic responses to institutional processes', Academy of Management Review, 16/1: 145-79. Reprinted with permission of Academy of Management.

Table 5.1 from D.E. Guest (1997) 'Human resource management and performance: a review and research agenda', International Journal of Human Resource Management, 8/3: 263-76. Reprinted with permission of Taylor and Francis Ltd. (http://www.tandfonline.com).

Table 5.2 From Subramony, M., *A meta-analytic investigation of the relationship between HRM bundles and firm performance*, Human Resource Management, 48/5: 745-68. Copyright © 2009 by John Wiley Sons, Inc. Reprinted by permission of John Wiley & Sons, Inc.

Textbox

Textbox 9.2 IKEA key values: togetherness from http://www.ikea.com/gb/en/this-is-ikea/working-at-the-ikea-group/who-we-are/. Reprinted by permission of IKEA.

ACKNOWLEDGEMENTS

The origins of Jaap's 2004 book entitled '*HRM and Performance. Achieving long term viability*', lay largely in a time of deep reflection, when Jaap, funded by the Netherlands Institute for Studies in Humanities and Social Science (NIAS), was able to spend time writing his personal ideas about HRM and performance. This was a time before Elaine and Jaap had even met, and actually the publication of the 2004 book largely coincided with when their collaborative work together began.

It is only fitting therefore that this new edition of the book builds off these strong foundations. The two of us have since worked together for many years, doing research, writing papers, travelling the globe for research interviews, presenting jointly at conferences, teaching students and training executives. We were at first both working at the same universities (Erasmus University and Tilburg University) but eventually found ourselves situated on opposite sides of the Atlantic (Pennsylvania State University, USA and Tilburg University, the Netherlands). Nevertheless, our collaboration did not wane with this change: With the benefit of being able to work across time zones, as Jaap's working day is almost over, Elaine's day is starting so she can pick up where Jaap leaves off! This has led to a substantial pipeline of papers.

Authoring a book, however, is a different ball game. We have been through a lengthy process of discussing every chapter, the necessary updates, different priorities, locating more up-to-date examples and cases that are relevant for a global readership, and, most importantly, engaging in a deep discussion of the whole philosophy and approach underlying the book. This has resulted – after a number of years – in an almost completely rewritten book, with new chapters, new cases and up-to-date theorizing, but most importantly still representing what is now our shared, deep-seated belief in the importance of a contextual best-fit approach to HRM at different levels of analysis (organization, sector, national, international), and how to make this work in practice.

We are indebted to many colleagues who in different ways acted as a source of inspiration. Many of them are included in our references. Yet, special reference needs to be made to fellow academics such as Veronica Hope Hailey, David Guest, Riccardo Peccei, Wayne Cascio, Peter Boxall, John Delery, Clare Kelliher, Paul Boselie, Patrick Flood, Marc van Veldhoven, Paul Sparrow, Graeme Martin, and Chris Brewster, and of course our colleagues with whom we formed the *Global Human Resource Research Alliance* back in 2004 (Philip Stiles, Shad Morris, Gunther Stahl, Jonathan Trevor, Patrick Wright) and travelled the globe with interviewing a range of top performing multinationals, from whom we learned a lot about the contextual nature of HRM systems.

Both being involved in the HR Division of the *Academy of Management* as elected members of the Executive Committee, we were lucky to be able to meet and talk with many leading HRM scholars on a regular basis, which stimulated our thinking and kept us up-to-date with new insights. Similarly, former graduate and PhD students/colleagues, Saahir Shafi, Michael Chiminec, Keimpe Schilstra, Corine Boon, Monique Veld, Judith van Dongen-van den Broek, Karina van de Voorde and Brigitte Kroon, also deserve our thanks as they contributed in various ways to developing our thinking behind this book, either through in-depth theorizing together, or by providing detailed case illustrations. We would also like to give our thanks to the many participants on executive development programs globally who participated in rolling out our theorizing, models and examples to practice.

Writing and editing a book is a time-consuming, enjoyable, but also at times frustrating affair, in addition to your other regular academic roles. Luckily there was sabbatical time for Jaap, spent happily at Pablo d' Olavide University in Seville, Spain. Thanks to Ramón Valle Cabrera and Alvaro López Cabrales, who together with their colleagues, offered great hospitality. Elaine also had an invaluable sabbatical experience back at Tilburg University in 2016, which ultimately facilitated this book being completed. Thank you to our respective universities for the opportunity to take this time, as well as to our wonderful hosts!

Another indispensable source of help stems from the student assistants at Tilburg University and The Pennsylvania State University who over the course of the years of writing rotated in and out of the project—Tessa Blok, Anke van Rossum, Caitlin van Mill, Erika Basabe—who assisted in many ways to completing this task: drafting case study reports, collecting articles, checking references, and ensuring the necessary permissions. Finally we would like to thank the editing staff at OUP, among whom we are especially grateful to Adam Swallow and Clare Kennedy for guiding us through this process.

In brief, we send our thanks to all family, friends and colleagues who have helped us in reaching this point today, as well as to you for reading this book. We are very much obliged to you all.

J.P. & E.F.

Woerden, the Netherlands/State College PA, USA
August 2017

■ CONTENTS

▣ LIST OF FIGURES

■ LIST OF TABLES

◼ LIST OF TEXTBOXES

1 Introduction

Human resource management (HRM) has been a hot topic in the management literature for some thirty years; it was introduced in the USA by the so-called Harvard (Beer et al., 1984) and Michigan (Fombrun, Tichy, & Devanna, 1984) models, and in the UK by Guest (1987), who presented it as a new approach to 'personnel management'. Since then, interest in the relationship between HRM and performance has exploded, with countless publications attempting to either demonstrate or question whether and how managing a firm's human resources can have an impact on bottom-line performance. As this field has expanded, we have become increasingly aware of some of the boundary conditions that surround this relationship, helping managers gain a better understanding of how to benefit from their 'most important asset'—their people.

Since the first edition of this book (published in 2004), the initial euphoria around making the connection between people and performance (with books such as *Competitive Advantage through People* (Pfeffer, 1994), *Living Strategy* (Gratton, 2000), and *HR Champions* (Ulrich, 1997)) appears to have settled down into a more evidence-based approach to exploring how HRM delivers value to organizations, with popular book titles more recently pointing us to a stronger, more professional HR function, including *HR from the Outside In: Six Competencies for the Future of Human Resources HR* (Ulrich et al., 2012), and *The Chief HR Officer: Defining the New Role of Human Resource Leaders* (Wright et al., 2011).

Does this mean that we have already learned everything we need to know about how HRM can deliver sustainable competitive advantage? As the 2004 edition of this book noted, the interest in HRM and performance can be traced to the seminal work by Huselid (1995), which claims that more advanced high-performance work practices were associated with a substantial increase in sales and market value per employee. Add to this the global popularity of Pfeffer's (1994) book *Competitive Advantage through People*, and the scene was set for an explosion in interest. Pfeffer (1994) emphasized the importance of what he described as sixteen best (human resource) practices. These human resource practices—later to be reclassified by Pfeffer (1998) into seven—would, if implemented, contribute to sustained competitive advantage.

So, by the mid-1990s, the topic of HRM and performance was not only popular amongst managers and consultants, but also demanded attention from academics on both sides of the Atlantic. By now numerous papers were being presented at a wide range of conferences and many of these were to find their way into special issues of respected academic journals. Amidst this expansion in interest and growth in publications, a number of papers began to emerge that attempted to present frameworks, set boundaries, and establish a landscape for other researchers to follow. Delery and Doty (1996), for example, developed the distinction between universalistic, contingency, and configurational approaches to understanding HRM practices. Guest (1997) discussed the idea of distinguishing between strategic, descriptive, and normative theories. Legge (1995) warned of the need to distinguish rhetoric from reality and made a plea for a more critical approach. She was not alone. Paauwe and Richardson (1997) and later Boselie, Paauwe, and Jansen (2001), following their reviews of the area, also emphasized the need for a more critical approach.

The search for the links between HRM and performance was, however, to continue unabated, culminating in a need for metrics. Can we, authors were to question, prove—in relation to daily business life—that human resources do indeed matter, and can this proof be expressed in terms of the hard currency of business? Once again a number of best-selling books were to set the scene. This time, however, the emphasis was not only on understanding the relationship between HRM and performance, but also on how we could measure progress and how we could put metrics around the strategic contribution of HRM practices to performance. Books like *The HR Scorecard* (Becker, Huselid, & Ulrich, 2001), *Predictive HR Analytics: Mastering the HR Metric* (Edwards & Edwards, 2016), and *The HR Scorecard: Measuring the Return on Investment* (Phillips, Stone, & Phillips, 2001) represent just a few of the titles that were, and still are, emerging on this topic.

Since the publication of the 2004 edition of this book, the latest conversations have built on a more critical approach, advocating a 'balanced' perspective on HRM and performance. What do we mean by 'balanced'? This requires managers to walk the delicate line between achieving hard, financial outcomes for the firm alongside softer, well-being outcomes for employees and society as a whole, or balancing the need to stay ahead of the competition with the need to maintain legitimacy within the firm's operating environment.

This need for a more balanced approach is the result of the many years of studies of HRM and performance, leading to mixed results—does HRM make a difference to the bottom line or not? Some argue for a universalistic, 'best practice' formula (such as Pfeffer 1994, 1998), arguing that as long as an organization has all practices in place, high firm performance will ensue. But what type of performance (shareholder or broader stakeholder performance), and is it really feasible to suggest that a high-tech knowledge worker firm (e.g. an internet-based services provider) should have the same HRM practices in place as a production facility (e.g. a food manufacturer), or even a hospital or a school? We argue in this book that the reason why the empirical evidence to date has been mixed regarding HRM's contribution to firm performance, is precisely because both the type of organization and the desired performance criteria can vary. We therefore side more with those who advocate a 'best fit' or 'contingency' approach to HRM (Boxall & Purcell, 2015; Delery & Doty, 1996).

These developments of the HRM literature essentially represented the birth of 'strategic human resource management' (SHRM). By adding the word 'strategic', we are acknowledging that the approach to HRM adopted in a firm is intended to be aligned with the overall goals of the firm, that is, its strategy. In this book, we differentiate between strategy, HRM, and performance in order to explain how these three elements are integrated in organizations. This is often described as a 'macro' perspective, for example, an organizational-level perspective of strategy, HRM, and performance.

Reflecting on all this activity, we propose that, to date, we have been blinkered by a predominantly universalist, profit-driven perspective on the HRM–performance relationship, largely driven by the USA-based academics who first started the debate. There has been a lack of attention to HRM 'in context'. What do we mean by this? As you will see throughout this book, we do not believe than HRM is a simple formula, that is, if you implement steps one to seven, the end result will be better firm performance. Our belief lies in the often frustrating statement 'it depends'! In other words, making the connection between HRM and performance centres in on the need to understand the setting in which an organization is operating in order to know what approach to HRM will be most effective. Addressing the profit motive behind much of the early HRM and performance writing—again, largely born of its US roots—the concept of performance has often been defined from a financial-economic perspective, such as productivity, return on investment, and shareholder value. Of course, that is important, but it is a rather narrow approach to what the concept of performance should imply, and we advocate adopting a more balanced perspective that includes broader performance outcomes than organization financial success alone.

It is little wonder, despite the plethora of books, articles, recommendations, and insights into the area of HRM and performance, that there is much still to be learned and considerable doubt surrounding whether the real picture is being adequately captured. There are, it seems, important elements absent when HRM and its contribution to performance are discussed. For example, do different organization contexts show different patterns of HRM practices? What sort of performance and for whose sake? Similarly, if performance is defined only in financial-economic terms what is this saying about how we view those who work in organizations? Is it that the only goal of HRM is to increase shareholder value? This book proposes a more nuanced approach based on the following four precepts.

a **Human resources are more than just resources**

Human resources are active individuals with past experiences, internalized values, and norms not necessarily matching those of the employing organization. They belong to a range of different communities both inside and outside the organization and their behaviour is only partially governed by the institutions for which they work. So we go beyond seeing employees as a means to an end (instrumentalism) and take a humanist perspective that employees are an end in themselves, worthy of being developed and nurtured. Interestingly, this does not have to come at the cost of the profit motive of employees as resources, as you will read.

b The HR function is not solely concerned with financial performance

The HR function, as one of the major organizational functions, has a financial imperative, but it also has a professional and social responsibility. It ensures that the organization is in compliance with all relevant national legislation, international guidelines, and trade union agreements, in addition to upholding professional values. It also plays a role in developing a sense of corporate citizenship among all who work within the organization. This is a tall order, but one that can be achieved. The focus for the HR function is on creating an appropriate balance between the (financial) welfare of the organization as a whole, and of each of its individual employees, while at the same time making a contribution to societal challenges such as participation, diversity, sustainability, and inclusion.

c HRM focuses on the exchange relationship between employee and employer

The exchange relationship between employee and employer not only involves labour and time in exchange for money, but also, for example, exchanges of competencies, knowledge, and information, for learning, participation, and well-being. People frequently spend at least eight to ten hours a day involved in an organization, so they are heavily influenced by this exchange relationship. The number of hours spent at work is often more than the number of hours they can consciously spend with their family and friends. So being involved in shaping that exchange relationship is a crucial task that does not solely revolve around economic rationality.

d The shaping of the employment relationship takes place in an arena of continuous tension between added value and moral value

Added value represents the harsh world of economic rationality, but HRM is also about moral value. It is about achieving fairness and legitimacy. *Fairness* relates to the exchange relationship at an individual level. People want to feel they have a fair (equitable) balance between what they contribute to the organization and what they receive back from it in return. Substantial research in this field has confirmed that perceived fairness leads to more positive employee attitudes and behaviours (Cohen-Charash & Spector, 2001). Once more this involves more than just the exchange of money for time and labour. *Legitimacy* refers to the exchange relationship at a more collective level and relates to the relationship between the organization and society at large (also referred to as 'corporate social responsibility'). It is about the organization attaining legitimacy in the eyes of relevant stakeholders, such as the government, shareholders, works councils and trade unions, customers, and employees, ultimately giving the organization its 'licence to operate'.

The two sides of the same 'value' coin (financial versus fairness and legitimacy) can also be distilled from the very concept of 'human resource management'. 'Resource' refers to the necessity of generating added value and contributing to productivity, profitability, and increasing shareholder value, hence safeguarding the continuity of the firm. However, there is also the concept of 'human', which refers to human beings who want to be treated humanely. This is where we enter the domain of moral values: Moral values that are ingrained by institutions such as family, church, school, education, culture, trade unions, and legislation. Given that our focus is on the employment relationship, we limit ourselves here to moral values of fairness and legitimacy related to the workplace, but these can easily be extended with values like sustainability, participation, solidarity, and trust. In Table 1.1 we schematically depict this tension between added value and moral value.

At first sight, added value and moral value might appear contradictory. However, the argument we develop throughout this book is that these two can be aligned in such a way that the unique blending (unique because it will be custom-made for every organization) results in sustainable competitive advantage. We do not consider moral values as an

Table 1.1 Added value versus moral value

Added value	Moral value
1. Economic rationality: the exchange of as little money/resources as possible for the maximum gain in labour, time and output	1. Relational rationality: the development and maintenance of sustainable relationships with all relevant stakeholders inside and outside the organization
2. Shareholders dominant	2. Multiple stakeholders
3. Instrumental focus: employees are a means to an end, fulfilling basic human needs	3. Humanistic, developmental approach: employees are an end in themselves with needs such as learning, participation and well-being
4. Focus on financial performance: productivity, profitability, shareholder value, etc.	4. Multiple performance outcomes: profit, well-being, etc.
5. Strategic use of resources to achieve efficiency and effectiveness	5. Abiding by relevant regulations and legislation to achieve legitimacy, fairness, trust and sustainability

impediment to a firm being economically successful. On the contrary, the creative and unique blending of the two sets of values can contribute to sustaining the competitive advantage and viability of the organization in the long term. That is the thesis of this book. We are not alone in making this plea. For example, Paine (2003: xi) argues in her book *Value Shift* that the superior performers of the future will be those that can satisfy both the social and financial expectations of their constituencies.

Based on this vision of HRM, the central theme of this book is the development of a newly revised *Contextual Strategic Human Resource Management (SHRM) Framework*. Building on the 2004 *contextually based human resource theory* (CBHRT), we also continue to advocate for a more pluralistic perspective on the concept of performance, distinguishing goals beyond those related to productivity, profitability, and shareholder value. We further include goals such as agility (Dyer & Shafer, 1999; Nijssen & Paauwe, 2012), social legitimacy (Boxall & Purcell, 2015), and individual and societal well-being (Beer, Boselie, & Brewster, 2015).

1.1 Outline of chapters

Chapters 2 to 5 serve as theoretical building blocks for the development of the Contextual SHRM Framework, which is presented in Chapter 6. Chapter 2 starts by explaining what strategy is, and highlights the relevance of strategy to the link between HRM and performance, emphasizing a 'best fit' rather than 'best practice' approach. We summarize the development of thinking in the strategic management field, moving from top-down, rationally planned classical approaches to strategy, to more emergent strategy concepts that include the role of power, politics, culture, and environment. We synthesize thinking in this field, comparing what has happened in parallel in HRM. The chapter also presents a number of useful diagnostic tools that HR and line managers can apply in their organization.

The aim of Chapters 3 and 4 is to examine the *context* of HRM in detail. We begin in Chapter 3 by building on the relationship between strategy and HRM, exploring the many forms of 'fit' or alignment that are required to ensure effective HRM. After a detailed examination of five types of fit (strategic, internal, organizational, environmental, and macro–micro), we explain how they reinforce each other to enhance the HRM and performance relationship. Chapter 4 then questions whether the different classical approaches to HRM give sufficient recognition to the context within which HRM is played out. Because of the close relationship between HRM and industrial relations (IR), we explore the contribution made by this association and conclude that institutional theory offers a sound theoretical base for the inclusion of context (such as labour market, industry, or country) in the study of HRM.

Chapter 5 is the last of our theory-based building blocks and focuses on the very concept of *performance* itself. We start with an assessment of the impressive amount of research in the area of HRM and performance, highlighting the latest review studies that attempt to synthesize much that we have learned to date on this topic. As a result of our overview we point to what is a fundamental concern of this book: the missing elements in the present debate on HRM and performance. We address some of the challenges in the field by unpacking the 'black box' research (including individual, organizational, and societal levels of analysis). Following an overview of the HRM systems perspective linked to performance (i.e. bundles of HRM practices rather than individual practices in isolation), we discuss the development of a more holistic concept of performance, balancing both employee well-being and financial performance.

These four chapters represent the design criteria for the core of the book (Chapter 6), which builds on Paauwe's (2004) CBHRT, developing a new Contextual SHRM Framework. This framework aligns the strategic dimension and the institutional perspective to create the contextual conditions within which strategic HRM operates. The framework takes into account the interplay between added value and moral value, encompassing different rationalities, both economic and relational. The result is a multidimensional view of performance emphasizing both financial and well-being goals. The Contextual SHRM Framework can be applied to analyse the shaping of HRM systems at different levels of analysis—organizational, sectoral, and international—as the later chapters demonstrate.

Chapter 7, using a series of case studies, illustrates analysis at the *organizational level*. We apply the Contextual SHRM Framework to six different organizations (a temporary work agency, a theme park, a consumer goods firm, an automotive producer, a mail delivery firm, and a retailer), to analyse how the HRM system and its resultant performance is linked to contextual factors. Chapter 8 outlines the importance of the sectoral level by presenting work from four *contrasting industries* (health care, call-centres, agriculture, and a contrast between the metal manufacturing and the information technology (IT) industry), highlighting in particular how competitive, institutional, and organizational constraints interplay to affect employment practices in different organizational settings. Chapter 9 deals with the *comparative international level of analysis*. Here we home in on the 'best practice' versus 'best fit' debate, and compare internationally operating firms. Explorations of IBM, IKEA, and Procter & Gamble (P&G) highlight the differential impact of institutional settings on multinational corporations (MNCs) facing similar global challenges.

After this empirical tour, Chapters 10 and 11 progress to consider the implications of strategy, HRM, and performance specifically for the HR function. We emphasize the added value of HR professionals in terms of their ability to implement and deliver HR services. While Chapter 10 focuses on the different roles that HR professionals play in organizations, Chapter 11 shifts our attention to establishing an appropriate HR architecture to deliver HR services, as well as a system of metrics that can provide evidence on how well delivery is taking place.

We conclude with Chapter 12, which synthesizes our thinking throughout the book, drawing out key themes and ideas to take the field forward. We consider what we have learned to date about strategy, HRM, and performance, and what challenges the field still faces. Our final thoughts are on the future of work, the future of HRM work, and the future of the HR function in organizations as part of the HRM and performance phenomenon.

Fellow academics and students with a thorough understanding of strategic management, alignment theories, institutional theory, and the HRM and performance debate may only read the conclusions of Chapters 2 to 5 before proceeding to Chapter 6 where our Contextual SHRM Framework is developed. Applying the framework at different levels of analysis (organizational, sectoral, and international) can be traced via the cases presented in Chapters 7 to 9. We recommend that practitioners (including participants in executive training programmes) with less theoretical underpinning read Chapters 2 to 5 to understand the developments in the area of strategic management, alignment theories, institutional theory, and the HRM–performance debate. After reading Chapter 6—the heart of the book—outlining the Contextual SHRM Framework, and Chapters 7–9 for the illustrative cases, HR professionals in particular are encouraged to proceed to Chapters 10 and 11 to learn more about the role of the HR function in the HRM–performance relationship. Of particular interest to practitioners are the various tools presented, particularly in Chapters 2 and 6, to assist in carrying out organizational analyses, based on the principles of the theoretical frameworks provided.

2 HRM and strategy

2.1 Introduction

Given the best fit/best practice and universalistic/configurational/contingent debates in human resource management (HRM) (Delery & Doty, 1996) as highlighted in Chapter 1, and the related mixed empirical evidence, we might legitimately ask 'does strategy matter' and if so, in what sense does it matter with respect to the linkage between HRM and performance?

To answer these questions, we first need to understand what strategy is. In Section 2.2, we present an overview of the various approaches in the strategic management field that have evolved since the term strategy was first introduced in the study of management and organization. Starting with the classic approaches based on a top-down, rationally planned concept of strategy, we end with the importance of factors such as power, politics, culture, and environment, which represent a far more emergent and interactive concept of strategy. The implications of these different approaches for HRM are highlighted in Section 2.3. The broad variety of approaches has given rise to fragmentation, and so it is not surprising therefore that academics have begun a search for synthesis, the topic of Section 2.4.

Based on developments in strategic management thinking, we can see a clear parallel with the developments in the HRM field. We first discuss the classic strategy models, which attempt to present planned and prescriptive approaches creating a close fit between strategy and HRM policies and practices (Section 2.5). More recent insights (and empirical evidence), however, present a far less clear linkage between HRM and strategy. Critically, we put the strategy–HRM–performance linkage into practice in Section 2.6, presenting a number of (diagnostic) tools that human resource (HR) managers can apply in their organization. Finally, in Section 2.7, we summarize our main insights in the area of strategy and strategic management that are relevant to the field of HRM and performance.

2.2 What is strategy?

Strategy outlines an organization's goals, including different performance indicators (e.g. market share, sales, competitive positioning, profit, growth, and return on investment) and the means to achieve those goals (e.g. finance, technology, and human resources). Especially in larger organizations a distinction is being made between corporate strategy and business strategy. Corporate strategy deals with the overarching strategy in large organizations (such as multinational corporations—MNCs), which are composed of various business units operating in different markets, each with their own business strategy. The business strategy is most important for achieving competitive advantage as this is focused on a specific market, which requires different goals and resources in order to achieve competitive positioning.

In this chapter, we highlight the concept of (business) strategy and how it relates to human resources/employees, HRM as a policy area, and the HR function. We also discuss HRM strategy, that is, 'the processes, decisions and choices the organization makes regarding its human resources and how they are organized' (Cascio & Boudreau, 2012: 18–19). We do this at a conceptual level, as well as providing a number of practical tools to guide line management and the HR function in creating alignment between strategy and the workforce.

The vast strategy literature finds its roots in military strategy. Bracker (1980) relates it to the Greek General 'Strategos', which in turn means 'army' or 'lead' (Whittington, 2001). Generally speaking, strategy is about achieving a fit between an organization and its environment, or developing a course of action for achieving an organization's purpose (De Wit & Meyer, 2010). Since its conception, different perspectives on strategy have been developed. The most well-known, and still dominant in strategic management textbooks, is the rational planned approach, also referred to as the 'classical' approach. Its main characteristics still strongly connote the military background (Mintzberg, Ahlstrand, & Lampel, 2009; Whittington, 2001): a controlled and conscious process of thought directly derived from the notion of rational economic man, for which the prime responsibility rests with the chief executive officer, who is in charge of a fully-formulated, explicit, and articulated decision-making process, in which there is a strict distinction between formulation and implementation.

In sum, the classical approach relies heavily on the readiness and capacity of managers to adopt profit-maximizing strategies through rational long-term planning, as Whittington (2001) critically remarks. Early HRM work bears a striking resemblance to this classical approach. For example, Hendry and Pettigrew (1986) state that the plea for strategic HRM implies: the use of planning; a coherent approach to the design and management of personnel systems based on an employment policy and manpower strategy, often underpinned by a philosophy; HRM activities being matched to some explicit strategy; and the people of the organization being seen as a strategic resource for achieving competitive advantage.

In reality, however, the concept of strategy has many guises. One of the first to demonstrate this was Mintzberg (1987), who distinguished five meanings of strategy (see also: Mintzberg, Ahlstrand, & Lampel, 2009):

- Strategy as a plan (intended): a direction, a guide, or course of action into the future, focused on looking ahead.

- Strategy as a pattern (realized): consistency in behaviour over time, focused on looking at the past.
- Strategy as a ploy: a specific manoeuvre intended to outwit an opponent or competitor.
- Strategy as a position: the way in which the organization positions its products and or services in particular markets in order to achieve a competitive advantage.
- Strategy as a perspective: an organization's fundamental way of doing things, including the way in which the members of the organization perceive their environment and their customers.

The different meanings of the concept of strategy are representative of the enormous variety of approaches, including incrementalism, entrepreneurialism, bounded rationality, learning, and coevolution. It is no wonder that several authors have, therefore, attempted to synthesize and integrate the field's enormous diversity (Meerveld, 2001; Mintzberg, 1998; Volberda & Elfring, 2001; Whittington, 2001). Using a jungle analogy, Mintzberg, Ahlstrand, and Lampel (2009) offer a guided tour through the 'wilds' of strategic management by presenting a clear overview of the field in ten 'schools'. Table 2.1 presents the first three schools, which are more prescriptive in nature.

The *design* school sees strategy formation as a deliberate process of conscious thought (MacMillan & Tampoe, 2000). The well-known and often applied 'SWOT' (strengths, weaknesses, opportunities, threats) analysis is part of this school. The *planning* school also sees strategy as a formal process, and entails a stepwise approach to creating an all-encompassing strategy. This school can be considered as a more formalized and detailed version of the design school. The *positioning* school perceives strategy mainly from an industrial economics perspective. The competitive position of an organization in its industry/market is analysed using economic models and techniques. Porter (1980, 1985) in particular made important contributions to this school, which dominated the strategic management field in the 1980s. His well-known concepts include the five forces model for competitive analysis, the value chain, and generic strategies (cost leadership, differentiation, and focus). Consultants also contributed to this school, including the Boston Consulting Group, which developed a growth-share matrix and experience curve.

Table 2.1 Three prescriptive schools of strategy

School	Characteristic of the process	Key player	Environment	Strategy	Dominant discipline
Design	Conception	CEO	Opportunities/threats	Explicit perspective	None
Planning	Formal planning	Planners	Stable and controlled	Explicit plan	System theory/cybernetics
Positioning	Analysis	Analysts	Can be analysed	Explicit generic position	Economics

Source: Meerveld (2001).

The underlying assumption of these three schools is that the environment is more or less stable and can be studied objectively in order to distil changes and opportunities for strategy. This kind of approach towards strategy and strategy development has been labelled an *outside-in* approach (Stopford & Baden-Fuller, 1994). The environment, namely the marketplace, is the starting point for analysis and the subsequent development of appropriate strategic responses in order to achieve the desired strategic positioning.

The positioning school has especially stimulated researchers in the field of HRM to link HRM policies and practices to a certain strategic positioning in order to achieve the required (role) behaviours. For example, Schuler and Jackson (1987) linked employee role behaviours to the three generic strategies of Porter (1980), while authors like Ackerman (1983), Storey (1995), and Guest (1997) discussed the applicability of Miles and Snow's (1984) typology (prospectors, defenders, analysers, reactors) to strategic HRM. Even Guest's (1997) model linking HRM to performance still makes use of the generic strategy types developed by Porter (1980, 1985). More recent insights, such as that by Schultz, Bennett, and Ketchen (2015), assess the degree to which the Miles and Snow (1984) typology is related to a specific set of HRM practices in an empirical study of small firms. The results are, however, disappointing, as they do not present a clear picture of the relationship between strategy and performance.

The next group of schools (depicted in Table 2.2) are more descriptive in nature. The *entrepreneurial* school emphasizes the important role of a visionary leader who is actively engaged in a search for new opportunities in order to speed up the company's growth (emanating originally from Schumpeter, 1934). The *cognitive* school considers strategy formulation as a cognitive process that takes place in the mind of the

Table 2.2 Six descriptive schools of strategy

School	Characteristic of the process	Key player	Environment	Strategy	Dominant discipline
Entrepreneurial	Vision	Leader	Can be influenced	Implicit perspective	None
Cognitive	Mental process	Mind	Hard to understand	Mental perspective	Psychology
Learning	Emergent	Everyone who learns	Demanding	Implicit patterns	Psychology
Power	Negotiation	Everyone with power	Can be moulded but difficult	Positions, ploys	Politics
Cultural	Collective process	Collectivistic	Incidental	Collective perspective	Anthropology
Environmental	Reactive process	Environment, stakeholders	Dominant and deterministic	Specific position	Biology

Source: Meerveld (2001).

strategist. Strategies thus emerge as perspectives (frames, mental maps, schemes) that shape how people deal with inputs from the environment. These inputs are subject to many distorting filters before they are decoded by cognitive maps (Mintzberg, Ahlstrand, & Lampel, 2009: 162). Simon (1947, 1957) made an important contribution to this school with his notion of 'bounded rationality' (see also March & Simon, 1958).

The starting point for the *learning* school relates back to Lindblom (1959), with his disjointed incrementalism, better known as the science of 'muddling through'. Strategy formulation is seen as a stepwise incremental process. Change and direction are the result of mutual adjustment between the different actors involved and between outside events and internal decisions. Strategy-making is, above all, a collective learning process over time, in which it is hard to distinguish between formulation and implementation (Mintzberg, Ahlstrand, & Lampel, 2009: 217). In addition to contributors like Quinn (logical incrementalism, 1980), commentators such as Argyris and Schön (single and double loop learning, 1978), Senge (the fifth discipline, 1990), and Prahalad and Hamel (dynamic capabilities, 1990) are also considered to be part of the learning school.

The *power* (or *political*) school regards the formation of strategy as a bargaining process between power blocks both inside the organization and between organizations. It emphasizes the use of power and politics to negotiate strategies that favour particular interests (Mintzberg, Ahlstrand, & Lampel, 2009: 242). The *cultural* school considers strategy formulation as a process of social interaction, based on the beliefs and shared understandings of the members of the organization. This results in a perspective that is reflected in the patterns by which deeply embedded resources (capabilities) are protected and used for achieving competitive advantage (Mintzberg, Ahlstrand, & Lampel, 2009: 281).

The *environmental* school focuses on the environment as the central actor to the strategy-making process. The organization must respond to the forces of the environment, otherwise it will be 'selected out' (Mintzberg, Ahlstrand, & Lampel, 2009: 304–5). This school has its roots in contingency theory, but gained popularity particularly through the writings of Hannan and Freeman (1977) on the population ecology of organizations using a biological analogy. Finally, the tenth school (*configurational*) emphasizes that there is no one best way of organizing and strategy formulation, but that specific circumstances will make a certain configuration of context, strategy, structure, and process effective. In Section 2.4, we explore this school of thought further.

2.3 **Implications for HRM and performance**

What do these ten schools tell us about the relationship between strategy, HRM, and performance? Primarily, they reveal that there is no universally agreed best way of strategy formulation and subsequent organizing, including with regard to the shaping of HRM policies. The field of strategic management is characterized by different streams and approaches. The field's plurality, however, enables us to learn important lessons about the relationship between strategy, HRM, and performance. The different schools highlight the importance of taking multiple factors into account, including the role of the entrepreneur, cognitive processes, incrementalism, power, culture, and institutional forces. We explore each of these in turn.

2.3.1 THE ROLE OF THE ENTREPRENEUR

Very often the founder and owner of the company. He/she likely plays an important role in shaping HRM policies and creating a related culture. Some companies, for example, have been founded by an entrepreneur (still active as the CEO) with a dislike for specialist staff departments (see: Flood, Gannon, & Paauwe, 1996: 220), and aside from the accounting department (which arises out of the necessity to comply with accounting standards and principles), there might be no specialist HR department at all. In small companies, this is no surprise (see, for example, Kroon & Paauwe, 2014), but in a large shipyard company employing 450 people this is indeed unusual. In the area of HRM, this means a lack of explicit HRM practices creating space for flexibility, but also leaves ample room for favouritism (Flood, Gannon, & Paauwe, 1996: 215–16).

2.3.2 COGNITIVE/FRAMING PROCESSES

Due to bounded rationality, cognitive processes distort filters and (de)coding processes, resulting in differences in the mental maps of the participants involved, which in turn may give rise to divergent opinions on how to shape HRM strategies, policies, and practices. For example, in the event of an economic slowdown, the threat of dismissals or factory closure might arise, and would undoubtedly give rise to divergent opinions among the main stakeholders concerning the severity of the economic slowdown and the kind of measures to be taken (see also Chapter 6, which discusses the role of key decision-makers in formulating HRM systems).

2.3.3 INCREMENTALISM/LEARNING

Due to the different parties involved (both inside and outside the organizational boundaries), formulating HRM strategy can be considered an emergent and stepwise iterative process with feedback loops, making it increasingly difficult to understand cause and effect linkages, and also difficult to distinguish formulation and implementation. In order to understand the shaping of HRM strategy and how it has an effect on perform-ance, research can best be aimed at describing change processes longitudinally. Taking such an approach, Stiles and colleagues (2015) describe how a newly implemented centralized performance management system affects routines in the organization over time, ultimately linking to performance outcomes.

2.3.4 POWER AND RESOURCES

The power position of the parties involved is often neglected in HRM and performance research. This neglect also includes the kind of resources the parties can mobilize through their networks in order to enforce and strengthen their HRM demands (explained by the resource dependency perspective: Pfeffer & Salancik, 1978). This is peculiar, as, in the related industrial relations (IR) field, these very issues are at the heart of the matter (Kaufman, 2014), and everybody knows how crucial power positions and resources (e.g. rate of unionization, workforce positions related to the core work processes being high in the case of air traffic flight controllers) are in shaping both collective bargaining agreement (CBA) outcomes and HRM policies (Kaufman, 2012, 2014) (see also Chapter 8 for a sector-specific example).

2.3.5 CULTURE/IDEOLOGY

The way in which collective perspectives and intentions develop over time will undoubt-edly have an (albeit often unconscious) effect upon the shaping of HRM policies. It will likely also affect the way in which the effectiveness of both HRM and employees themselves are perceived by other members of the organization, and the degree to which related values and perceptions are shared (see also process theory: Bowen & Ostroff, 2004; attribution theory: Nishii, Lepak, & Schneider, 2008; organizational climate: Schneider, Ehrhart, & Macey, 2013). For example, the top management of a large financial service company that opts for value-based management and shareholder value as the final criterion for judging effectiveness might encounter resistance among its employees if its values were based more upon a stakeholder conception of the firm, in which the interests of customers, employees, and shareholders were carefully balanced.

2.3.6 ENVIRONMENTAL AND INSTITUTIONAL FORCES

Environmental forces, stemming from trade unions, tripartite (governments, employers' federations, trade unions) and bipartite consultative bodies at the national level, and subsequent guidelines, can have a large impact upon an organization's HRM strategy and policies. Essentially, these forces are sources of societal pressure to which manage-ment must react in order to achieve legitimacy and not be selected out (see also Chapter 4 for a description of neo-institutional theory).

2.4 **In search of synthesis**

The ten schools are a rich source of inspiration and demonstrate quite clearly the different perspectives in the field of strategic management. At the same time, they also demonstrate the apparently increasing degree of fragmentation and ongoing diversity among academics representing different sub-disciplines.

As noted in Section 2.2, Mintzberg, Ahlstrand, and Lampel (2009) offer their tenth school (the *configurational* school) as an approach to synthesize the previous nine. The configurational school emphasizes that there is no single best way of organizing and formulating strategy, but that it depends on the specific circumstances. Collectively, these circumstances combine to produce a certain effective configuration of context, strategy, structure, and process. Periods of stability for a given configuration will occasionally be interrupted by a transformation process, resulting in a quantum leap to a new configuration. Mintzberg, Ahlstrand, and Lampel (2009) admit that this integrative approach is, however, only one among many. Volberda and Elfring (2001: 11–12) discuss the causes of fragmentation, presenting a synthesis distinguishing three schools, including configurational. Each school has a related set of theories, a cluster of challenges, and accompanying problem-solving tools (see Table 2.3; Volberda, 2004: 38).

Mainardi and Kleiner (2010) present a useful synthesis based on a number of influential authors and publications on strategy, including Mintzberg, Ahlstrand, and Lampel (2009), Kleiner (2008), and Kiechel (2010). Kiechel, a former Fortune managing editor, reflects in his 2010 book on the prevailing theories of business strategy over the past fifty years. Mainardi and Kleiner (2010) summarize the different schools of thought regarding how to achieve competitive advantage through corporate strategy (see Figure 2.1). Based on a matrix that balances a present or future orientation with whether few or many are involved in making major strategy decisions, they suggest four options: Position, execution, adaptation, and concentration. We explore each in turn.

Position-based strategy (future-oriented, top-down formulation) refers to organiza-tions undertaking a comprehensive analysis of internal capabilities and external markets/needs to position themselves appropriately to take advantage of both. This school of thought relies on detailed collection of data and formal strategic planning processes, which in themselves can be costly and slow processes. In contrast, *execution-based* strategy (present-oriented, collective decision-making) focuses more on operational excellence than strategic planning, redesigning processes to be more quality-focused or

Table 2.3 Three modes of strategy synthesis

The 'boundary' school	The 'dynamic' school	The 'configurational' school
Questions		
Where to draw the boundary	With whom and how do firms compete	What are the contingencies
How to manage across the divide	How do they sustain their competitive advantage over time	Which strategy configurations are effective
		What are the underlying dimensions of strategy configurations
Base disciplines/theories		
Agency theory (economics/ psychology)	Resource-based theory of the firm (economics)	Social sciences
Transaction costs theory	Entrepreneurship (economics)	History
Industrial organization	Innovation theories (organization theory)	Equilibrium models (biology)
Control theories (sociology)	Learning theories (organizational behaviour)	Catastrophe theories (mathematics)
Decision-making theories (psychology)		
Problem-solving tools		
The strategy sourcing process (Venkatesan, 1992)	The roots of competitiveness (Prahalad & Hamel, 1990)	Archetypes (Miller & Friesen, 1980)
Porter's value chain (Porter, 1980)	The capability matrix (Schoemaker, 1992)	Strategic types (Miles & Snow, 1978)
		FAR method (Volberda, 1998)
New directions		
Strategizing	Coevolution of capabilities and competition	Conceptually derived typology
Joint value creation	Managerial dimensions of dynamic capabilities	Empirically based taxonomies
Building trust		Configurations as sources of competitive advantage
Learning across boundaries		

Source: Volberda (2004: 38).

to reduce costs, for example. The drawback of this approach is that it focuses on improving current processes, but not on deciding the future business that the firm should be conducting.

Adaptation-based strategy (future-oriented, collective decision-making) refers to continual experimentation and renewal of ideas, rather than focusing on analysis and planning. This strategy, however, as suggested, is highly unstructured and can lead to excessive diversity in the firm's products or processes. Finally, *concentration-based* strategy (present-oriented, top-down formulation) is appealing as this focuses on

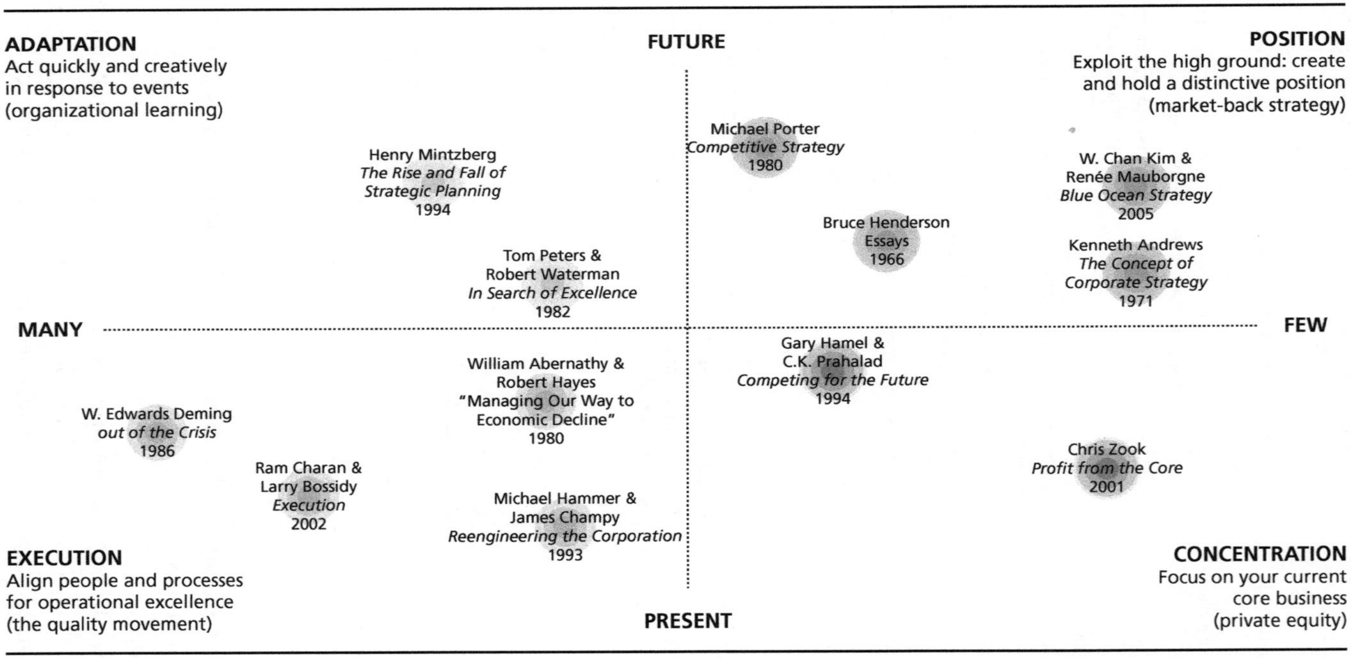

ADAPTATION
Act quickly and creatively
in response to events
(organizational learning)

POSITION
Exploit the high ground: create
and hold a distinctive position
(market-back strategy)

W. Chan Kim &
Renée Mauborgne
Blue Ocean Strategy
2005

Kenneth Andrews
*The Concept of
Corporate Strategy*
1971

Chris Zook
Profit from the Core
2001

CONCENTRATION
Focus on your current
core business
(private equity)

FEW

Bruce Henderson
Essays
1966

Michael Porter
Competitive Strategy
1980

Gary Hamel &
C.K. Prahalad
Competing for the Future
1994

Henry Mintzberg
*The Rise and Fall of
Strategic Planning*
1994

Tom Peters &
Robert Waterman
In Search of Excellence
1982

FUTURE

MANY

William Abernathy &
Robert Hayes
*"Managing Our Way to
Economic Decline"*
1980

Michael Hammer &
James Champy
Reengineering the Corporation
1993

PRESENT

W. Edwards Deming
out of the Crisis
1986

Ram Charan &
Larry Bossidy
Execution
2002

EXECUTION
Align people and processes
for operational excellence
(the quality movement)

Based on: Walter Kiechel, *The Lords of Strategy*, Art Kleiner, *The Age of Heretics*, Henry Mintzberg, Bruce Ahlstrand, and Joseph Lampel, *Strategy Safari*

Figure 2.1 A landscape of strategy concepts

Source: Mainardi and Kleiner (2010).

developing the core competencies of the firm to achieve success. Its present orientation, however, means that only current competencies are developed, foregoing the opportunity to innovate and expand into new areas of product development or services.

In summary, different schools of thought can be applied to develop corporate strategy to achieve competitive advantage, but while they all have their advantages, they can also have limitations in terms of how they balance focusing on emergent strengths compared to potential future needs, and whether or not it is advantageous to leave strategic decision-making to a select few or to adopt a more bottom-up approach. This balancing act is symptomatic of the inherent tension of business realities: that competitive advantage is transient but, simultaneously, the need to change is not easily met due to corporate inertia (Cascio & Boudreau, 2012).

Finally, we present the overview by De Wit and Meyer (2010). Unlike the aforementioned syntheses, De Wit and Meyer's (2010: 14) main goal is to present an overview of inherent tensions in the field of strategic management theory and practice, which gives rise to different perspectives. For example, the tension between logic and creativity is related to the strategic perspectives of rational thinking versus generative thinking. The tension between deliberate and emergent processes is related to the strategy perspectives of planning and incrementalism. The perspectives we have encountered as schools of thought in Mintzberg, Ahlstrand, and Lampel's (2009) overview are applied by De Wit and Meyer (2010) to distinguish ten tensions in strategy. We focus here on those tensions that extend the thinking presented so far and that are relevant to the relationship between strategy, HRM, and performance.

The first tension is the between markets and resources, related to the *outside-in* versus *inside-out* strategy perspectives. We have already encountered the outside-in approach when discussing Porter's (1980, 1985) contribution. The inside-out perspective is represented by the resource-based view (RBV) of the firm (e.g. Barney, 1991), in which the (internal) resources are presumed to be the key to organizational success. These inside-out approaches emphasize the importance of unique organizational resources (e.g. financial resources, human resources) for the development of strategies to achieve sustainable competitive advantage (Paauwe & Boselie, 2005b). In strategic HRM, the more classic models are dominated by the outside-in perspective, whereas the inside-out perspective based in RBV theory is dominant in more current HRM models. These two perspectives can be considered paradoxical, as a situation in which two seemingly contradictory, or even mutually exclusive, factors appear to be true at the same time. If we accept that both are true, this has implications for HRM. On the one hand, HRM is dependent on the strategic positioning of the firm as it attempts to fit with the market environment (outside-in approach); on the other hand, (human) resources can be cultivated and developed in order to enable strategies that will result in a sustainable competitive advantage (inside-out approach). In Chapter 3, we will deal with this issue of alignment in greater depth when discussing strategic fit.

A related tension is that between profitability and responsibility, related to the strategy perspectives of *shareholder value* versus *stakeholder values*. In USA-based HRM models, the shareholder perspective historically dominated (see also Chapter 5): HRM strategies, policies, and practices serve only one goal, which is to increase shareholder value. In contrast, in European (especially Continental European) models there are more stakeholder-oriented approaches, balancing the needs, interests, and aspirations of various stakeholders both inside and outside the organization. Most recently, there has been a shift in USA-based writing that pays greater attention to an organization's context and stakeholders beyond shareholders (e.g. Beer, Boselie, & Brewster, 2015; Jackson, Schuler, & Jiang, 2014; Schuler, 2013; Schuler & Jackson, 2014). Table 2.4 presents De Wit and Meyer's (2010) overview of the characteristics of these two opposing perspectives.

It is interesting to note that both tensions and related perspectives (outside-in/inside-out and shareholder/stakeholder) also relate to what has become known as an alternative stream in organizational theorizing—coevolution (Aldrich, 1999; Futuyma & Slatkin, 1983). In an excellent overview, Aldrich (1999) describes the origins of evolutionary theory and the related concept of coevolution. Referring to authors such as Baum and Singh (1994) and Roughgarden (1983), he states: 'Evolutionary theorists have coined the term coevolution to describe situations in which organizations and populations not only respond to influence from their environments, but also affect their environments' (Aldrich, 1999: 38).

In a special issue of the journal *Organization Science*, Lewin and Volberda (1999) sketch the contours of this coevolution framework for research in the area of strategy and new organizational forms. Normally the environment is considered to be an exogenous variable, but they focus on the way in which organizations systematically influence their environments and how organizational environments (inclusive of populations inside

Table 2.4 Overview of shareholder and stakeholder value perspectives

	Shareholder value perspective	Stakeholder values perspective
Emphasis on	Profitability over responsibility	Responsibility over profitability
Organizations seen as	Instruments	Joint ventures
Organizational purpose	To serve owner	To serve all parties involved
Measure of success	Share price and dividends (shareholder value)	Satisfaction among stakeholders
Major difficulty	Getting agent to pursue principal's interests	Balancing interests of various stakeholders
Corporate governance through	Independent outside directors with shares	Stakeholder representation
Stakeholder management	Means	End and means
Social responsibility	Individual, not organizational matter	Both individual and organizational
Society best served by	Pursuing self-interest (economic efficiency)	Pursuing joint-interests (economic symbiosis)

Source: De Wit & Meyer (2010).

organizations) influence those organizations in turn (Lewin & Volberda, 1999: 520). The origins of this issue of *adaptation and selection* can be found in a range of disciplines, including sociology, economics, strategy, and organization theory. Following an excellent review of these sources of inspiration, they define coevolution as:

[T]he joint outcome of managerial intentionality, environment and institutional effects. Coevolution assumes that change may occur in all interacting populations of organizations. Change can be driven by direct interaction and feedback from the rest of the system. In other words, change can be recursive and need not be an outcome of either managerial adaptation or environmental selection but rather the outcome of managerial intentionality and environmental effects. (Lewin & Volberda, 1999: 526)

The relevance of these remarks can easily be related to the way in which changes in HRM come about. For example, an expected labour market shortage due to population aging might give rise to abolishing early retirement schemes at the industry level and subsequently create more attention for career management, job crafting (Kooij, Tims, & Kanfer, 2015; Wrzesniewski & Dutton, 2001), and idiosyncratic I-deals (Kroon, Freese, & Schalk, 2015; Rousseau, 2005) for older workers within companies. Despite its relevance, the concepts of coevolution and related theoretical frameworks have not been extensively applied in strategic HRM research. Researchers seem to prefer the institutional perspective (as we will discuss in depth in Chapter 4). Since its inception, coevolution research, which also makes use of institutional theory, has become increasingly focused at the industry level of analysis, exploring populations of organizations interacting with their ecosystems (Geels, 2014; Murmann, 2013).

The overview of schools and the syntheses by Mintzberg, Ahlstrand, and Lampel (2009), Mainardi and Kleiner (2010), and De Wit and Meyer (2010) together offer important clues for the relationship between strategy, HRM, and performance. Before drawing conclusions with respect to our own way of modelling this relationship, we first present an overview of the classical strategic approaches in the HRM field.

2.5 Classical strategic approaches in HRM

In describing the traditional strategic approaches in the HRM field, we need to distinguish between process and content models. The *process* of strategy refers to the way strategies come about, whereas the *content* is concerned with the product or 'what' of strategy. In addition to this well-known distinction, De Wit and Meyer (1998: 5–6) also emphasize the *context* of strategy, referring to the set of circumstances in which both the process and content of strategy are shaped, developed, or simply emerge.

The process of strategy formulation includes considering the consequences of a firm's chosen strategic direction (at business or corporate level), which can be

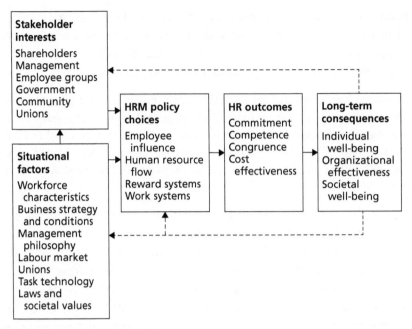

Figure 2.2 The Harvard model of strategic HRM

Source: Beer and colleagues (1984).

analysed with respect to cost constraints and staff requirements. The content and context of the strategy then need to be considered by monitoring the external environment and analysing the current human resources both with respect to quantity and quality. Questions regarding the present and required human resources can be raised, such as: Do we have the necessary talent and competences to carry out the chosen strategy, or can we obtain these? Are the costs involved in recruiting, retaining, and/or developing the necessary talent in line with the assessment of cost constraints? If the answers are positive, the chosen strategic direction can be adopted. If not, an alternative strategic direction needs to be selected, and the whole process starts again.

The Harvard model of strategic HRM (see Figure 2.2) developed by Beer and colleagues (1984) is one of the most well-known models in HRM theorizing that combines process, content, and context. Thirty years on, the model has been reviewed (Beer, Boselie, & Brewster, 2015); the conclusion was that it has lost nothing of its relevance, which is quite an achievement. Alongside market and strategic considerations, the Harvard model purposely takes into account the interests of various stakeholders in both the external and internal organizational environment. The model outcomes do not focus solely on performance in its strict economic sense, but also pay attention to individual well-being and societal consequences. In this way, the model is both descriptive and prescriptive. It provides a clear overview of the factors that are important in

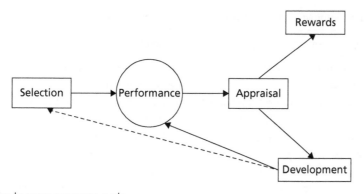

Figure 2.3 The human resource cycle

Source: Fombrun, Tichy, and Devanna (1984).

shaping HRM policies, but at the same time it is quite conclusive in prescribing to what kind of outcomes these choices—once made—should lead.

Fombrun, Tichy, and Devanna (1984) (the competition from Michigan Business School) published their approach in the same year as their counterparts from Harvard (see Figure 2.3). According to this model, achieving a tight fit between strategy, structure, and HRM policies takes place amidst economic, political, and cultural forces. More focused on the functional level of HRM itself, the Michigan authors emphasized the 'human resource cycle', which can be considered to be one of the first 'content' models. In their cycle, performance is dependent upon selection, appraisal, rewards, and development.

The final classic model (if we are allowed to use the word 'classic' in the still rather infantile discipline of HRM) is the model by Schuler and Jackson (1987). Using Porter's (1980) generic strategies as a point of departure, they developed a repertoire of role behaviours for each type of strategy (cost-effectiveness, innovation, and quality). Subsequently, HRM policies and practices were used to stimulate or even enforce the required role behaviours. In Table 2.5 we present an overview of the range of possible role behaviours.

The role behaviours required for each distinct competitive strategy differ, and these can be stimulated by a consistent set of HRM practices. For example, in the case of a firm pursuing an innovation strategy, the profile of employee behaviour includes (Schuler & Jackson, 1987: 209):

- A high degree of creative behaviour
- A longer-term focus
- A relatively high level of cooperative, interdependent behaviour
- A moderate degree of concern for quality
- A moderate concern for quantity
- An equal degree of concern for process and change

Table 2.5 Employee role behaviour for competitive strategies

Non-competitive strategy	Competitive strategy
1. Highly repetitive predictable behaviour	Highly creative, innovative behaviour
2. Very short-term focus	Very long-term behaviour
3. Highly cooperative, interdependent behaviour	Highly independent, autonomous behaviour
4. Very low concern for quality	Very high concern for quality
5. Very low concern for quantity	Very high concern for quantity
6. Very low risk-taking	Very high risk-taking
7. Very high concern for process	Very high concern for results
8. High preference to avoid responsibility	High preference to assume responsibility
9. Very inflexible to change	Very flexible to change
10. Very comfortable with stability	Very tolerant to ambiguity and unpredictability
11. Narrow skill application	Broad skill application
12. Low job (firm) involvement	High job (firm) involvement

Source: Schuler & Jackson (1987).

- A greater degree of risk taking, and
- A high tolerance of ambiguity and unpredictability.

Based on the kind of required role behaviours, the following HRM practices can be used to stimulate appropriate employee behaviour for an innovation strategy (Schuler & Jackson, 1987: 213):

- Job designs that stimulate close interaction and coordination among groups of individuals;
- Performance appraisals that are more likely to reflect longer-term and group-based achievements;
- Jobs that allow employees to develop skills that can be used in other positions in the firm;
- Compensation systems that emphasize internal equity rather than external or market-based equity;
- Pay rates that tend to be low, but that allow employees to be stockholders and have more freedom to choose the mix of components (salary, bonus, stock options) that make up their pay package;
- Broad career paths to reinforce the development of a broad range of skills.

According to Schuler and Jackson (1987), these practices are aimed at facilitating cooperative interdependent behaviour that is oriented towards the longer term and foster exchange of ideas and risk-taking. They follow the same kind of reasoning for the quality and low-cost strategies, and in this way they are able to present three hypotheses concerning the relationship between competitive strategy, required role behaviours, and related HRM policies and practices (Schuler & Jackson, 1987: 213). In this respect, one could say that they were among the first to present clearly how strategy and HRM policies could be interrelated. They offered a concrete insight into the possible linkages between the content of a certain strategy and what kind of HRM policies would help to implement that strategy.

In reality, however, distinctive competitive strategies are not really so clear-cut. Nowadays, given the fierce competition, companies need simultaneously to be cost-effective, innovative, and offer high quality. Moreover, one company or one business can have more than one strategic orientation, dependent on the range of business units and related business strategies. In such a case, the required role behaviours are highly mixed. Actual company practice has overtaken this way of modelling. Over recent decades, we have experienced an enormous rise in 'high performance/high involvement work systems', which have successfully been applied in a range of industries and which do not distinguish between different strategies. This touches on the issue of the universalistic approach of 'best practices' versus the contingent approach of 'best fit', which we discuss in detail in Chapter 5.

Both the Harvard and Michigan models are nonetheless still relevant (see the special issue of *Human Resource Management* published on the occasion of the thirtieth anniversary of these models in May/June 2015). They remain relevant because they take into account the importance of context, and specify these factors in their respective frameworks. Schuler and Jackson's (1987) model is likewise still applicable as it focuses on achieving strategic goals, emphasizing the importance of the linkage between organizational requirements based on strategic imperatives and role behaviours with related HRM practices. However, nowadays the words are different: in order to realize the business strategy, a firm needs to have specific organizational capabilities or core competences (such as speed, logistics, design, marketing, innovation) at the level of the organization. The next step is to translate these organizational capabilities into team or individual-level competences, combining knowledge, skills, and abilities (KSAs). HRM practices can help to recruit, develop, and reward these.

2.6 **Practical strategic HRM tools**

As this chapter has so far discussed, we are interested in exploring strategy because of the fundamental requirement in organizations that HRM should support this strategy to achieve high firm performance. The questions then arise as to how we know whether or not the HR function is delivering added value, and, specifically, how well aligned the HR function's activities are with the overall organization strategy. The first part of this question focuses on the fundamental link between HRM and performance, specifically exploring value creation through HRM activities. The second part focuses on the issue of 'fit', which we will explore in depth in Chapter 3. For now, we will focus on presenting some tools that help us to think about the HRM–strategy linkage, and opportunities for the HR function to deliver organizational performance.

In the appendix to this chapter, we provide details of four models that address the HRM–strategy relationship. The first, the *Kano model*, focuses on value creation, emphasizing the importance of the different levels of impact that the HR function can have in supporting corporate strategy. The second model focuses on the related notion of *line of sight* as a critical way in which alignment is achieved through creating a shared mind-set among employees (not only in terms of understanding what the strategy is all about, but also knowing how to actually contribute to it). The third model offers insight in the *different categories of employees* based on their degree of uniqueness for the organization and their possibility to add value. This kind of segmentation can help to build an appropriate HR architecture. Our fourth model, the *HR value chain*, is sometimes referred to as a 'stepwise' approach: Ensuring a clear linkage through the organization, starting from its vision all the way through to the HRM practices put in place ultimately to support this. Building on the first three models, the HR value chain allows HR professionals to explore potential gaps or breaks in the linkages from corporate vision through to HRM practices.

Overall, these models provide suggestions for ways in which strategy can be linked with HRM, as well as tools to help implementation in organizations. Chapter 11 also provides further suggestions related to implementation, focusing on how to structure the delivery of HRM to support the organization strategy, as well as providing a review of HR metrics as a means of recognizing whether or not HRM is delivering added value.

2.7 **HRM and strategy: Lessons learned**

This overview of strategy and the different approaches both in strategic management as well as in the field of HRM has generated a number of insights. These will be useful in modelling the relationship between strategy, HRM, and performance in the following chapters in this volume.

First, it is important to draw the conclusion that simplistic reasoning based on distinguishing a range of strategy types and subsequent HRM policies and practices has its limitations. Becker and Huselid (in Wood, 1999: 377) rightly state that: 'The HRM system should be highly idiosyncratic and tailored to each firms' individual situation.' Yet, even in unique situations, it is important to be able to map the various factors and variables that play a role in shaping HRM policies and practices. It is therefore important to remember the insights that have been generated throughout this chapter, including:

- Process, content and context approaches are important in establishing the relationship between HRM and strategy.

- Both outside-in (Porter-like) and inside-out (resource-based view) approaches are of relevance and can be combined on the basis of a co-evolutionary perspective.
- In addition to rationally planned strategies, (disturbing) cognitive processes, politics, and related power positions and resources also play a role, which leads to an emergent and interactive approach to strategy development. The process of strategy formulation itself is characterized by an interactive, iterative, and thus incremental nature, especially in the field of HRM, where a range of stakeholders (with their ideology and—to a certain degree—shared values) has an interest in the outcomes.
- The entrepreneur him/herself—as a key decision-maker—can play an important role in shaping HRM policies and bringing about an ideology and culture that is quite determinant in subsequent shaping of HRM policies.
- As well as competitive market forces, the social, legal, and cultural environment is important. Legislation, social partnership (between employers, federations, and trade unions), agreements, and directives can and will guide the shaping of HRM policies and practices in companies.
- Shareholders are not the only stakeholders interested in the outcomes of strategic HRM. Customers, employees, and their representative bodies also have an important voice (whether one likes it or not) in all matters related to HRM.

A crucial element at the heart of this chapter has been the importance of creating balance in connecting strategy to HRM in order to achieve high firm performance. In Chapter 3, we focus explicitly on the process of alignment, exploring different types of 'fit' in HRM strategy formulation and highlighting the importance of context.

▰ APPENDIX

A2.1 **Value creation: The Kano model**

Originating in the field of marketing, the Kano (1995) model aims to map the characteristics of a service or product in relation to its customer appreciation. As the HR function also has customers, both internally (managers, employees, other business support functions, trade union representatives, and works council members) as well as externally (end customers, trade unions, labour market intermediaries, society at large), this model is also useful and relevant here.

Kano (1995) distinguishes three characteristics:

- *Threshold characteristics*: These refer to the bare minimum requirements that one expects from a product or service. For example, when buying a car one expects the brakes to function. In the field of HRM, when appointing somebody, one expects

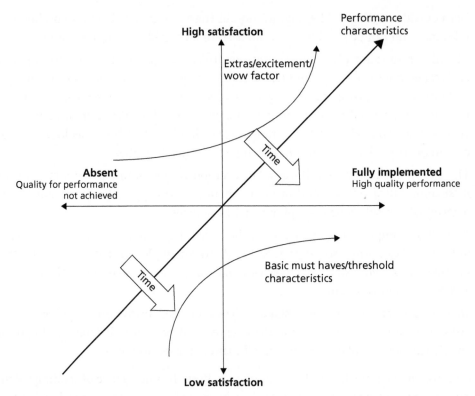

Figure A2.1 The Kano model

Source: Kano (1995).

the labour contract to specify what both employer and applicant/employee have agreed upon. If the threshold characteristics are not present the customer/employee will be very dissatisfied, however, if present, these threshold characteristics will not generate additional appreciation or satisfaction. They are simply taken for granted.

- *Performance characteristics*: The more these characteristics are present in the product or service, the happier the customer is. For example, the more fuel-efficient a car is, the more this will be appreciated by the customer. As far as HR is concerned, the better the quality of a training programme, the more the employee will be appreciative of it. If these factors are not present, they may cause dissatisfaction for the customer, but may not necessarily be a reason for rejecting the product or service.

- *Excitement characteristics or 'wow' factors*: The product or service provides characteristics that one had not expected in advance, but, once present, they generate additional satisfaction (they 'delight' the customer), whereas their absence will not cause lower levels of appreciation. Again, the car example: You take your first ride in your brand-new car and you discover that all the pre-sets of your favourite radio stations have been programmed in and even in the right ranking order. That is indeed a pleasant surprise!

A similar example of a 'wow' factor in the realm of HRM is the HR function delivering an analysis of performance data to a manager (without having to ask for it), which gives her or him a clear overview of high achievers and underperformers in the unit. The manager is then highly satisfied with her or his experience with the HR function.

The Kano model (see Figure A2.1) clearly shows the three possible categories of product or service attributes and how they contribute (or not) towards achieving competitive advantage. Moreover, Figure A2.1 also shows that, over time, performance attributes tend to be considered as basic 'must haves' and that the excitement characteristics have the tendency to become performance attributes. We are therefore in need of continuous product/service innovation. Applying this framework to the HR function requires an innovative attitude with a central and continuous focus on the (unforeseen) needs and expectations of the various internal and external customers in order to generate a 'wow' feeling among customers/ employees. Being sensitive to external trends (e.g. market, demographic, technological) is crucial for achieving this kind of product and service development in the field of HRM.

A2.2 **Line of sight**

A business strategy can only live up to its promises once complemented by a supportive organization model, including an appropriate structure, culture, and related systems and operating procedures that determine how work is actually performed in an organization. How can we be sure that employees at all levels in the organization understand what the strategy is, and are capable of translating this into operating in such a way as to support strategy implementation? For this, we need a 'line of sight' (Boswell & Boudreau, 2001).

'Line of sight' refers to a shared mind-set among all employees, which can enable an organization to reach its goals. However, a shared mind-set alone is not enough. Employees who understand the strategy, also need to understand how to act based on that strategy: 'employee understanding of the organization's objectives and how to contribute to those objectives' (Boswell & Boudreau, 2001: 851). The line of sight framework therefore distinguishes two dimensions:

- Accuracy of understanding the direction of the strategy (accurate or inaccurate).
- Level of understanding of actions/contributions aligned with the strategy (deep or shallow).

This is summarized in Figure A2.2. Quadrant 1 represents those employees who have an accurate understanding of the strategy and also deep insight into how to contribute towards achieving those strategic goals. Quadrant 2 depicts the employees who contribute appropriately, yet do not have an accurate understanding of what the strategy is all about. Although not as sound as quadrant 1 employees, these quadrant 2 employees are moving the organization forward. The problem areas are those employees in quadrants 3 and 4, where they either have an accurate understanding of the strategy but do not know

	Accurate	Inaccurate
Deep	1	2
Shallow	3	4

Figure A2.2 Employee understanding of strategic organizational objectives

Source: Boswell and Boudreau (2001).

how to contribute (quadrant 3), or, even more serious, have no understanding of the strategy and also do not know how to contribute (quadrant 4).

The first step for the HR function is to assess how employees are distributed across the four quadrants. This can be achieved with the help of line management or through employee involvement surveys. The next step is then to develop interventions (such as communication, training, incentives, and voice) in order to ensure that employees in quadrants 2, 3, and 4 are better informed and equipped to make the right contribution.

Boswell and Boudreau (2001) carried out research in four organizations to find out more about: (a) the determinants of line of sight (what moves alignment); (b) how it can be established whether people have line of sight (defining and detecting line of sight); and (c) what are the positive and negative consequences of increased levels of line of sight. Figure A2.3 presents a schematic overview of their findings.

Overall, the positive outcomes of line of sight are increased morale, commitment, and retention. In contrast, however, being better able to understand the complexities of the organizational strategy, and what it takes to make a difference, might also result in more work stress and having more difficulty in finding the right work–life balance (Boswell & Boudreau, 2001: 858). There is also the question of whether having line of sight is important for all employees or only for a select group? The preferred answer might be that it is important for all employees, but that will take some time and effort to achieve. In so far as this has not yet been achieved, preference should be given to those employees or departments that are working in the core organizational processes (service delivery, product development) or working in close proximity with the (end) customers/clients. If these employees have full line of sight, the customer will notice the difference.

A2.3 **Segmenting the workforce: Frameworks for differentiation**

There are several reasons why organizations differentiate between their employees, including with respect to types of labour contract (permanent or temporary workers), or degree of investment in training and development. One prominent reason is, of course, fluctuations in economic cycles. Some industries, such as construction, truck manufacturing, and the automotive industry in general, are very sensitive to these fluctuations. These organizations simply cannot afford to offer everybody a permanent

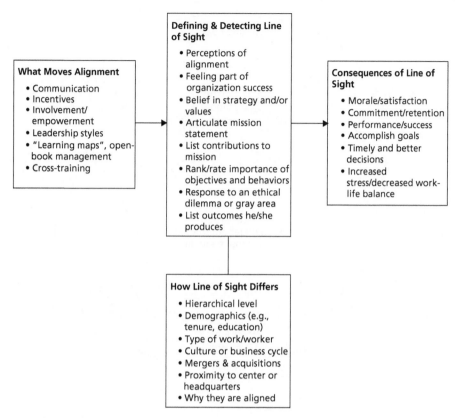

Figure A2.3 Line of sight

Source: Boswell and Boudreau (2001).

contract. So, they employ a core group of workers with a permanent contract in addition to a number of peripheral (ring) workers who are employed on a temporary contract in order to cope with the ups and downs of the economic cycle. This model became known as the 'core-ring' strategy (Atkinson, 1984), and is summarized in Figure A2.4.

Another reason for differentiating the workforce is related to how important employees are for achieving sustainable competitive advantage. Sustainability implies that competitive advantage is based on unique capabilities that cannot be easily imitated by competitors (see Section 2.4 on the resource-based view of the firm). In this respect, Lepak and Snell's (1999) framework offers a useful distinction between workers based on two dimensions:

- *Degree of added value of human capital*: Based on the resource-based view of the firm, resources are valuable according to Lepak and Snell (1999: 35): 'when they enable a firm to enact strategies that improve efficiency and effectiveness, exploit market opportunities and/or neutralize potential threats'. Considering employees as resources implies that they differ in the degree in which they are able to contribute to the competitive advantage or core competences of the firm. As such, they can be classified as either core or peripheral as Atkinson (1984) also argued.

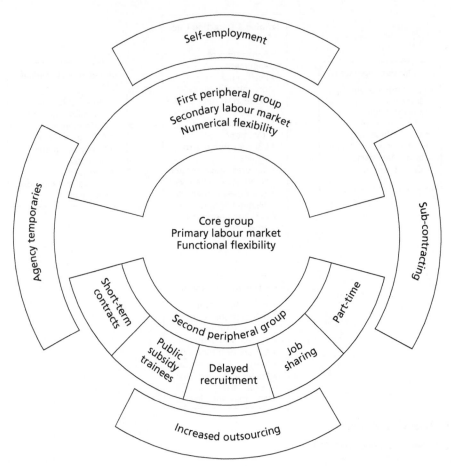

Figure A2.4 Segmenting the workforce

Source: Atkinson (1984).

- *Degree of uniqueness of human capital*: Again, using resource-based view arguments, the degree of uniqueness or firm specificity will differ per resource, and thus per employee. According to Lepak and Snell (1999), this may be due to unique operational procedures, interdependent arrangements, or team-based production, which will lead to increased social complexity and causal ambiguity. This will also generate tacit knowledge, which again contributes to uniqueness. Moreover, as 'these skills often involve idiosyncratic learning processes, firms are not likely to find these skills in the open labour market' (Lepak & Snell, 1999: 35). In the case of uniqueness, the focus will be on developing resources internally, whereas in the case of low or absent uniqueness, this kind of theorizing implies relying on the external labour market.

To summarize, the value and uniqueness of human capital will give rise to different employment modes and related HRM policies/configurations, as indicated in Figure A2.5.

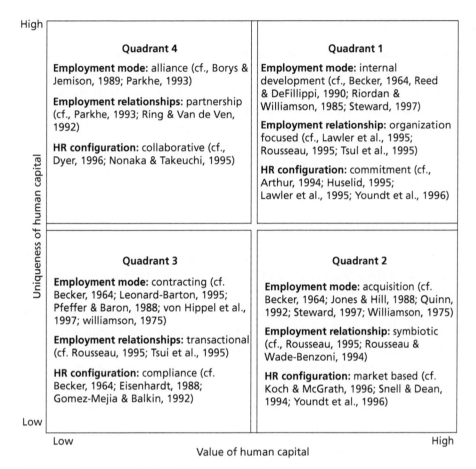

Figure A2.5 Uniqueness and value of human capital

Source: Lepak and Snell (1999).

Here, we provide a short description of each quadrant in Figure A2.5. (For a more extensive discussion, refer to Lepak and Snell (1999) on which these excerpts are based.)

QUADRANT 1 (HIGH VALUE AND HIGH UNIQUENESS)

The focus is on internal development of those employees that possess valuable and unique, organization-specific capabilities and skills. The company desires long-term commitment from these employees. Both the organization and the employees aim for mutual investment in order to cultivate and grow critical firm-specific skills. The HR configuration is based on establishing commitment through HRM practices such as extensive training, career development, and participation. The HR configuration for this quadrant resembles to a large degree the HRM practices that make up high performance work systems (HPWSs) (see Chapter 5).

QUADRANT 2 (HIGH VALUE AND LOW UNIQUENESS)

Although these employees also add value to the organization, they are widely available in the labour market as they do not possess organization-specific skills. Instead of focusing on investment and internal development, the main employment mode is acquisition, that is, 'buying' employees from the labour market who are instantly ready to contribute to the firm and who do not need to be invested in as their valuable skills have already been developed elsewhere. The HR configuration for this quadrant is mainly focused on staffing (recruitment, selection, on-boarding) and, compared to the first quadrant, there is far less emphasis on training and development.

QUADRANT 3 (LOW VALUE AND LOW UNIQUENESS)

The human capital in this quadrant is of less strategic value and of a generic nature. In essence, it can be treated as a commodity and can easily be purchased from and returned to the labour market (Lepak & Snell, 1999: 39). The employment mode is focused on contracting and is transactional in nature: It simply focuses on short-term economic exchanges. As far as the HR configuration is concerned, the main emphasis is on securing compliance with the terms and conditions of the agreed-upon contract. There will be barely any investment in training or development activities and performance appraisal, and rewards will be job-based, with a narrow focus on the quality and quantity of the work as agreed (Lepak & Snell, 1999: 40).

QUADRANT 4 (LOW VALUE AND HIGH UNIQUENESS)

Albeit that this kind of human capital is unique, it does not directly contribute to added value. This might have to do with its limited use by the firm (for example, hiring in a lawyer for a specific issue), or due to the fact that, for value to be generated, parties need to work together in order to generate a jointly shared outcome. Lepak and Snell (1999: 41) use the concept of alliance to refer to a kind of hybrid employment mode that blends externalization and internalization. As working together implies combining knowledge, sharing information, trust, and reciprocity, the employment relationship is based on partnership. The HR configuration consists of activities such as team building, process facilitation, communication, exchange programmes, job rotation, and mentoring in order to improve trust and encourage information sharing.

We present here a third and final model that focuses on differentiation. This model identifies 'A', 'B', and 'C' functions and players. As indicated, employees differ in their contribution towards implementing the business strategy, realizing strategic objectives, and hence achieving or helping to maintain sustainable competitive advantage. To put it more colloquially: Some employees provide a bigger bang for the company's buck than others. Huselid, Beatty, and Becker (2005) built upon the theorizing of Lepak and Snell (1999) by identifying systematically the strategically important 'A' positions, which preferably should be filled by 'A' players.

In line with this thinking, Huselid, Beatty, and Becker (2005) developed a portfolio approach to workforce management by identifying first the strategic positions (A positions)—those positions that contribute most to strategy and competitive advantage—and making sure that these are being fulfilled by the best possible employees (A players) and, secondly, that these are accompanied by good performers (B players) in essential support positions (B positions). The final step is making sure that non-performing employees (C players) and positions/jobs (C positions) that do not add value are eliminated.

The question then arises: How to identify those A positions? As indicated by Huselid, Beatty, and Becker (2005: 2), economists and HR managers differ in that respect. Economists simply base this on the wages that someone is earning; thus, the most important jobs are those held by the most highly paid employees. That situation is, however, a reflection of the past and might not be correct for the (near) future, and that is what strategy is all about. As far as HR managers are concerned, they also consider the level of skill or education, position in the hierarchy, and responsibility. Yet again, however, this is a reflection of the past. In order to identify an appropriate and future-oriented identification of A positions, Huselid, Beatty, and Becker (2005) recommend the following procedure.

First of all, HR managers need to have a clear idea of the organization's strategy. Is the firm aiming for cost leadership, quality, service, or a niche strategy? Based on the chosen strategy, management needs to identify the organization's critical capabilities, also called core competences. These encompass finance, logistics, technology, information, and skills, and are needed to convert the chosen strategy into a living reality. Based on this, the following question can then be posed: 'what jobs are critical to employing those capabilities in the execution of the strategy?' (Huselid, Beatty, & Becker, 2005: 2). Secondly, those jobs identified should be characterized by a high degree of performance variability, as this represents potential for improving performance as well as the risk of not being able to perform well as a company. Examples of these include sales positions or the position of the purchasing manager in a low-cost retail chain. In both cases, performance can vary greatly either positively or negatively. As far as the B positions and B players are concerned, they are important as well as they support the A positions. The various positions and their defining characteristics are presented in Table A2.1.

A2.4 **HR value chain: A diagnostic tool**

Our final practical HR tool takes a very broad perspective, diagnosing the (mis)connections between the various stages in the process of achieving alignment between business

Table A2.1 Positions and characteristics

	A Position STRATEGIC	B Position SUPPORT	C Position SURPLUS
DEFINING CHARACTERISTICS	Has a direct strategic impact AND Exhibits high performance variability among those in the position, representing upside potential	Has an indirect strategic impact by supporting strategic positions and minimizes downside risk by providing a foundation for strategic efforts. OR Has a potential strategic impact, but exhibits little performance variability among those in the position	May be required for the firm to function but has little strategic impact
Scope of authority	Autonomous decision making	Specific processes or procedures typically must be followed	Little discretion in work
Primary determinant of compensation	Performance	Job level	Market price
Effect on value creation	Creates value by substantially enhancing revenue or reducing costs	Supports value-creating positions	Has little positive economic impact
Consequences of mistakes	May be very costly, but missed revenue opportunities are a greater loss to the firm	May be very costly and can destroy value	Not necessarily costly
Consequences of hiring wrong person	Significant expense in terms of lost training investment and revenue opportunities	Fairly easily remedied through hiring of replacement	Easily remedied through hiring of replacement

Source: Huselid, Beatty, & Becker (2005: 3).

strategy and HRM strategy, practices, and their possible impact on HRM outcomes (such as turnover, productivity) and firm performance. The HR value chain analysis enables an HR manager to gain feedback on how HRM is experienced by a range of important internal stakeholders (top management, front-line managers, colleagues, and employees), and it helps explain the different stages of the HR value chain, identifying critical organizational success and failure factors. Figure A2.6 presents the stages in the analysis, ranging from distinguishing the business strategy all the way through to desired firm performance, identifying the various HRM steps along the way.

The HR value chain © is based on Wright and Nishii's (2007) process model, in which they distinguish intended, actual, and perceived HR practices and the subsequent reaction of employees in terms of attitude and behaviour. Boselie and Paauwe (2010) have extended this and developed into a diagnostic tool. Based on the various steps of the HR value chain presented in Figure A2.6, possible stakeholders are identified for each stage and used as

Figure A2.6 Conceptual model of the HR value chain ©

Source: Boselie and Paauwe (2010).

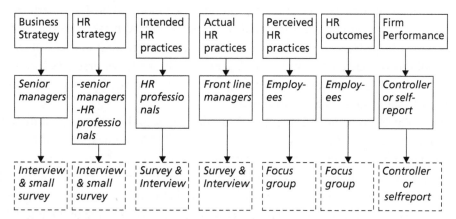

Figure A2.7 Research design, respondents, and techniques for data collection

Source: Boselie and Paauwe (2010).

respondents to collect data by means of a survey, interviews, and discussions in focus groups. See Figure A2.7 for a more detailed overview of the data collection process.

Benchmarking or contrasting with other organizations or among divisions of the same organization is recommended as this helps to put one's own outcomes in perspective. This also enables a discussion of differences in outcomes, which can lead to propositions regarding underlying causes and possible solutions. The HR value chain diagnostic tool can help—especially through comparing and contrasting with other companies/divisions—to gain a better insight into:

- The linkage between the business strategy and the HRM strategy;
- The alignment of HRM with line management;
- The cost-effectiveness of HRM delivery channels;
- HRM qualities and competences;
- The quality of front-line management leadership;
- The HRM outcomes perceived by employees; all in relationship to
- General company data (for example, employee turnover, sales, and size).

3 The more fits the better

3.1 Introduction

Fit!?[1] What does 'fit' have to do with human resource management (HRM)? The reality is that 'fit' is an absolutely crucial concept in our discussion of HRM and performance. 'Fit' refers to the notion of alignment. HRM should be aligned firstly with the corporate or business strategy (see Chapter 2), otherwise we cannot even start to speak of strategic HRM. But this vertical alignment is insufficient in itself: the HRM practices and policies should also be aligned with one another, aligned with the nature of the organization, and aligned with the institutional environment.

In the following section (3.2) we introduce the origins and background of these four traditional forms of fit. In the subsequent sections (3.3–3.6) we deal with each of these in turn in greater detail, including the latest insights concerning these traditional fits. In Section 3.7 we introduce a new form of fit, the macro–micro fit. As indicated in Chapter 1, this book is mainly focused on a macro, that is, organizational-level perspective of strategy, HRM, and performance. Yet we need also to be aware of the micro level, that is, individual perspective. By introducing concepts such as person–environment (PE) fit, the distinction between intended, actual, and perceived HRM practices, and applying signalling theory, the importance of the macro–micro fit becomes clear.

Reflecting on the realities of fit in practice, Section 3.8 explores what priority should be given to the different levels of fit; how they reinforce or support each other; and the need for dynamic forms of fit to suit agile organizations. We discuss how different phases can be distinguished in achieving the various forms of fit, with a view to exploring the impact on organization performance aimed at achieving sustained competitive advantage.

3.2 Traditional forms of fit

The concept of fit assumes that the effectiveness of HRM practices is context-specific. This approach is often contrasted with the 'best practice' or universalistic approach, which argues that certain HRM practices will be effective in any context (e.g. Delery & Doty, 1996; Pfeffer, 1994, 1998). The 'best fit' approach, mainly rooted in the strategic

---

[1] This chapter is partly based on Paauwe et al., 2013.

contingency approaches of the 1970s and 1980s, emphasizes the importance of internal and external organizational context for the shaping of HRM in an organization (e.g. Miles & Snow, 1978; Paauwe, 1989; Porter, 1985). A number of studies have shown evidence for the best fit approach (e.g. Gooderham, Nordhaug, & Ringdal, 1999; Jackson & Schuler, 1995; Marchington & Grugulis, 2000; Toh, Morgeson, & Campion, 2008). Later in this book, when we discuss HRM and performance from an international perspective (see Chapter 9), this 'best practice' versus 'best fit' debate becomes critical, but for now we will explore what these approaches mean for HRM in general.

Beer and colleagues (1984), as discussed Chapter 2, were among the first to apply fit to strategic HRM in their Harvard 'map of the HRM territory'. In their model, situational factors (for example, workforce characteristics, task technology, laws, and societal values) and stakeholder interests (those of shareholders, management, employee groups, government, and trade unions) are proposed to affect HRM policy choices and organizational performance. Organizational success is achieved through optimal alignment (fit) between the situational factors and HRM policy choices, and between stakeholder interests and HRM. These situational factors gave rise to two kinds of fit:

- Strategic fit, also known as vertical fit;
- Internal fit, also known as horizontal fit.

In addition to these two original forms of fit, Wood (1999) later added two more forms:

- Organizational fit, which focuses on the link between the HRM system and other relevant systems in the organization including technological systems, production systems, and control systems;
- Environmental fit, which focuses on the link between the HRM strategy and the external institutional environment.

In total, therefore, we have four basic fits, as depicted in Figure 3.1. The following sections detail each of these four kinds of fit.

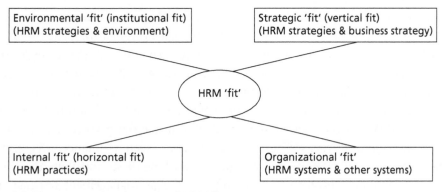

Figure 3.1 The component elements of HRM fit

3.3 **Strategic fit**

Strategic (or vertical) fit is aimed at aligning a set of HRM practices to the business strategy of an organization, which will help to implement strategy effectively and achieve optimal organizational performance (Boxall & Purcell, 2008; Huselid, 1995). The nature of the link between strategy and HRM has been a central issue to strategic HRM (SHRM). The basic premise underlying SHRM is that organizations adopting a particular strategy require HRM practices that may differ from those required by organizations adopting alternative strategies (Delery & Doty, 1996), assuming an important link between organizational strategy and the HRM practices that are implemented in that organization. The assumption is that HRM systems, which 'simultaneously exploit the potential for complementarities or synergies among such practices and help to implement a firm's competitive strategy, are sources of sustained competitive advantage' (Huselid, 1995: 636).

In exploring strategic fit, most researchers used the 'classical' strategy typologies of Porter (1985) or Miles and Snow (1978) to operationalize strategy (e.g. Schuler & Jackson, 1987; Montemayor, 1996; Youndt et al., 1996). For example, Schuler and Jackson (1987) were among the first to present ways in which strategy and HRM policies could be related. They used a classic approach to test strategic fit using Porter's generic strategies (cost-effectiveness, innovation, and quality), and linked each of these strategies to a repertoire of role behaviours (see Chapter 2). Subsequently, HRM policies and practices are used to reinforce the required role behaviours. The role behaviours required for each distinct competitive strategy differ and can be stimulated by a relevant and consistent set of HRM practices. For example, for an innovation strategy, HRM practices, such as variable pay rates and broad career paths, facilitate cooperative interdependent behaviour that is oriented towards the longer term and fostering the exchange of ideas and risk-taking. In sum, these studies offer a concrete insight in the possible linkages between the content of a certain strategy and what kind of HRM policies would help to implement that strategy.

Many of these classical models of strategic HRM reflect what is known as an outside-in approach (Baden-Fuller & Stopford, 1994): Strategic decisions are made based on the external environment (see also Chapter 2). This corresponds with the strategic contingency theory (i.e. Lawrence & Lorsch, 1967; Mintzberg, 1979), which argues that the 'best' model of organization depends on reacting to elements of the environment. In the 1990s, a shift in strategic thinking was presented by the introduction of the resource-based view (RBV) (Barney, 1991), representing an inside-out perspective. The starting point in this approach focuses on internal resources (such as finance, organizational systems, and physical assets as well as people) and how these contribute to achieving sustained competitive advantage. This shift in strategic management has had major implications for the field of HRM. Wright (who was then working closely together with Barney) states:

This RBV of competitive advantage differs from the traditional strategy paradigm in that the emphasis of the resource-based view of competitive advantage is on the link between strategy and internal resources of the firm. The RBV is firm-focused whereas the traditional strategic analysis paradigm has had an industry-environment focus. (Wright & McMahan, 1992: 300–1)

This inside-out approach uses (human) resources as a starting point. The unique strengths and capabilities of the employees determine the range of possible business strategies to be implemented: 'The resource-based view may demonstrate the fact that strategies are not universally implementable, but are contingent on having the human resource base necessary to implement them' (Wright & McMahan, 1992: 303). The RBV states that internal resources (such as human resources), which are scarce, valuable, inimitable, and non-substitutable, serve as the basis for sustained competitive advantage, and instead of just adapting to the environment (as in the outside-in approach), it might even be possible to adapt the kind of environment in which the organization is operating (see Weick (2009) on enactment). For a comparison of the outside-in and inside-out perspectives, see Table 3.1.

These two perspectives appear contradictory; however, an overview of HRM and performance research published between 1994 and 2003 by Boselie, Dietz, and Boon (2005) shows that both are relevant to strategic HRM. On the one hand, HRM is dependent on the strategic positioning of the firm as it attempts to fit within the market environment; on the other hand, human resources can be cultivated and developed in order to enable strategies that will result in sustainable competitive advantage. Both strategic contingency theory and RBV have been widely used as theoretical frameworks underlying strategic HRM models, and rank among the top three theories most used in strategic HRM and performance research (Boselie, Dietz, & Boon, 2005). The third is the so-called AMO theory, which draws our attention to the importance of a bundle of

Table 3.1 Outside-in versus inside-out perspectives on strategy

	Outside-in perspective	Inside-out perspective
Emphasis on	Markets over resources	Resources over markets
Orientation	Opportunity-driven	Strength-driven
Starting point	Market demand/industry structure	Resource base and activity system
Fit through	Adaptation to environment	Adaptation of environment
Strategic focus	Attaining advantageous position	Attaining distinctive resources
Strategic moves	External positioning	Building resource base
Tactical moves	Acquiring necessary resources	External positioning
Competitive weapons	Bargaining power and mobility barriers	Superior resources and imitation barriers

Source: De Wit & Meyer (2004: 255).

HRM practices which focuses on abilities, motivation, and opportunity to participate in order to improve performance (for more details on AMO theory, see Chapter 5 on performance).

3.3.1 PROBLEMS WITH STRATEGIC FIT

Conceptually, the idea of strategic fit is convincing, which is why it continues to play an important role in strategic HRM research (Becker & Huselid, 2006; Gerhart, 2004). However, initially, only limited empirical support for the impact of fit existed. Instead, more evidence has been found for the counterpart of the 'fit' approach, the so-called 'best practice' approach. This touches on the debate between the universalistic approach of 'best practices' versus the contingent approach of 'best fit'. While the 'best fit' approach assumes that the effectiveness of human resource (HR) practices is context-specific, the 'best practice' approach assumes that certain HR practices universally outperform others and acknowledges that a set of 'best practices' exists which will lead to organizational effectiveness regardless of the organization in which it is implemented. Over the last two decades much attention has been paid to high-performance, high-involvement work systems which have been successfully applied in a range of industries and which do not distinguish between different strategies (see Chapter 5 for further details).

Researchers who tested both the 'best practice' and the 'best fit' hypothesis in the 1990s consistently found stronger evidence for 'best practice' (e.g. Becker & Huselid, 1998; Delery & Doty, 1996; Huselid, 1995). To date, only modest evidence has been found for 'best fit', which may appear difficult to believe as the argumentation behind the 'best fit' hypothesis seems to be stronger than for the 'best practice' hypothesis. After all, we have evidence that HRM is highly context-dependent based on differences in sector, industry, related institutional arrangements, and differences in culture, both at the sectoral and national level. This is due to the embeddedness of HRM in the dominant system of industrial relations (IR). See, for example, Veld, Paauwe, and Boselie on HRM in hospitals (2010), Batt, Holman, and Holtgrewe (2009) on HRM/IR in call centres, MacDuffie (1995) on car manufacturing, and Kroon and Paauwe (2014) on HRM in agriculture.

So, how can we explain the lack of empirical support so far for strategic fit in these early studies? The reason is that measurement instruments used to test 'best fit' have a number of deficiencies which have resulted in the real nature of fit not being captured. For example, as we mentioned in the introduction to Section 3.3, most researchers have used the 'classical' strategy typologies of Porter (1985) or Miles and Snow (1978) to operationalize strategy (e.g. Montemayor, 1996; Schuler & Jackson, 1987; Youndt et al., 1996). In using these typologies, strategy is oversimplified into static constructs that do not capture the full breadth of business strategies in contemporary organizations

(Boxall & Purcell, 2008; Paauwe, 2004). In reality, competitive strategies are not really that clear-cut. Organizational strategies are typically more complex and tend to consist of more elements than those captured in these classic strategy typologies (Paauwe, 2004). Moreover, one company or one business can have more than one strategic orientation related to a variety of product market combinations (Vloeberghs, 1997: 77). In such a scenario, the required role behaviours are highly diverse.

Strategy typologies are thus unable to capture the uniqueness of business strategies. Yet, this uniqueness is seen as the potential source of sustainable competitive advantage (Becker & Huselid, 2006). So there is a lot of criticism on the operationalization and measures of strategic fit as they do not do justice to the complexity of the fit concept; the approaches used are seen as too superficial (e.g. Boxall & Purcell, 2003; Gerhart, 2004). Becker and Huselid (2006: 910) argue that fit is 'inherently multidimensional and not easily captured by simple bivariate statements'. Gerhart (2004: 10) notes a 'troublesome lack of progress on this front'. Boxall and Purcell (2003) formulate three main critiques on the 'classical' approaches for measuring strategic fit: They overlook employee interests, lack sophistication in their description of competitive strategy, and devote insufficient attention to dynamics. Moreover, empirical studies mainly do not take into account time lags; it takes twelve to eighteen months for an HRM strategy to be developed and implemented, and another three to four years before a relationship with performance could be observed (Paauwe & Boselie, 2005a; Wright & Haggerty, 2005).

3.3.2 'BEST FIT' IN STRATEGIC HRM AS THE WINNER?

Recent research evidence is more conclusive on the battle between 'best fit' and 'best practice', which, according to Boxall and Purcell (2011: 94), results in a clear win for the 'best fit' approach. A study by Toh, Morgeson, and Campion (2008), based on evidence from 661 US firms, finds major variation in HRM models across different contexts. So they conclude: 'Any prescription for a set of universal HR "best practices" must be informed by the contextual factors that surround their use' (2008: 877). Various authors present evidence on the difference in HRM between public and private sector (Bach & Kessler, 2007; Kalleberg et al., 2006), and for the private sector there are marked differences between manufacturing and services (see, for example, Combs et al., 2006). In addition, there are also big differences in HRM between high knowledge services like consulting and engineering and low-cost routine services like fast-food, cleaning, call centres, and so on. And, even within the same sector, there are marked differences in HRM, dependent on the kind of customers we want to serve. For example, compare a Michelin star restaurant to a fast-food chain restaurant, or a five star hotel to an almost fully automated roadside hotel chain. In all these cases there will be marked differences in recruitment and selection practices, the education level of employees, and, related to that, the kind of training required, levels of pay, degrees of employee autonomy, and so on, dependent on the kind of market segment in which the firm is operating and the kind of business strategy it is pursuing in order to gain sustainable competitive advantage.

The problem with all these contextually based studies, however, is that they demonstrate that HRM practices or HRM systems differ due to the context, yet do not explicitly make the link to performance, so this implies that there is not yet a winner, as no best fit studies have mastered the art of linking HRM to performance based on measuring the specific context.

3.3.3 TWO SIDES OF THE SAME COIN: PRINCIPLES VERSUS POLICIES AND PRACTICES

If we distinguish HRM between principles, systems, policies, practices, and tools (cf. Arthur & Boyles, 2007; Beijer, 2014; Wright, Dunford, & Snell, 2001), then we might see a way to unify the 'best fit' and the 'best practice' approach to understand better how strategic fit works. After all, in every HRM system or set of practices the underlying philosophy is based on a set of principles. For example, it will always pay off to select and recruit employees carefully, and it will always be wise to pay attention to how to motivate and reward employees appropriately. These principles are what Boxall and Purcell (2015: 80) call the *underpinning* level of general principles of HRM. However, the specific practices you put in place to recruit and select people, or motivate and reward them, is dependent upon the specific situation or context in which you are operating. Boxall and Purcell (2015: 80) call this the *surface* level of HRM policies and practices, which are heavily influenced by the economic, technological, and socio-political context. Figure 3.2 illustrates these two layers of HRM principles and practices.

Having established a clearer understanding of what strategic fit entails for HRM, both at the universalistic principle level and the context-dependent practice level, it remains important to consider *how* the linkage between strategy and HRM is actually

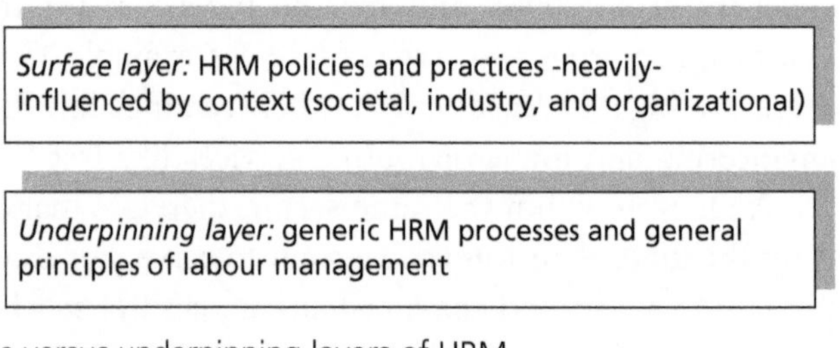

> *Surface layer:* HRM policies and practices -heavily-influenced by context (societal, industry, and organizational)

> *Underpinning layer:* generic HRM processes and general principles of labour management

Figure 3.2 Surface versus underpinning layers of HRM

Source: Boxall & Purcell (2015: 80).

achieved. We do this here from four perspectives: the notion of strategic capability in implementation; the role of the HR function in the process of strategy development; how corporate decision-making affects HRM strategy; and the long-term versus short-time linkages between corporate and HRM strategy.

3.3.4 STRATEGIC CAPABILITY: FOCUS ON IMPLEMENTATION

The field of strategic management has witnessed an increased emphasis on implementation, which is no longer seen as the process that automatically follows strategy formulation. Instead, strategy formulation and implementation are co-dependent: 'A strategy that is formulated without regard to its implementation is likely to be fatally flawed' (Grant, 2015: xii). RBV commentators identify that 'the ability to implement strategies is, by itself, a resource that can be a source of competitive advantage' (Barney, 2001: 54). So, under the influence of the RBV, the concept of strategic capability (defined as the set of capacities, resources, and skills that create a long-term competitive advantage for an organization) became en vogue (Johnson, Scholes, & Whittington, 2009).

This shift in focus has also influenced theorizing and research in SHRM, especially since, traditionally, SHRM mainly focused on intended HRM policies rather than the enactment of these policies (Boselie, Dietz, & Boon, 2005; Guest, 1999; Legge, 2005; Purcell, 1999; Wright & Boswell, 2002; the distinction between intended, actual, and perceived HRM is also discussed in Chapter 5). This new perspective has been adopted by, amongst others, Becker and Huselid (2006), who make a plea for a strong focus on the role of key strategic business processes in HRM implementation: HRM strategies can only be successfully implemented through an ideal *HR architecture*, which consists of the systems, practices, competencies, and employee performance behaviours that reflect the development and management of the firm's strategic human capital (Becker & Huselid, 2006: 899).

According to Becker and Huselid (2006), strategic fit of HRM not only plays a role at the organizational level, but also at the shop floor level. Strategy implementation includes strategic, tactical, and operational elements to make HRM work in practice. For example, an organization with an extensive training and development infrastructure not only has the HRM instrument known as training, but also the structure to make it work. In combination with a general culture for continuous employee development, this organization would possess an implementation strategy that can be a source of superior performance. From another perspective, the degree to which employees participate in the objective setting process, in other words adding a bottom-up process to implementation, can foster desired employee behaviours, which in turn link to firm performance (Gratton Hope-Hailey, Stiles, & Truss, 1999). Thus, consistent implementation of strategy through appropriate HRM practices is also necessary for HRM to be linked with firm performance.

3.3.5 THE ROLE OF THE HR FUNCTION IN ACHIEVING STRATEGIC FIT

In the early strategic HRM literature, Golden and Ramanujam (1985) distinguished various linkages between HRM and strategy; however, their emphasis was not so much on the *content* of HRM practices (as had been the case with the previous studies we have discussed in the introduction to Section 3.3, such as the model of Schuler and Jackson (1987), as on the involvement of the HR function in the whole *process* of strategy development and implementation. They distinguish four different linkages, which represent increasingly closer involvement of the HR function with corporate or business strategy:

- *Administrative linkage*: This kind of linkage (more accurately: barely any linkage!) reflects the traditional and administrative role of the HR function (e.g. Tyson and Fell's (1986) 'clerk of works' framework: see Chapter 10 on HR roles), in which there is little interest in establishing a relationship between the strategic orientation of the organization and HRM policies and practices. We still encounter this linkage in firms facing less or no competition, or in sectors/organizations which still lag behind in terms of strategic HRM.
- *One way linkage*: Once the strategy has been formulated, the specialist HR function becomes involved in order to design policies and practices that will help to implement the strategy. The HR function itself does not participate in the process of strategy formulation. Some authors label this as the reactive role of HR (Kydd & Oppenheim, 1990).
- *Two-way linkage*: The relationship between corporate strategy and HRM strategy is a balanced and reciprocal one. There are formal processes in place which enable both to influence each other, and the HR function really contributes to the process of strategy formulation.
- *Integrative linkage*: The relationship between corporate strategy and HRM strategy is one characterized by a strong degree of interaction, both formally and informally. Both managers and HR specialists operate in the same networks. They have a mutual influence on each other and responsibility for HRM is intricately interwoven with responsibility for overall corporate strategy and policies.

Lengnick-Hall and Lengnick-Hall (1988) are strongly in favour of developing reciprocal interdependence between strategy development and the HR function for the following reasons. First, an integrated approach offers a broader range of solutions to complex organizational problems. Secondly, integration assures that human, financial, and technological resources are given consideration simultaneously in setting goals and assessing capabilities for implementation. Thirdly, integration forces organizations to explicitly take into account the individuals who compromise them and who have to implement strategies. Fourthly, reciprocity and integration limits the subordination of HR preferences to strategic considerations, and also limits the neglect of human resources as a vital source of organizational competence and competitive advantage.

Here we already see a first indication of what would eventually become a very important stream in HRM thinking, that is, the RBV. With a special focus on strategic decision-making in the multi-divisional company, Purcell and Ahlstrand (1994) distinguish between *first order strategies*, concerned with the enterprise's basic goals and range of businesses and markets served; *second order strategies*, which focus on the decisions on internal operating procedures; and finally employee relations (ER) and HRM strategies as *third order strategies*. Their modelling includes both downstream (from first to third order) and upstream (from third to first order) patterns of decision-making, but they admit that the dominant mode in the empirical reality is still the downstream pattern of decision-making. Hence they conclusively state: 'Thus an understanding of human resource strategy can only come about by looking at the opportunities and constraints imposed by first and second order strategies' (Purcell & Ahlstrand, 1994: 48). HRM, whatever the rhetoric, is being seen as a third order activity, shaped greatly by the bigger decisions of strategy and structure (Purcell & Ahlstrand, 1994: 80).

In addition to these insights, findings from in-depth case-study research among large companies in the UK (including Hewlett-Packard, Glaxo Welcome, and Citibank) have facilitated a deeper understanding of the processes that link business strategy to the performance of individuals and the organization (Gratton et al., 1999). The study argues that it is important to balance the need for continuity and consistency in the long term with the challenge of momentary change. For HRM strategies in particular, it is important to emphasize the long-term perspective, because the time cycle for changing people resources is often longer than those for financial or technological resources. There must be a vision of the future and a focus on concerns (such as building leadership, skills, and competences) that are broader, more long-term oriented, and less problem-centred than the short-term delivery of business goals (Gratton et al., 1999: 21–2). Nevertheless, the case firms have the majority of their HRM activities focused on a short-term linkage with corporate strategy (e.g. individual/team goal setting, training, and reward). Long-term linkages between corporate and HRM strategy only occur in the area of leadership development and high-potential top talent (Gratton et al., 1999: 25).

3.4 Internal fit: The strength of interaction among HRM practices

Internal (or horizontal) fit focuses on ensuring that individual HRM practices are aligned together consistently and coherently, such that the HRM practices work together as a system to achieve organizational objectives and enhance performance (Delery, 1998). The assumption is that 'certain HR practices blend better than others do, and it is sensible to select practices in conjunction with and not in isolation from each other'

(Wood, 1999: 368). The strength (or weakness) of the aligned practices is defined in terms of the type of connections that exist between individual HRM practices, as it is important to know how HRM practices support each other (Baron & Kreps, 1999; Delery, 1998), as we shall discuss.

Different HRM practices can be additively, or interactively (synergistically), related. In an *additive* relationship, HRM practices have independent effects on outcomes. For example, teamwork and pay for team performance may both stimulate team perform- ance, but in different ways. In an *interactive* relationship, the effectiveness of one practice depends on the level and nature of the other practices (Delery, 1998). Becker and colleagues (1997) make a distinction between two types of *interactive* relationships between HRM practices: powerful connections, which represent a positive synergy, and deadly combinations, which represent a negative synergy. Powerful connections represent combinations of HRM practices, such as employee involvement and extensive employee development, which strengthen each other and can create a high performance work system (HPWS) in an organization. An HPWS stimulates employee abilities and motivation and provides opportunities to participate (Boxall & Macky, 2009), which enhances employee job performance (e.g. through organizational citizenship behaviour) and organizational performance (e.g. through high levels of cost-effectiveness) (Boselie, Dietz, & Boon, 2005). (You can read more about HPWSs in Chapter 5.) So-called 'deadly' combin- ations reveal a negative synergistic connection between individual HRM practices. Here, combining practices such as teamwork and pay for individual performance, leads to unin- tended negative consequences. Therefore, the impact of a deadly combination is most likely to be negative for the individual employee and the organization as it can cause frustration, low motivation levels, and low levels of trust. Internal fit models assume the effectiveness of powerful connections as opposed to deadly combinations (Becker et al., 1997: 43).

Linking to the notion of strategic fit, literature on HRM systems and internal fit also stresses the importance of a focus on dominant business goals (Baron & Kreps, 1999). HRM practices communicate messages from the employer to employees: the higher the consistency and clarity of these messages, the higher their effectiveness (Baron & Kreps, 1999; Bowen & Ostroff, 2004; Rousseau, 1995). In other words, creating an HRM system with dominant, consistent messages is likely to be effective in accomplishing a dominant business goal as employees are selected, trained, developed, and rewarded. Bowen and Ostroff (2004) label this the 'strength' of the HRM system, which is associated with a strong climate. They distinguish three characteristics (distinctiveness, consistency, and consensus) of a 'strong' situation, which bring across the kind of messages HRM wants to convey meaningfully and distinctly (Bowen & Ostroff, 2004). Boxall and Purcell (2008) remark that usually not one, but several desirable themes can be communicated through the HRM system. Sometimes these goals can be competing, forcing a trade-off between goals within the HRM system. HRM systems thus need a clear focus, but this focus is rarely a single goal, and is more often a set of goals or themes because of the complexity involved. For example, hospitals nowadays are faced with potentially competing goals such as efficiency, high-quality care, and the need to be innovative (Veld, Paauwe, & Boselie, 2010) (see also Chapter 8).

Different models propose that an HRM system is most likely to be effective when it is focused on dominant consistent messages that have both strategic (vertical) and internal (horizontal) fit. Most authors agree that alignment with dominant business goals and alignment between the HRM practices are needed in order to achieve a strong HRM system. This suggests that 'internal fit without external fit will have little strategic value' (Becker & Huselid, 2006: 909). If the HRM system as a whole supports strategic business processes, this automatically implies that this HRM system is internally aligned (Becker & Huselid, 2006).

3.5 Organizational fit: Alignment with organizational systems and work systems

As noted in Section 3.2, Wood (1999) first introduced the notion of organizational fit in HRM research, focusing on the link between the HRM system and other relevant aspects of the organization, including technological systems, production systems, and control systems. Since then, researchers have agreed that an organization should align its HRM practices and employees' skills and motivation with organizational structures, systems, and processes (Wright, Dunford, & Snell, 2001), and integrate the HRM system with strategically important business processes (Becker & Huselid, 2006). In order to be effective, 'an HR bundle or system must be integrated with complementary bundles of practices from core business functions' (MacDuffie, 1995: 198).

Studies in HRM covering the relationship between organizational systems, structures, and processes have focused predominantly on the issue of technology. Research in the manufacturing sector has shown that HRM is affected by the dominant technology used in the sector and firm (Appelbaum et al., 2000; MacDuffie, 1995; Youndt et al., 1996). For example, Snell and Dean (1992) focused on alignment between advanced manufacturing technology, total quality management, just-in-time management, and HRM. Shaw, Gupta, and Delery (2001) examined the interactive relationship between integrated manu-facturing and compensation practices and found moderate support for the effectiveness of this congruence model. Cooke (2007) found that alternative workplace strategies differed with regard to the degree of integration of technological and human capital. These studies indicate the effectiveness of aligning different types of systems used in manufacturing with HRM practices and strategies, and the same is found in other sectors (e.g. Verburg, Den Hartog, & Koopman, 2007). (For a broader discussion of the link between HRM and performance at the sector level, please refer to Chapter 8.)

More recently, commentators have made a plea for more explicitly incorporating the relevance of an organization's inherent work design and work systems alongside focus on other organizational systems. Cordery and Parker state that a work system is 'a particular configuration of interacting subsystems, including work content, technology, employee capabilities, leadership style, and management policies and practices' (2007: 188–9). Organizational fit from a work system and design perspective highlights the relevance of alignment with: (1) the HRM systems in place; and (2) the broader organizational context (e.g. culture, technology, and production techniques). For example, MacDuffie (1995) studied HRM practices and work system practices, such as work teams, problem-solving groups, job rotation, and decentralization of quality-related tasks. However, until recently, the majority of HRM research paid little attention to these work systems (Boselie, Dietz, & Boon, 2005), until Boxall and Macky (2009: 7) revived this thinking, indicating that 'any HRM system encompasses the management of some work domain and the management of people who do the work in question'. They thus clarify the distinction between work practices (anything to do with how work is organized, e.g. allowing for problem solving, degree of autonomy, self-managing teams, quality circles) and HRM practices (e.g. training, recruitment, selection). Later, in Chapter 5, when discussing HPWSs, we will see that very often they include a mixture of both employment and work practices.

3.6 Environmental fit: Applying an institutional perspective

Environmental fit, described by Wood (1999) as the link between the HRM strategy and the external environment, has to be similar to the concept of institutional fit in order to be perceived by different stakeholders as legitimate (Paauwe, 2004; Paauwe & Boselie, 2003). Although the institutional context is widely acknowledged, particularly in European HRM models, to be important, few empirical studies take it into account when looking at the relationship between HRM and performance (e.g. Boon et al., 2009; Boselie, Paauwe, & Richardson, 2003; Van Gestel & Nyberg, 2009). An exception to this is Paauwe and Boselie's (2003) work in which they present an HRM model based on DiMaggio and Powell's (1983) institutional mechanisms for organizational isomorphism, namely coercive, normative, and mimetic mechanisms. In this model, institutional fit and thus legitimacy is achieved when the HRM strategy and policies are aligned with legislation, regulations, and the interests of social partners (coercive mechanisms); the values of professionals, professional bodies, and professional development networks (normative mechanisms); and/or the adoption of HR fads and fashions to mimic what is popularly being used (mimetic mechanisms).

Environmental fit in HRM may positively affect organizational performance, for example if an organization should be better and faster in adopting institutionalized HRM practices than competitors (Boon et al., 2009). These HRM 'leaders' (Mirvis, 1997) can benefit from the first mover advantage and strengthen their reputation towards stakeholders, including (potential) employees, customers, suppliers, government, financiers, and social partners (e.g. trade unions). Perhaps even more important is the risk of institutional misfit in HRM, potentially causing negative media attention and reputation damage (Paauwe & Boselie, 2005b). A more extensive treatment of institutional theory and related mechanisms will be discussed in Chapter 4.

3.7 Macro–micro fit: Aligning the organizational and individual level

Most research in the area of HRM and performance dating from the 1990s has been carried out at the organizational level, establishing a link between HRM practices and some measure of organizational performance. In the industrial and organizational psychology (I/O psychology) and organization behaviour (OB) fields, this level is referred to as the *macro* level of analysis. Since 2000, attention has shifted towards trying to understand the mechanisms through which this macro-level relationship takes place (see also Chapter 5 for an overview of theories addressing this 'black box' mystery). The way in which employees perceive and experience HRM practices is very important in this respect. Thus, alongside the organizational, macro level of analysis, we also need to include the individual, *micro* level of analysis.

Nowadays multi-level research designs set the stage for more advanced HRM and performance research (see, for example, Nishii, Lepak, & Schneider, 2008). An important contribution in this respect has been made by Wright and Nishii (2013). Their starting point is what they define as 'intended' HRM practices. These intended practices are the outcome of a process in which organization members have developed an HRM strategy that will help implement and execute the business strategy. However, intended practices are transformed into 'actual' HRM practices. In other words, not all intended practices will be implemented; moreover, it is possible that the degree and nature of implementation, especially through the involvement of line management, will differ per unit, group, or department within the organization. This means there might be a discrepancy between 'intended' and 'actual' HRM practices, which, of course, might lead to a difference in impact on corporate strategy.

However, we cannot determine the full impact of intended or actual practices without understanding 'perceived' HRM practices. Experienced and interpreted by

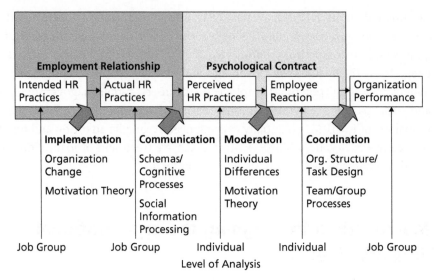

Figure 3.3 Intended, actual, and perceived HRM practices and performance

Source: Wright & Nishii (2013).

the employees, perceived practices shift the level of analysis to the individual, micro level (Wright & Nishii, 2013). The reasoning here is that employees will react based on how they perceive the HRM practices (regardless of how they were intended or actually carried out), and these reactions may differ per individual or group. Wright and Nishii (2013) distinguish three categories of reactions: Affective (attitudinal: e.g. job satisfaction, commitment), cognitive (e.g. increase in knowledge or skill), and behavioural (e.g. task performance, productivity, discretionary behaviour). So far, we have identified positive outcomes, but these can also be negative or counterproductive depending upon the way the HRM practices are perceived. For example, a new performance-related pay practice designed to speed up productivity and increase fairness might be implemented in such a way that some employees become suspicious and react in terms of withholding effort. Figure 3.3 represents the relationship between intended, actual, and perceived HRM practices.

Where the notion of implementation mainly focuses on the macro-level HRM strategy and the need for processes and infrastructure to support implementation, this notion of intended, actual, and perceived HRM practices emphasizes the importance of the actors involved at the micro level, and the need for them to act consistently in order to strengthen fit. This closely resembles the observations of Bowen and Ostroff (2004), who emphasize consistency as an important element of the strength of the system (see also Section 3.8 on the 'realities of fit').

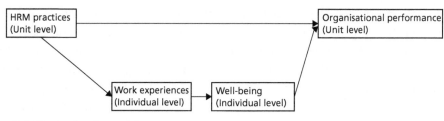

Figure 3.4 The bath tub model

Source: Van Veldhoven (2012).

3.7.1 THE BATH TUB MODEL

Based on Coleman (1990), a similar line of thinking has been developed by Van Veldhoven (2012). He also distinguishes the macro and micro level in HRM and highlights the different levels in his 'bath tub' model (see Figure 3.4).

The top level of the bath tub represents the organizational (macro) level, where we encounter the HRM practices, aimed at creating the right AMO for employees to carry out their work in order to achieve the goals and related performance at the organizational level. This process, however, takes place through the discretionary effort of individual employees, who—based on their personal characteristics, attitudes, abilities and perceptions, and degree of experienced well-being—are more or less inclined to perform and thus contribute in differing extents towards achieving those goals.

This brings us to the related notion of PE fit, which refers to the extent to which certain types of people fit with certain types of organizational environments (Bretz & Judge, 1994; Van Vianen, 2000). Research, mainly in the area of recruitment and selection in the I/O psychology and OB fields, shows that PE fit positively affects employee attitudes and behaviours (Kristof-Brown et al., 2005). The two most studied types of PE fit are person–organization (PO) fit and person–job (PJ) fit. PO fit focuses on the alignment between the individual employee and the organization's values, culture, and goals. PJ fit focuses on the alignment between employees' skills, abilities, and needs and characteristics of the job (Kristof-Brown et al., 2005). Only recently have HRM researchers started to include the PE fit in strategic HRM research (e.g. Boon, Den Hartog, Boselie, & Paauwe, 2011).

3.7.2 SIGNALLING THEORY

Finally, we refer to signalling theory as a way to illustrate further the importance of the link between macro and micro levels of analysis. Signalling theory suggests that people (employees, customers, shareholders, etc.) need tangible information to help them understand the organization's interests or future prospects (Biron, Farndale, & Paauwe, 2011). The information gathered is often used to form inferences about what issues are important in the organization and may thus serve to guide or strengthen relevant behaviours (Murray, 1991; Srivastava & Lurie, 2001). We can apply this theory here to understand how HRM practices are indicative of management concerns for the importance of displaying certain behaviours (e.g. being customer oriented or proactively taking safety precautions) in order to contribute to the goals of the organization. In other words, signalling exists when the organization promotes certain practices which are perceived by employees as signals (Rousseau, 1995; Spence, 1973). Signalling assumes an interaction between organizations and their members, which results from the way organizations choose, design, and implement their practices. Signalling in this way is considered to be a means by which an organization (macro level) influences the attitudes and behaviour of the employee (micro level). This can be done both informally (for example, through the organizational culture to set expectations that guide members' behaviour) or through formal HRM practices that drive members' attention towards performance-related issues that are important from the standpoint of the employer. These practices can be seen as structural signals or 'vehicles people use to convey commitments and offer inducements for present and future behaviour' (Rousseau, 1995: 169).

3.8 Is 'fit' enough?

In first instance, the main aim for organizations is to achieve a basic level of fit across the five areas we have identified in this chapter: Strategic fit covers both content and process approaches; internal fit covers the interaction between HRM practices; organizational and environmental (institutional) fit are included to incorporate the importance of alignment of HRM with organizational systems and the institutional environment respectively; and macro–micro fit ensures that employee perceptions of the HRM activities are as intended, and thus that employees fit the needs of the organization. Focusing on achieving these five types of fit enables the formulation of a strong HRM system, which should lead to safeguarding organizational continuity.

However, achieving fit across these five domains simultaneously is probably difficult to achieve. It is therefore likely that some elements of fit need to be achieved first, as a basic condition or hygiene factor for organizational survival. For example, achieving environmental fit by complying with legal and collective bargaining agreement (CBA) requirements might be one of these first steps to avoid serious consequences for the organization. Other elements of fit may not be basic requirements, but could be implemented or realized later in order to achieve a sustained competitive advantage;

for example, aligning a competence management system with the job characteristics and requirements of a service delivery work system.

Even if all of these fits can be achieved, we can wonder if this will be enough. The notion of 'fit' implies achieving a stable link between one system and another related system. However, in a dynamic world, additional gains might be achieved if alignment is combined with an ability to take into account dynamics and change (either internally or externally). After all, organizations are not static entities. On the contrary, they face change and dynamics, both internally as well as externally. So the impact of dynamics emphasizes the need for the HRM system to be focused on both strategy and flexibility in order to achieve sustained competitive advantage (Wright & Snell, 1998). Thus, while achieving fit can lead to short-term success, a dynamic fit is needed to cope with changes in order to continue achieving fit in the long run.

Secondly, it is important that the different types of fit identified here are aligned (i.e. a 'fit between the fits') rather than being counterproductive. Alignment at all levels should aim for the same overall goals, which makes it more likely for an organization to achieve a sustainable competitive advantage. Wright, Dunford, and Snell (2001) apply the RBV to HRM and highlight the importance of 'dynamic capabilities' for HRM. Dynamic capabilities can add value to HRM as they function as a renewal component for resources: 'Such dynamic capabilities require that organizations establish processes that enable them to change their routines, services, products, and even markets over time' (Wright, Dunford, & Snell, 2001: 712). Wright and Snell (1998: 758) use the term flexibility, referring to 'a firm's ability to quickly reconfigure resources and activities in response to environmental demands'. While, as we have seen in Section 3.3, strategic fit focuses on the match between an internal (HRM practices) and an external characteristic (strategy) and is therefore strategy focused, flexibility can be labelled as predominantly internally driven, encompassing employees as well as organizational systems (Wright & Snell, 1998: 757). Flexibility can be stimulated in employees and integrated in the HRM system, which can lead to successful adaptation to organizational change (Wright & Snell, 1998). Wright and Snell (1998) argue that both strategy-focused and flexibility-focused HRM practices should be present in an HRM system, in order to achieve both fit and flexibility simultaneously. See also Nijssen and Paauwe (2012) for a more extensive treatment of this topic.

Empirical evidence shows that HRM flexibility is associated with superior firm performance (Beltrán-Martín et al., 2008; Bhattacharya, Gibson, & Doty, 2005). HPWSs, if appropriately designed, can help develop flexibility of the workforce (Beltrán-Martín et al., 2008). HRM flexibility implies adapting employee characteristics, such as knowledge, skills, attitudes, and behaviour to a changing environment (Bhattacharya, Gibson, & Doty, 2005). Essential characteristics of flexibility or dynamic fit are:

1. The firm's ability to integrate and reconfigure internal and external competences to rapidly address changing environments.

2. The extent to which both strategy-focused and flexibility-focused HRM practices are present.

3. The extent to which employee attributes are adapted to changing environmental conditions (based on Teece, Pisano, & Shuen, 1997).

3.8.1 FIT AND PERFORMANCE

Achieving fit, that is, achieving the various forms of fit, is ultimately intended to improve performance. In order to understand how this might be achieved, we are still in need of further research in this field. We need an integrated perspective on fit (Paauwe et al., 2013), which takes into account:

- how the different approaches to fit are related (forming a unique configuration);
- the ranking order and hierarchical relationships between the different types of fit;
- and the importance of dynamic rather than static fit, dependent upon the degree of dynamism in the sector in which the organization is operating;
- as well as the relationship between fit and the kind of performance it is aiming at.

These realities regarding achieving HRM fit are summarized in Figure 3.5.

In Chapter 6 we will show how our Contextual SHRM Framework deals with a number of fits simultaneously in order to achieve performance in its multidimensional meaning—encompassing competitive advantage as well as individual well-being and societal legitimacy.

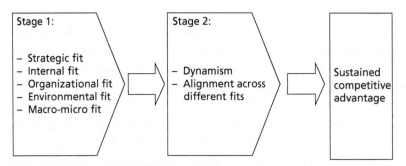

Figure 3.5 A two-stage framework for fit in SHRM

3.9 **Conclusions**

This chapter has taken a detailed look at the different types of fit that align HRM strategy, systems, and practices with various aspects of the organization and context in which they are being implemented. The dominant discourse surrounds the first type of fit: Strategic (or vertical) fit. As we have seen, strategic fit refers to how HRM strategy can be aligned with corporate strategy, either through an outside-in approach (based in strategic contingencies theory), or through an inside-out approach (based in the RBV of the firm). An important distinction was also highlighted here: HRM principles versus HRM practices. We argue that although HRM principles may be considered universal across organizational contexts, HRM practices must fit within the given organizational operating environment for maximum effect. It was also noted that it is important not only to achieve fit between HRM and corporate strategies, but also to consider the challenges of implementation: Does the firm have the necessary strategic capability to implement the aligned strategies, and can the HR department and organizational decision-making processes support this implementation?

The second type of fit discussed was internal (or horizontal) fit, which refers to the interdependencies between individual HRM practices, for example, does the selection process align with the training and development process in terms of achieving an appropriate balance between bringing in people with appropriate skills versus training them on the job. This is about gaining synergy from aligning HRM practices, and, as a result, developing a strong HRM system which projects clear signals to employees regarding desired attitudes and behaviour for high performance. This last point is important as it links internal fit to strategic fit: the value of having all HRM practices aligned with each other and, simultaneously, this integrated system being aligned with corporate strategy.

The third and fourth types of fit refer to the internal and external organizational environments. Organizational fit focuses on linking the HRM system to other internal organizational systems and processes. In particular, technology was identified as a key factor to consider when developing an HRM system: Achieving integration between technological and human capital is associated with higher levels of firm performance. Work systems are another important element here—work systems focus on the way that work is organized, which needs to be aligned with the people management practices in place to support this work. Environmental (or institutional) fit focuses on the external rather than internal environment of the organization. This is about ensuring that a firm's HRM system is aligned with relevant regulations, recommendations, traditions, and latest insights to ensure maximum integration with this broader context.

The fifth area of fit discussed in this chapter was macro–micro fit. This is best summarized by reference to intended versus perceived HRM practices. In other words, there needs to be alignment between what the organization envisaged when establishing its HRM system (macro-level, intended HRM) and how employees ultimately experience this system (micro-level, perceived HRM). A lack of fit here would imply the occurrence of unintended consequences of the HRM system, which may negatively impact firm performance.

Finally, we highlighted some of the realities of achieving these five types of fit in organizations today. First, we raised the issue of how firms may need to prioritize these different types of fit, especially if any are found to be conflicting. Secondly, we highlighted the importance of not only focusing on achieving fit (which implies a relatively static state), but simultaneously achieving flexibility in the HRM system to cope with the dynamic environment of most organizations today.

This chapter has particularly highlighted the importance of both the internal and external organizational context to HRM. In Chapter 4, we continue our examination of the context of HRM.

4 HRM in context

An institutional perspective

4.1 Introduction

In Chapter 3, we demonstrated the alignment between human resource management (HRM), strategy, and subsequent performance. This chapter continues on the theme of examining the context of HRM. We start by taking a closer look at the field of HRM itself (Section 4.2). Do different HRM models consider the importance of context? Researchers in the field of industrial relations (IR) perhaps have the greatest experience in this regard. For example, Dunlop's (1958) modelling of IR systems is an example of a method that considers economic, technological, and socio-political contexts.[1] The field of IR (Section 4.3) thus provided the motivation for our application of institutional theory to build a sound theoretical base that could encompass context in a study of HRM (Section 4.4).

Institutional theory has often been criticized that is places too much emphasis on stability, that it is deterministic, and that it stresses the conservative and conserving nature of institutions too greatly. In response to these criticisms, we show how institutional theory is able to encompass change, as well as the role of agency and the processes of deinstitutionalization (Section 4.5). Finally, we summarize our main discussion points and indicate how they can be used to build a more integrated perspective on HRM (Section 4.6).

4.2 HRM modelling: Why does context matter?

Looking back at the classic HRM models of Beer and colleagues (1984) and Fombrun, Tichy, and Devanna (1984), we see that they observed how context affected HRM policies and practices. Fombrun's model (also known as the Michigan model) refers to context in terms of economic, political, and cultural forces. Beer and colleagues' model

---

[1] 'Economic' includes ownership and control, organizational size and structure, the growth path of an organization, industry structure, and markets. 'Technological' includes skills, work organization, and labour force requirements of technologies. 'Socio-political' includes the institutional framework, particularly the national education and training systems.

(also referred to as the Harvard model) is more explicit in that it recognizes a wide range of contextual factors ranging from stakeholder interests to situational factors. Alongside shareholders and management, Beer and colleagues' model also acknowledges stakeholders such as employee groups, government, community, and unions. Situational factors that have an impact on the stakeholders include labour markets, technology, laws, and societal values.

Since the models developed by Fombrun, Tichy, and Devanna (1984) and Beer and colleagues (1984), research has continued in the field of HRM and performance. As noted in Chapter 3, a key discussion centres around how many boxes (sets of variables) should be in a model linking *strategic HRM* and *performance* (see Becker et al., 1997; Guest, 1997) in order to account sufficiently for the relationship between strategy, HRM, and performance. As part of this discussion, less explicit attention has been paid to context in current research. Nevertheless, almost every piece of empirical research incorporates control variables, which include contextual features either at the organization level (such as the degree of unionization, industry/sector) or at the individual level (e.g. education level, gender, and nationality) (for a summary of a number of research projects and the kind of control variables used see Paauwe & Richardson, 1997: 260). Delery and Doty (1996) characterize HRM theories under three headings: Universalistic, configurational, and contingent. The latter is especially interesting for our purposes. Contingency theory states that the relationship between the relevant independent variables (HRM policies and practices) and the dependent variable (performance) will vary according to contingency variables such as company size, age, technology, capital intensity, degree of unionization, industry/sector, ownership, and location.

The concept of '*fit*' (see Chapter 3) is also used in HRM theorizing to achieve a better understanding of the impact of context. Traditionally, we only distinguished two kinds of fit: *Horizontal (internal) fit*, which relates to the coherence and consistency among a set of related HRM practices, and *vertical (strategic) fit*, which relates to the relationship between HRM strategies and business strategy. Wood (1999), however, goes further in his review article on HRM and performance, distinguishing two additional types of fit:

- *Organizational fit*: Is the coherent fit between sets of HRM practices (HRM systems/bundles) and other systems within the organization.
- *Environmental fit*: Is the fit between HRM strategies and the organization's context.

Environmental fit is the focus of this chapter.

However, observing and labelling fit is insufficient in itself. We need a theory to assess the relationship between a set of HRM policies and practices, and to explore how these policies and practices relate to each other, interact, or are influenced by the context. Moreover, how do we define 'context'? How can we develop a theory that will make it possible to generate hypotheses about the relationship between HRM and its wider context?

In comparing USA-based HRM approaches to the situation in Europe, Brewster (1993), later complemented by Gooderham and Nordhaug (2011), discuss a range of differences and conclude with a plea to develop a 'European' model of HRM. According to these commentators, in the USA the HRM concept is based on notions of organizational independence and autonomy. However, in most European countries organizational autonomy is constrained at the national level by culture and legislation, at the organizational level by patterns of ownership/corporate governance, and at the HRM level by trade union involvement and consultative arrangements such as works councils (Brewster, 1993; Gooderham & Nordhaug, 2011). Therefore, what is needed is a model of HRM that considers such factors. Brewster proposes a European model, but with certain reservations because Europe cannot be conflated into a single entity: the differences between the European countries are sometimes greater than the difference between, for example, Germany and Japan or between the UK and USA (see Harzing & Sorge, 2003). Similarly, Gooderham and Nordhaug (2011) suggest that a dual-level framework is required to understand European-level HRM, particularly because of differences between organizations within countries too. They propose that HRM is affected both at an institutional level (culture, legislation, role of the state, trade union influence) and at a firm level (corporate strategy and HRM strategy).

What may be desirable in our increasingly global context is a universally applicable model, a way of theorizing that can be applied in any context: a theory that can accommodate the enormous variety of HRM policies and practices, as well as the various contextual factors involved. Commentators have attempted to achieve this. For example, Poole (1990) has criticized a number of HRM models, Beer and colleagues' model among others, suggesting adding the factors of globalization, power, and strategic choice. Hendry and Pettigrew (1990) proposed broadening HRM models by including economic, technical, and socio-political topics, which include a range of factors that influence strategic decision-making in HRM. Of course, all these authors emphasize that they do not want to fall into the trap of contingent determinism. There is, and there should be, leeway for the actors involved to make strategic choices. These notions are explicit in the field of IR, which has a tradition and a well-developed range of theoretical models for carrying out context-dependent comparative research. This leads us to explore the IR field in greater detail to inform our understanding of HRM.

4.3 **The interaction between HRM and IR**

From its inception, the concept of HRM and its relationship with and implications for the area of IR have received a lot of attention (see de Nijs, 1996; Guest, 1987; Poole, 1986; Storey, 1989; Storey & Sisson, 1993). We are especially interested in what we can learn from IR theory, and modelling in particular, for the development of an integrated framework for HRM that explicitly considers context. The classic Dunlop IR model is based on systems thinking and distinguishes not only context but also actors and shared ideologies. Context, which, according to Dunlop (1958: 48), is decisive in shaping the rules established by the actors in an IR system, is subdivided into the following three domains:

- technological characteristics of the work place and community;
- product and factor markets and/or budgetary constraints;
- political domain or the locus and distribution of power in society.

The term 'actors' refers to hierarchies of managers (and their representatives), hierarchies of workers (and their representatives), and specialized governmental agencies. Shared ideology is defined as a set of ideas and beliefs commonly held by the actors to bind or integrate the system together as an identity (Dunlop, 1958: 53). According to Dunlop (1958: ix), the task of a theory in IR is 'to explain why particular rules are established in particular industrial relations systems and how and why they change in response to changes affecting the systems'. The roles of actors are limited to how they adapt the rules to changes that occur within the three domains. The model can be applied at different levels of IR: National, industry sector, and organizational.

4.3.1 CONSTRUCTIVE CRITICISM

Over the years, Dunlop's IR model has served as a focal point both in practice as well as in terms of the criticism and suggestions for modification it has provoked. The assumptions upon which Dunlop's model is based (pluralism, positivism, and functionalism) have particularly aroused much criticism. Based on an overview by Schilstra (1998: 20), we highlight the main criticisms of Dunlop's systems thinking:

- Behavioural factors are virtually absent from Dunlop's framework. Although he emphasizes actors and their interactions, he neglects to analyse behavioural factors and treats interaction as a black box.
- Dunlop concentrates on rules and procedures as output, as dependent variables of the system. He does not explain the dynamic interactions, the process of how and when actors determine the rules (Schilstra, 1998: 20; see also Bain & Clegg, 1974: 92; and Blain & Gennard 1970: 403). This means that the emphasis is on the product, the web of rules, and not on the process of rule-making itself.
- Behaviour is mainly considered to be adaptive. It almost exclusively results from the context and changes therein (Schilstra, 1998: 22).
- Dunlop's focus on rules implies a focus on the output of the system. The idea of a 'web of rules' and the subsequent focus on job regulation seems to reflect a conservative bias.

The approach only concentrates on accommodation and equilibrium, not on conflict and change (Schilstra, 1998: 23).

4.3.2 THE NOTION OF STRATEGIC CHOICE

In his search for comparative frameworks in order to analyse IR in different contexts, Poole (1986: 11) states that the main thrust of his theoretical position is that variations in IR institutions and practices have their roots in the strategic choices of the parties in the employment relationship. The first application of the concept of strategic choice (Child, 1972) to the field of IR can be traced back to authors such as Walker (1969), Poole (1986), and Kochan, McKersie, and Cappelli (1984). Kochan and colleagues (see Figure 4.1) extensively adapted and added to Dunlop's original framework. Their amendments included the following:

- They saw a more active, as opposed to merely adaptive, role for management by introducing the notion of strategic choice. Of course, all parties involved can make strategic decisions but Kochan, McKersie, and Cappelli (1984: 17) consider management to be the dominant party in this respect.

- They included more and interrelated levels of IR. Next to the functional level of collective bargaining itself, they also included strategic and workplace levels in their analysis. The strategic level, by definition, concerns long-term and high-level planning and encompasses, from a management point of view, the strategic role of human resources. In much of their work, the strategic level is considered on a par with the corporate level. Kochan, McKersie, and Cappelli (1984: 21) explicitly stress that theory should allow an exploration of both content and the process of strategy formation. The workplace level relates to factors such as supervisory style, worker participation, job design, and work organization (Kochan, Katz, & McKersie, 1986: 17).

- They consider that the concept of strategy in IR is only useful if actors have some discretion over decisions. As this is usually the case, there is no place for environmental determinism of the kind suggested by Dunlop (1958).

- They say that the various levels interact and because different ideologies dominate each level, instability and conflict are inevitable. However, it is only at the functional level, the level of collective bargaining, that there is a need for a common ideology to bind the system together.

4.3.3 DIFFERENT RATIONALITIES

According to Poole (1986: 13), the concept of strategy encapsulates, at a more abstract level, the idea of overall design within social action—an overall design based upon

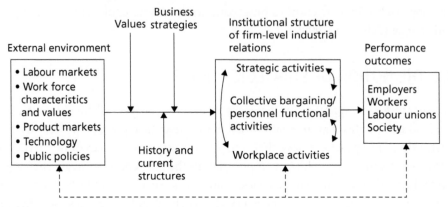

Figure 4.1 General framework for analysing IR issues
Source: Kochan, Katz, and McKersie (1986: 11).

rationality and calculus in the pattering of decisions. Following this line of reasoning, he associates the concept of strategy with the general categories of social action as follows:

- Instrumental-rational refers to the means to utilitarian ends (reflecting material interests and the will to power). Weber (1946) labels this 'zweckrationalität'.
- Value-rational refers to ethical, aesthetic, religious, political, or other ideals (involving identification and commitment). Weber (1946) labels this 'wertrationalität'.
- Affect/emotional refers to the actor's specific affects and feelings (sentiments and emotions can enhance value rational commitments).
- Traditional refers to ingrained habits (the institutionalization of previous strategic decisions of either a utilitarian or an idealistic character).

In the field of HRM, these four kinds of social action and their related rationalities and values are particularly relevant in shaping policies and practices. From an economic and managerial perspective, very often only the instrumental-rational perspective is taken into account. Yet, especially when involved in the shaping of employment relationships, other categories of social action, based on values, affect, and traditions, are at stake.

Kochan, Katz, and McKersie (1986) also attach importance to the role of values, which stems from different rationalities, and the role of the history and processes of institutionalization. The framework presented in Figure 4.1 summarizes their conceptualization.

Summarizing, we conclude that the related field of IR has a lot to offer. What have we learned so far?

- The importance of the context subdivided into the economic, technological, and political domain.
- The notion of strategic choice and discretion.

- That different levels of analysis interact and do not necessarily share the same kind of ideology.
- That there are different types of rationality.
- The importance of values and ideology.
- It is vital to include actors and a social action perspective alongside a systems perspective.
- The importance of history and processes of institutionalization, that gives us a sound theoretical basis for the inclusion of context in the study of HRM and a way to explore the effect of context on strategy, HRM, and performance.

4.4 **Institutionalism and HRM**

The idea that organizations are deeply embedded in wider institutional environments suggests that organizational practices are often either direct reflections of, or responses to, rules and structures built into their larger environments (Powell & DiMaggio, 1991). Jaffee (2001: 227), in a clear introduction to institutional theory, states that:

[V]iewing organisations as institutions means that organisations have a history, a culture, a set of values, traditions, habits, routines and interests. This contrasts with the economic or bureaucratic view of organisations that views organisations as formally rational instruments for the realization of clearly defined objectives. Calling organisations 'institutions' means that they are not simply black boxes that produce goods and services, but human organisations driven by emotion and tradition . . .

Thus, institutional theory combines a rejection of the optimization assumptions of rational actor models popular in economics with an interest in institutions as independent variables (Powell, 1998: 301). The process of institutionalization itself can be defined as 'the processes by which societal expectations of appropriate organizational action influence the structuring and behaviour of organizations in given ways' (Dacin, 1997: 48). Selznick, one of the founders of institutional theory, used the term institutionalization in order to refer to the organizational policies and practices that become 'infused with value beyond the technical requirements of the task at hand' (Jaffee, 2001: 227).

In general, institutional theory shows how the behaviour of organizations is a response not solely to market pressures, but also to institutional pressures (e.g. from regulatory agencies, such as the state and professional bodies and from general social expectations and the actions of leading organizations) (Greenwood & Hinings, 1996).

In the beginning of the eighties, a group of USA-based sociologists presented themselves as *new* institutionalists (Meyer & Rowan, 1977). Academics such as Selznick, Meyer, Rowan, Scott, DiMaggio, Powell, and Zucker can be considered as the founding fathers (or, in the case of Lynne Zucker, mother) of neo-institutionalism. According to Greenwood and Hinings (1996), neo-institutionalism assumes that organizations conform to contextual expectations in order to gain legitimacy and increase their probability of survival. For an extensive treatment of the differences between old and new institutionalism we refer to Powell and DiMaggio (1991).

With respect to our topic, the embeddedness of the relationship between HRM and performance, the contribution made by DiMaggio and Powell (1983) is important. They state that rational actors make their organizations increasingly similar as they try to change them (homogenization). The concept that best captures the process of homogenization is isomorphism. DiMaggio and Powell (1983) say that *isomorphism* is a constraining process that forces one unit in a population to resemble other units that are exposed to the same set of environmental conditions.

There are two types of isomorphism: Competitive and institutional. *Competitive isomorphism* assumes a system of rationality, which emphasizes market competition, niche change, and '*fit*', and is most relevant where free and open competition exists. However, for a more complete understanding of organizational change, DiMaggio and Powell (1983) focus more on an alternative perspective and that is *institutional isomorphism*. Three institutional mechanisms are said to influence decision-making in organizations: *Coercive mechanisms*, which stem from political influence and the problem of legitimacy; *mimetic mechanisms*, which result from standard responses to uncertainty; and *normative mechanisms*, which are associated with professionalization. Coercive influence refers to the formal and informal pressures exerted by other organizations upon which a firm is dependent, as well as to the cultural expectations held in society. No wonder neo-institutionalism is linked to the resource dependency theory (e.g. Pfeffer & Salancik, 1978; Oliver, 1991; Zucker, 1977) and population ecology theory (e.g. Hannan & Freeman, 1977; Trist, 1977). In 2008, Scott proposed three pillars of institutions, which are similar to the institutional mechanisms DiMaggio and Powell (1983) discuss. He identifies the regulative, normative, and cultural cognitive pillars, which are closely related to, respectively, coercive mechanisms, normative mechanisms, and mimetic mechanisms.

Lammers, Mijs, and Noort (2000) state that neo-institutionalism criticizes the 'functionalistic contingency approaches' of the sixties, as these approaches assume that actors are rational. According to the authors, neo-institutionalists believe in the 'non-rationality' of processes at all levels in society, that is, the micro (individual and organizational), meso (sector or industry), and macro levels (national or international). The central theme in new institutionalist approaches is the study of processes of cognitive and normative institutionalism, whereby people and organizations conform to social and cultural influences *without thinking* (Lammers, Mijs, & Noort, 2000). Without thinking, in the sense that these normative influences are *taken-for-granted* assumptions (Zucker, 1977) that actors perceive as being part of their objective reality.

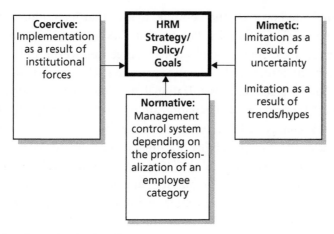

Figure 4.2 HRM and new institutionalism

Source: Paauwe & Boselie (2003).

Coercive mechanisms in our field of enquiry (HRM) include, amongst others, the influence of social partners (the trade unions and works councils), labour legislation, and government. Mimetic mechanisms refer to imitations of the strategies and practices of competitors as a result of uncertainty or fashionable fads in the field of management. Organizations' current (2017) interest in abandoning annual performance appraisals (e.g. Buckingham & Goodall, 2015) could be a typical example of a mimetic mechanism in the field of HRM. Normative mechanisms refer to the relationship between management policies and the background of employees in terms of educational level, job experience, and professional networks. According to Powell and DiMaggio (1991), these networks, in particular, encourage isomorphism. Professional networks consist of, for example, universities and professional training institutes that develop and reproduce (taken-for-granted) organizational norms among professional managers and staff specialists in the different functional areas of finance, marketing, accounting, and HRM.

In Figure 4.2 we schematically give an overview of the way in which the three mechanisms, identified by Powell and DiMaggio (1991), have an impact upon HRM.

4.5 **Institutional theory and change**

Institutional theory has often been criticized as only being able to explain the persistence and the homogeneity of phenomena. Another critique is that it does not explain the role of interest and agency in shaping action (Dacin, Goodstein, & Scott, 2002: 45–7). Research by people such as Greenwood and Hinings, Oliver and contributors to the special issue of *Academy of Management Journal* (edited by Dacin, Goodstein, & Scott,

2002) convincingly demonstrate the opposite, that is, that institutional theory can also account for change. The work by Powell and DiMaggio (1991), discussed in the Section 4.4, demonstrates how organizations change due to the influence of coercive mechanisms, mimetic forces, and normative pressures. However, these pressures imply that organizations in a specific organizational field (sector) will become more alike (i.e. isomorphism, homogeneity). Therefore, although Powell and DiMaggio (1991) are able to account for change, it is change in the same direction, and their approach does not take into account the possibility of uniqueness due to specific interests and human agency. Greenwood and Hinings (1996) explore this problem. They start from the premise that a major source of organizational resistance to change derives from the normative embeddedness of an organization within its institutional context. In order to be able to account for change, they explore the interaction between context and (strategic) choice. More specifically, they focus on the link between organizational context, intra-organizational dynamics, and the role of individuals in making choices. They state that change—unique change—can only occur if an organization decouples itself from the institutional context and reformulates its internal interpretive scheme. An organization's interpretative scheme consists of:

- Assumptions about the appropriate domain in which the organization should operate.
- Beliefs and values about the principles of organizing.
- Defined performance criteria to assess success.

Decoupling from the institutional context depends on an organization's internal dynamics, which include:

- The kind and degree of commitment to change.
- The power structures and coalitions favouring or opposing organizational change.
- The capacity to implement change: Greenwood & Hinings (1996: 1039) define this capacity as the ability to manage the transition process from one template to another.

In this respect, Kostova and Roth (2002) distinguish between implementation and internalization of practices. They state that: 'Implementation is expressed in the external and objective behaviours and the actions required, or implied, by the practice. Internalization is that state in which the employees at the recipient unit view the practice as valuable for the unit and become committed to the practice' (Kostova & Roth, 2002: 217). According to these authors, internalization is an important predictor of the persistence of the practice over time.

Oliver (1991) complements this dynamic perspective and makes it possible to account for change in the institutional framework by showing how organizations can respond to institutional processes and by discussing the antecedents of deinstitutionalization. Organizations use different strategies (options) to respond to institutional processes

Table 4.1 Strategic responses to institutional processes

Strategies	Tactics	Examples
Acquiesce	Habit	Following invisible, taken-for-granted norms
	Imitate	Mimicking institutional models
	Comply	Obeying rules and accepting norms
Compromise	Balance	Balancing the expectations of multiple constituents
	Pacify	Placating and accommodating institutional elements
	Bargain	Negotiating with institutional stakeholders
Avoid	Conceal	Disguising non-conformity
	Buffer	Loosening institutional attachments
	Escape	Changing goals, activities, or domains
Defy	Dismiss	Ignoring explicit norms and values
	Challenge	Contesting rules and requirements
	Attack	Assaulting the sources of institutional pressure
Manipulation	Co-opt	Importing influential constituents
	Influence	Shaping values and criteria
	Control	Domination institutional constituents and processes

Source: Oliver (1991).

ranging from acquiescence to manipulation. The scheme taken from Oliver (1991: 152) shown in Table 4.1 gives a full overview of the range of strategies/options.

A limitation of this overview is that the responses are formulated either in a conforming way ('acquiesce' and 'compromise') or in a negative way ('avoid', 'defy', 'manipulate'). If Oliver had also formulated positive and more constructive strategic responses such as 'lead', 'initiate', 'develop', the scheme would provide a more complete overview of strategic responses.

Oliver (1992: 564) went on to introduce the idea of deinstitutionalization and defined it as the process by which the legitimacy of an established or institutionalized practice is eroded or discontinued. In identifying the various factors that contribute to this process of deinstitutionalization, and thus to change, she distinguishes two different groups of determinants. Based on a summary by Jaffee (2001), these two groups can be described as follows:

- *Intra-organizational determinants*: 'Pressures may arise within the organization as new members are recruited, performance declines, power alignments shift, goals are more clearly defined or the organizational structure is transformed owing to diversification or mergers. These rather common events can conceivably threaten, or at least call into question, institutionalised patterns of organization and behaviour and stimulate change' (Jaffee, 2001: 235; Oliver, 1992: 579).

- *External environmental forces*: 'These might include increasing competition or environmental turbulence, changes in government regulations, shifts in public opinion, dramatic events or crises and changes in task environment relationships' (Jaffee, 2001: 235; Oliver, 1992: 579).

Colomy (1998) introduced human agency and interests into the debate on institutionalism and change. He rightly drew attention to the role of human agency in transforming the normative, cognitive, and regulative aspects of institutions (see also Jaffee, 2001: 236). Moreover, Dacin, Goodstein, and Scott (2002) summarize a range of studies (for example Kraatz & Moore, 2002; Sherer & Lee, 2002; Townley, 2002; Zilber, 2002) that explicitly pay attention to the roles of power, interests, and agency in determining how organizations interpret and respond to institutions: Actors are not passive, they make choices based on the interpretation of the meaning put forth (Dacin, Goodstein, & Scott, 2002: 47).

A more recent and less well-investigated area of institutional theory that accounts for the role of agency in (institutional) change processes is related to institutional logics (Friedland & Alford, 1991; Thornton, Ocasio, & Lounsbury, 2012). According to Scott and colleagues (2000: 170), institutional logics can be defined as 'the belief systems and associated practices that predominate in an organizational field'. These logics determine the suitability of managerial practices, such as HRM practices, in certain contexts and situations (Greenwood et al., 2010). As Ocasio (1997) explains, institutional logics are capable of guiding the attention of organizational decision-makers to specific issues and influencing decisions such that they will be coherent with the logic (Van den Broek, Boselie, & Paauwe, 2013). Therefore, this perspective accounts for change and agency in organizations due to the presence of institutional logics (Thornton, Ocasio, & Lounsbury, 2012). Often organizations are confronted with multiple and sometimes even conflicting institutional logics (Pache & Santos, 2010; Thornton & Ocasio, 2008), referred to as

---

TEXTBOX 4.1 CASE STUDY 'PRODUCTIVE WARD: RELEASING TIME TO CARE'

Similar to hospitals in other countries, Dutch hospitals are confronted by the challenge of needing, simultaneously, to enhance the quality and reduce the cost of care. Several scholars (e.g. Kitchener, 2002; Reay and Hinings, 2009; Ruef & Scott, 1998; Scott et al., 2000) acknowledge this development by indicating shifts in institutional logics in the health-care field, from a professional logic to a market logic. The traditional professional logics mean that factors such as prestige and technical quality determine the legitimacy of services (Kitchener, 2002), while the market logic primarily views cost reduction as an important parameter (Reay & Hinings, 2009). Nowadays, both professional and market logics seem to be affecting the health-care industry, for example, by influencing decision-making and implementation processes around the adoption of HRM-related innovations.

In a longitudinal case study ('Productive Ward: Releasing Time to Care'), insights into the adoption, decision-making, and implementation process of an apparently hybrid innovative practice were explored. Semi-structured interviews, focus groups, document studies, and observations were conducted to gather data. The case involves a quality improvement programme that aimed to empower nursing staff in order to improve the care processes in their wards, the aims being to release more time for direct patient care ('Releasing Time to Care'), a higher quality of care, more satisfied patients and nurses, and a decreasing amount of waste ('Productive Ward'). This is an interesting innovation to study in the health-care context, because, at first glance, the programme seems to combine the two logics with which hospital organizations are confronted. The title of the case alone suggests its hybrid nature, incorporating both a nursing professional logic ('Releasing Time to Care') and a market logic ('Productive Ward').

Initially, the findings demonstrated that respondents referred to both types of logic when discussing the programme. The labelling and communication of the programme throughout the organization seemed to play an important role in this. Overall, however, the findings indicated that although appearing to incorporate both logics, in practice, the main goals were to accomplish those aims that suited the market logic rather than both logics simultaneously. In addition, internal presentation of the programme as fitting the professional logic of nurses did not deliver intended results, partly because of the suspicion that was created among nurses due to the double labelling of the programme.

Source: Van den Broek, Boselie, & Paauwe (2013).

institutional complexity. Textbox 4.1 presents a case study of the adoption and implementation of an HRM-related innovation process in such an institutionally complex field, health care.

4.5.1 TOWARDS A SYNTHESIS

So far, we have outlined:

- The process of institutionalization that aims at bringing about stability, legitimacy, and homogeneity.
- The range of strategic responses open to organizations in reacting to institutional pressures.
- The process of deinstitutionalization (due to environmental and/or intra-organizational forces).
- The role of human agency in changing institutions.

The great variety of perspectives of institutional theory put forward by different authors that we have reviewed so far requires some kind of synthesis. Scott (1994) produced such a synthesis and this is presented in the schematic overview of the cyclical and iterative process by which institutions develop, reinforce, *and* change (see Figure 4.3).

As can be seen, institutions are made up of three components:

- meaning systems and related behaviour patterns, which contain
- symbolic elements, including representational, constitutive, and normative components, that are
- enforced by regulatory processes.

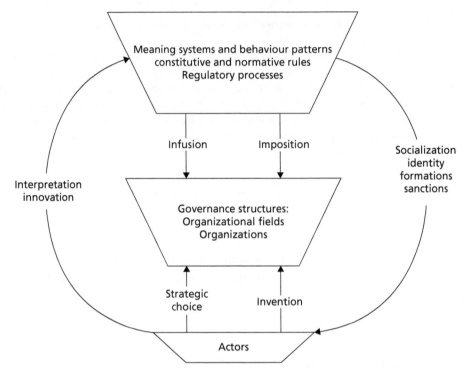

Figure 4.3 Institutions: A layered model

Source: Scott (1994).

Meaning systems refer to the creation of shared meanings, which are indispensable in collective activity. Meaning systems give rise to organizations as well as to distinctive fields of organizations. As meanings arise, they are preserved and modified by human behaviour, making related actions and patterns of behaviour just as important. The importance of human agents is illustrated by the arrows linking institutional elements with actors (see Figure 4.3). A meaning system must incorporate different kinds of rules in order to qualify as an institution. Representational rules are used to formulate the collection of knowledge claims including empirically based observations and fundamental assumptions; for example, that water flows downhill and that foxes chase rabbits (Scott, 1994: 60). Constitutive rules describe the nature of actors and their capacity for action, defining their interests, rights, and capacities. Normative rules, finally, exist in the expectations others have of our behaviour and become internalized through socialization processes. Examples are that, as a citizen, one should vote or that one should not throw any waste out of the car window.

The regulatory processes are the enforcement mechanisms that back the institutional rules, either in formally designed and centralized form or in informally administered and decentralized shape. The regulatory processes can be defined on the basis of Powell and

DiMaggio's (1991) contribution; they distinguish three mechanisms (coercive, mimetic, and normative) for enforcing organizations to become more alike (institutional isomorphism), as outlined in Section 4.4.

Having defined institutions and regulatory processes, Scott moves on to the level of organizational fields, as can be seen in Figure 4.3. He states that institutional arguments are applied logically at the level of analysis of the organizational field, not at societal or individual organizational level. Powell and DiMaggio (1991: 64–5) define the concept of organizational field as 'those organizations that in the aggregate, constitute a recognised area of institutional life: Key suppliers, resource and product consumers, regulatory agencies, and other organizations that produce similar services and products'.

Having described how institutional arrangements might influence organizations, Scott discusses what organizational structures result from the influence. Based on different assumptions regarding the role of rationality and intentional action in organization design, he distinguishes two camps of authors and researchers. One camp builds on a bounded rationality model to describe how actors deal with economic choices and their known and assumed effects in designing organizational forms. The second camp sums up a number of reasons why this line of thought is incorrect. Current choices are constrained by existing structures, information is imperfect, outcomes often unanticipated, environments may change faster and more abruptly than expected, and dominant organizations may suppress the development of more efficient organizational forms. Related to HRM, Scott rightly draws our attention to the fact that both camps tell their part of the story and that we are in need of both.

4.6 **Summary and conclusion**

In this chapter, we have examined the context of HRM in detail. Our quest focused especially on finding appropriate theoretical frameworks for considering the context of HRM, since this is considered to be of importance when discussing the relationship between HRM and performance if we assume a debate between 'best practice' and 'best fit'. The best fit approach assumes a fit between HRM and a range of contingencies, including an organization's context.

HRM theorizing itself provided us with a range of clues. First of all there is the importance of environmental fit. The field of IR has a reputation for explaining differences in IR across countries on the basis of differences in context, be this politics, history, or differences in economic conditions. This comparative aspect has always been very important in the field of IR. Models can account for different systems of IR per country, but also per sector or industry. A short overview led to the following findings, which are relevant for the relationship between strategy, HRM, and performance:

• The context can be subdivided into the economic, technological, and political domain.

- Leeway, strategic choice, and discretion counteract a too deterministic perspective.
- National, industry sector, and corporate levels interact and do not necessarily share the same ideology.
- Different types of rationalities affect decisions in the fields of IR and HRM.
- Alongside a systems perspective, empirical reality demands an actor and social action perspective.
- History and processes of institutionalization are important.

Our quest ended in the realm of institutional theory, specifically neo-institutionalism. Discussing the contributions of a range of academics, we emphasized that, on the one hand, processes of institutionalization bring about stability, legitimacy, and homogeneity. However, on the other hand, organizations are subject to change, due to processes of deinstitutionalization, and human agency in selecting a range of strategic responses open to organizations that are reacting to institutional pressures. Having established the links between strategy and HRM, and the related importance of context, in Chapter 5 we move on to consider in greater detail the 'performance' element of the relationship.

5 HRM and performance

Achievements and challenges

5.1 Introduction

The association between human resource management (HRM) and performance has become a 'holy grail' or 'panacea' promising to link a new way of thinking about how people are managed in organizations with commensurate organizational goals. Guest's (1987) normative framework described the essence of HRM as moving away from 'personnel management' to a new way of managing people, which involved closer association to corporate strategy and business priorities. In turn, this meant more involvement of line management, and an increasing focus on HRM outcomes such as commitment, quality, and flexibility, which were expected to lead to improved job performance, and reduced turnover and absenteeism. As a result, 'human resources' could be used more cost-effectively, and became seen as more attractive sources of competitive advantage in firms.

'HRM' as a term has subsequently been adopted widely by practitioners and academics alike, and reached its heights of adoration to date when the first quantifiable evidence of the link between HRM and performance was published in the *Academy of Management Journal* in 1995 by Mark Huselid. Huselid (1995) demonstrated a significant positive correlation between human resource (HR) system sophistication and market value per employee among a range of publicly quoted firms in the USA. Following both praise and critique, many similar studies followed (e.g. Delery & Doty, 1996; Guthrie, 2001; Koch & McGrath, 1996; Wright, Gardner, & Moynihan, 2003), starting a surge of research in this field across both sides of the Atlantic (for a review, see Paauwe, 2009; Paauwe, Guest, & Wright, 2013). The HRM–performance relationship has, to date, been studied from many perspectives, ranging from organizational behaviour to sociology, from economics to industrial relations (IR). Studies incorporate various combinations of HRM practices, and focus on both the individual and organizational levels of analysis.

In the following sections, we guide you through this burgeoning research in the HRM–performance field. We first discuss what has been achieved to date (Section 5.2). Whereas in the past we have had to rely on individual studies (see Paauwe, 2004: 58–66), the field has now matured, and there are a number of review studies that have emerged since 2005. In fact, attempting to cite individual studies has almost become impossible: Since 1995, some 200+ empirical papers have been published on the HRM–performance relationship, demonstrating the prominence of the field amongst academics, consultants, and practitioners across the globe.

At the same time, there are many challenges still facing the field, such as missing elements; inappropriate theorizing with respect to the HRM and performance concepts; and a lack of insight in the underlying mechanisms and processes that explain *why* HRM practices and systems contribute to performance (the 'black box' phenomenon). These issues will be dealt with in Section 5.3. The following section (Section 5.4) then contributes towards solving the 'black box' problem by first exploring the various levels of analysis that come into play when we discuss the relationship between HRM and performance. Subsequently, we link each level of analysis (including individual, organizational, and societal) to possible solutions by describing theories that shed light on the underlying mechanisms.

Studies of HRM systems (bundles of HRM practices rather than individual practices) have become particularly prominent since 1995. Initially, a distinction was made between control- and commitment-oriented HRM systems (Walton, 1985), but a nuanced distinction between types of HRM systems, particularly high performance work systems (HPWSs) (e.g. Boxall & Macky, 2009; Messersmith et al., 2011; Subramony, 2009) has since flourished. This is the topic of Section 5.5. The various HRM systems emphasize different outcomes ranging from financial productivity markers to 'softer' indicators such as involvement, commitment, and well-being. The challenge here is how these 'hard' and 'soft' outcomes might be balanced. Based on a review of thirty-six studies (Van de Voorde, Paauwe, & Van Veldhoven, 2012), we explore whether a focus on both well-being and financial performance can be achieved simultaneously or whether these are competing goals. The outcome sets the stage for the discussion of a multidimensional perspective of performance in the final section (Section 5.6) of this chapter.

5.2 **Achievements to date**

The USA is the birthplace of HRM and performance research. Whilst academics in the UK were debating how personnel management was morphing into a more unitarist, managerialist HRM model (see, for example, commentators such as Legge, Guest, Storey, Purcell, Tyson, and Keenoy), US academics focused on finding evidence on how HRM could add value to the firm. The roots of HRM in the USA came from two well-known models: Beer and colleagues' (1984) Harvard model, and Fombrun, Tichy, and Devanna's (1984) Michigan school model. The former was considered more of a broader stakeholder model, and the latter as taking a more functional, managerial approach to HRM (for an overview of these two seminal works and its appreciation thirty years later see the special issue of *Human Resource Management*, May/June 2015).

Paauwe (2009) presents an overview of the empirical studies that were subsequently published on the HRM–performance link, with the ground-breaking work starting around 1994/5 (Arthur, 1994; Huselid, 1995; MacDuffie, 1995; Osterman, 1994). As this field matured, review studies started to emerge, one of the first of which was Paauwe and Richardson's (1997) summarizing framework. This framework started to clarify the difference between HRM outcomes (e.g. satisfaction, motivation, turnover) and organization outcomes (e.g. productivity, customer satisfaction, sales, profit). This raised one of the issues inherent in the field at that time: the need for greater conceptual clarity and theorizing in the HRM and performance relationship. By asking questions such as 'what does HRM mean', 'what does performance mean', and 'what is the level of analysis' (e.g. Guest, 1997), this gave rise to what became known as the 'black box' problem: What are the mechanisms that help to explain the link between HRM practices and policies on the one hand and organization performance on the other? Becker and colleagues (1997), Guest (1997), and Wright and Gardner (2001) started to develop models which included additional variables that helped to explain the linkage, such as motivation, creativity, and discretionary effort (see, for example, Table 5.1).

Progress in the HRM–performance field is therefore apparent, yet remains modest: the dominant review articles that have appeared draw cautious conclusions. Becker and Gerhart (1996) argue that the evidence to date suggests that HRM can be crucial, in the same way that Paauwe and Richardson (1997) suggest that HRM outcomes can in turn influence organization outcomes. Specifically, Huselid and Becker (2000) found that one standard deviation change in the HR system of a firm is associated with a 10–20 per cent increase in a firm's market value. As the rigor of studies in the field has continued to increase, more cautious notes have been sounded: Wright and Gardner (2003) still support the HRM and performance link, but comment that HRM practices are at least weakly related to firm performance. In this section, we discuss five critical review

Table 5.1 Linking HRM and performance

HRM strategy	HRM practices	HRM outcomes	Behaviour outcomes	Performance outcomes	Financial outcomes
Differentiation (Innovation)	Selection		Effort/ Motivation	High: Productivity Quality Innovation	Profits
	Training	Commitment			
Focus (Quality)	Appraisal		Cooperation		
	Rewards	Quality		Low:	Return on
Cost (Cost-reduction)	Job design		Involvement	Absence	investment
	Involvement	Flexibility	Organizational	Labour turnover	(ROI)
	Status and Security		citizenship	Conflict Customer complaints	

Source: Guest (1997: 270).

papers, published since 2005, which we believe help to summarize the achievements in the field to date.

Boselie, Dietz, and Boon (2005) analyse a comprehensive sample of 104 studies published in HRM, general management, and IR journals from 1994 to 2003. They explicitly focus on strategic HRM empirical studies, including multiple HRM practices and performance measures: 'HRM is conceptualized in terms of carefully designed combinations of such practices geared towards improving organizational effectiveness and hence better performance outcomes' (Boselie, Dietz, & Boon, 2005: 67). They conclude that much—though by no means all—of the empirical HRM research in its 'systems' form has been found to matter (in a positive sense) for organizational performance.

Performance itself can be measured in a multitude of ways. For example, Dyer and Reeves (1995) suggest three levels of outcomes:

- Financial (e.g. profit, sales, market share, Tobin's q, GRATE).
- Organizational (e.g. output measures such as productivity, quality, efficiency).
- HRM (e.g. employee attitudes and behaviours, such as satisfaction, commitment, intention to quit).

In their overview, Boselie, Dietz, and Boon (2005) conclude that financial measures are represented in half of all articles they studied. Profit is most common, followed by various measures of sales. This is, however, quite problematic. Financial indicators can be influenced by a whole range of factors (both internal and external to the organization) that have nothing to do with employees and their related skills or with the human capital pool. As noted by Kanfer (1994) and Guest (1997), the distance between some performance indicators (e.g. profit, market value) and HRM interventions can be too large and is potentially subject to other business interventions (e.g. research and development activities, marketing strategies, economic trends). There is, therefore, an argument to be made that we need performance indicators that are far more proximal that HRM practices can directly affect, such as changes in employee attitudes (motivation, commitment, trust) and behaviour (turnover, absence), associated with subsequent changes in outcomes at organizational level (e.g. productivity, quality of services and/or products).

Boselie, Dietz, and Boon (2005: 75) indicate that productivity (a more proximal indicator) is the most common and popular variable among the organization-level outcomes (Chang & Chen, 2002; Huselid, 1995; Ichniowski & Shaw, 1999; Kato & Morishima, 2002), followed by product and service quality (Jayaram, Droge, & Vickery, 1999; MacDuffie, 1995). As far as employee attitudes and behaviours are concerned, the most commonly used are employee turnover (Batt, 2002; Huang, 1997; Shaw et al., 1998) and absenteeism (Lowe, Delbridge, & Oliver, 1997), which can be determined by objective data. Subjective attitudinal measures of performance include job satisfaction (Guest, 1999; Hoque, 1999), commitment (Tsui et al., 1997), trust in management (Whitener, 2001), and negative outcomes such as stress and job–home spill over (Boselie, Dietz, & Boon 2005: 75).

The second study we focus on here, published by Wall and Wood (2005), was based on a selection of twenty-five mainly US-based top-journal studies. They conclude—even more cautiously—that the evidence for an effect of HRM on performance is promising but only circumstantial, due, for the most part, to inadequate research design. Thus, nineteen of the twenty-five studies they examined report some statistically significant positive relationships between HRM practices and performance. The effect sizes, however, are typically small, with the majority of studies also failing to pay sufficient attention to whether it is the HRM system as a whole generating the effects, or just specific components/individual practices (Wall & Wood, 2005: 453). Overall, therefore, they conclude that 'the existing evidence for a relationship between HRM and performance should be treated with caution' (Wall & Wood, 2005: 454).

The third important study to include in this overview is by Combs and colleagues (2006). The first two studies we included are review studies, whereas this is a meta-analysis, which means that all the evidence is statistically aggregated rather than just being described. Combs and colleagues (2006) carried out this meta-analysis to establish whether high performance work practices (HPWPs, or high performance work systems—HPWSs) have a higher impact on performance than individual practices, and if HPWSs are more effective in manufacturing than in service settings. They carried out their meta-analysis based on ninety-two recent studies (encompassing a total of almost two thousand organizations) on the HRM–performance relationship. They found that an increase of one standard deviation in the use of HPWSs is associated with a 4.6 per cent increase in return on assets, and with a 4.4 per cent decrease in turnover. Hence their conclusion that: 'HPWPs' impact on organizational performance is not only statistically significant, but managerially relevant' (Combs et al., 2006: 518). They also established that HPWSs have a stronger effect than individual HRM practices. The effect size among manufacturing firms was almost twice as large as among service firms. They explained that this may be due to the more complex man–machine/technology interfaces in manufacturing that require more training and instruction (Combs et al., 2006: 520). Another reason, according to Combs and colleagues (2006: 520) for the fact that HPWSs affect manufacturers more is: 'that whereas the full range of productive outcomes is largely under the control of manufacturers and thus potentially influenced by HPWPs, production outcomes among services are heavily influenced by customers' ability and willingness to participate (Bowen, 1986)'. 'Customers therefore limit the range of possible productive outcomes under the influence of HPWPs' (Combs et al., 2006: 520).

In our fourth study, Subramony (2009) carried out a meta-analysis focused on three different HRM bundles (see Table 5.2) and aimed at testing the value of bundling HRM practices on the basis of their empowerment, motivation, and skill-enhancing effects.

Table 5.2 The content of HRM bundles

Empowerment-enhancing bundles

Employee involvement in influencing work process/outcomes

Formal grievance procedure and complaint resolution systems

Job enrichment (skill flexibility, job variety, responsibility)

Self-managed or autonomous work groups

Employee participation in decision-making

Systems to encourage feedback from employees

Motivation-enhancing bundles

Formal performance appraisal process

Incentive plans (bonuses, profit-sharing, gain-sharing plans)

Linking pay to performance

Opportunities for internal career mobility and promotions

Health care and other employee benefits

Skill-enhancing bundles

Job descriptions/requirements generated through job analysis

Job-based skill training

Recruiting to ensure availability of large applicant pools

Structured and validated tools/procedures for personnel selection

Source: Subramony (2009: 746).

This approach to HRM relates to the 'AMO' theory of ability, motivation, and opportunity (Appelbaum et al., 2000), whereby the latter is defined by Subramony as 'empowerment enhancing'. In total, sixty-five empirical studies (239 effect sizes) are included, published from 1995 to 2008, which link HRM practices and bundles with business outcomes.

Subramony (2009) establishes that the three bundles have significant and positive relationships, with outcomes like employee retention, operating performance (e.g. labour productivity, reduction of waste), and financial performance. Moreover, the three bundles correlate more strongly 'with business outcomes than their constituent practices' (Subramony, 2009: 753), which confirms the conclusion by Combs and colleagues (2006) that bundles/systems have a stronger effect than individual HRM practices. In a similar vein, Subramony (2009) also confirms that the studies conducted in manufacturing samples show significantly larger effect sizes than those based on samples from the service sector.

The fifth and final study in this overview stems from Jiang and colleagues (2012). This meta-analytic study explores the mechanisms between HRM systems and both proximal outcomes (human capital and motivation) and distal outcomes (turnover, operational performance such as labour productivity, and financial performance). By including human capital and motivation as mediating variables/intermediate outcomes, the authors are able to reveal more about the underlying mechanisms through which HRM is associated with different organizational outcomes. As with Subramony (2009), Jiang and colleagues (2012) conceptualize HRM practices in terms of three distinct dimensions: Skill-enhancing, motivation-enhancing, and opportunity-enhancing. Skill-enhancing implies strengthening human capital, and motivation-enhancing HRM practices imply increasing the motivation of employees. These two sets are selected as 'the most critical mediating factors' (Jiang et al., 2012: 1276). By distinguishing different sets of HRM practices, the authors also shed more light on differential outcomes. For example, skill-enhancing practices mainly increase human capital and, to a lesser degree, have an impact on motivation. This study involves 116 papers and includes over 30,000 organizations in total.

Jiang and colleagues' (2012) findings reveal that all three HRM dimensions have significant and positive effects on human capital and motivation, and that, as hypothesized, skill-enhancing HRM practices explained the largest percentage of variance in human capital. Motivation-enhancing and opportunity-enhancing HRM practices had a significantly stronger effect on motivation than the skill-enhancing set of HRM practices, as was expected. The authors also found that operational- and employee-level outcomes had a mediating effect on the relationship between HRM practices and financial outcomes: 'In sum, these results support that human capital, employee motivation, voluntary turnover, and operational outcomes partially mediated the relationships between skill-enhancing and motivation-enhancing HR dimensions and financial outcomes and fully mediated the relationship between opportunity-enhancing HR practices and financial outcomes' (Jiang et al., 2012: 1275) (see Figure 5.1).

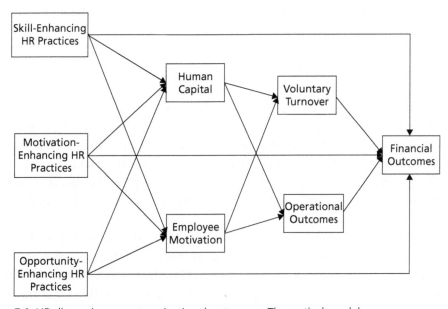

Figure 5.1 HR dimensions on organizational outcomes: Theoretical model

Source: Jiang and colleagues (2012: 1274).

To summarize, we can conclude that—in line with the studies presented and paraphrasing Wright and Gardner (2003: 312)—in the course of two decades evidence has mounted to show that HRM practices, be they individual or bundled in a system, are, at least to some extent, related to firm performance. Undoubtedly, though, there are still significant methodological and theoretical challenges with regard to furthering our understanding of this relationship. Some of these challenges are highlighted in Section 5.3.

5.3 Challenges in HRM and performance research

As we have seen in Section 5.2, no matter what perspective we take, there is definite evidence emerging of a link between HRM and performance, borne out by, if nothing else, the number of studies being undertaken and level of interest in the field. Yet, despite this evidence, many commentators remain sceptical of both HRM as concept, and of the HRM and performance link (see Fleetwood & Hesketh, 2010; Guest, 2011; Kaufman, 2015, Keegan & Boselie, 2006; Keenoy, 1997; Legge, 1995, 2005). Some make the argument that: 'empirical evidence for the existence of an HRM–performance link is inconclusive [...] a statistical association in, and of itself, constitutes neither a theory nor an explanation' (Hesketh & Fleetwood, 2006: 678). Meanwhile, Kaufman (2015: 400) refers to the fact that most regression studies are based on cross-sectional data, which makes it difficult to infer causality in the majority of studies, and so many people remain unconvinced. There are both theoretical and methodological issues at play here, as we discuss.

5.3.1 LEVELS OF ANALYSIS

A common problem, particularly in earlier HRM and performance research, has been confusing the levels of analysis in a study. Typically, a study will distinguish between both HRM practices and performance outcomes that can be measured at the individual and/or organizational level. These are two distinct levels of analysis and should be clearly identified; in the same way, we should not confuse measuring HRM in terms of individual practices or bundles/systems of practices. These are two fundamental ground rules for HRM and performance research.

At a theory level, analysing the content of 104 empirical articles, Boselie, Dietz, and Boon (2005) conclude that the three most commonly used theories are: Contingency theory, the resource-based view (RBV), and the AMO framework. Contingency theory and RBV are both situated at the organizational level, whereas the AMO framework focuses on the importance of taking into account variables at the individual level, in addition to the organization level, such as employee 'A'bilities (skills and competencies),

'M'otivation, and their 'O'pportunity to participate. These three theories reflect different traditions in HRM research: Contingency theory and RBV are mainly focused on the performance effects of HRM from a business perspective, whereas the AMO framework has its foundations in industrial and organizational psychology and can be applied both at the individual level of analysis as well as at the organizational level.

Wright and Boswell (2002) have contributed to this debate by distinguishing between macro (strategic, organization-level) and micro (individual-focused) HRM research. This highlights the importance of multi-level analysis to the field (see Klein & Kozlowski, 2000; Wright & Boswell, 2002: 266), as well as the application of appropriate theorizing that can combine organizational and individual level foci, such as AMO and psychological contract theory (Guest, 1999; Rousseau, 1995). An important point here is, as we discussed in Chapter 3 (Figure 3.3) when considering alignment or fit, that HRM practices can be considered from the perspective of how the organization intended them in their design, how they are actually implemented by line managers throughout an organization, or how an individual employee actually experiences the practice for himself or herself in the workplace. This differentiation between intended, enacted, and experienced (Nishii & Wright, 2008) is critical to understanding the HRM and performance link. As Guest (1999: 22) found, when HRM practices result in employees experiencing a high-involvement work climate, they are more likely to report a more positive psychological contract, and hence greater job satisfaction, job security, and motivation, and lower levels of work pressure.

In brief, in the exploration of the HRM and performance relationship, it is important not to forget about the employees! As suggested by Peccei, Van de Voorde, and Van Veldhoven (2013), there are many employee-related pathways that link HRM and organizational performance. Figure 5.2 summarizes some of these linkages. Nevertheless, too many studies that only consider the macro-level HRM strategies and the organizational-level

Figure 5.2 Employee-related pathways linking HRM and organizational performance

Source: Peccei and colleagues (2013: 19).

performance indicators, although valuable in showing added value, will limit our ability to explain the mechanisms by which those strategies convert into bottom-line outcomes, that is, through the attitudes and behaviours of employees. In other words, we also need studies that include more proximal, micro-level HRM measures and outcomes to help understand this HRM–performance relationship in greater detail. This also addresses the calls by critical theorists (e.g. Hesketh & Fleetwood, 2006, Keenoy, 1997; Legge, 1995) regarding the sometimes overly managerialist focus of HRM research (Paauwe, 2009).

Our radial overview of the HRM and performance literature has shown how the field has advanced from somewhat simplistic models when in its infancy in the 1990s, linking HRM practices directly with firm performance indicators, to far more advanced approaches to modelling the relationship. In this respect, Guest (2011) distinguishes the following phases in HRM and performance research: the *beginnings* (1980s) with conceptual frameworks linking strategy to HRM; *empiricism* (1990s) fuelled by Huselid (1995), Arthur (1994), and MacDuffie (1995); *backlash and reflection* (late nineties), especially focused on the methodological issues at play; *conceptual refinement* (more or less around the start of the new millennium), being inspired by expectancy theory, RBV, and institutional theory; *bringing the worker centre-stage* (overlapping with the previous stage), focusing on how workers respond to HRM practices; and finally *growing sophistication*, with contributions from Bowen and Ostroff (2004), who have drawn our attention to the importance of the processes that take place between design of HRM practices, their implementation, and how they are perceived by employees.

These more advanced approaches consider how organizational-level practices affect employee-level attitudes and behaviours, and, in turn, how these attitudes and behaviours affect aggregate-level HRM outcomes such as productivity, employee turnover, or well-being. Ultimately, these HRM outcomes are expected to influence bottom-line financial firm performance. This chain of effects is represented in Van Veldhoven's (2012) 'bath tub' model of HRM (see Chapter 3, Figure 3.4). This 'bath tub' approach involves multi-level forms of theorizing that explicitly seek to link phenomena across different levels of analysis: From the top of the tub at organizational level (e.g. systems of HRM practices), to the bottom of the tub at individual level (e.g. employee satisfaction and performance), and back again to the top at organizational level (e.g. productivity and financial performance). In Section 5.4, we deal more explicitly with these different levels of analysis and the theories available to help unravel the mysteries of the 'black box'.

5.3.2 CAUSAL ORDER

The issue of causality is a recurring theme as unfortunately most empirical papers exploring the relationship between HRM and performance are based on cross-sectional research. Cross-sectional research (i.e. all independent, intervening, and dependent variables are measured at the same moment in time) can only represent an association between HRM and performance rather than testing causality. Although appropriate theorizing can help draw conclusions in cross-sectional research with regard to causal order, this can become problematic, especially in the case of using distal financial indicators.

A literature review by Wright and colleagues (2005) identified sixty-six empirical studies that analysed the relationship between HRM practices and organization-level performance. The vast majority of these studies were actually found to have used a post-predictive research design, that is, 'it measures HR practices after the performance period, resulting in those practices actually predicting past performance' (Wright et al., 2005: 412). Only a small number of studies actually assessed HRM practices and related them to performance at a subsequent point in time (e.g. Huselid, 1995; Youndt et al., 1996). Causality is therefore a major assumption that has been ignored in many studies in this field (Cook & Campbell, 1979; Wright & Haggerty, 2005; Wright et al., 2005).

Future research will benefit from focusing on developing appropriate research designs that are able to link HRM practices both to past performance (to check for reverse causality) and subsequent performance. More recent studies have started to do so (e.g. Guest et al., 2003; Van de Voorde, Paauwe, & Van Veldhoven, 2010; Van Veldhoven, 2005; Wright et al., 2005), and have found significant relationships in both directions. Wright and colleagues (2005: 437) therefore warn that the results 'suggest caution among both academics and practitioners in making any causal inference'.

An associated problem with some HRM–performance studies is related to common method bias: When both the independent and dependent variables are collected from the same respondents, as well as potentially being collected at a single point in time. This can introduce bias in the results, so it is preferable that different respondents provide the dependent and independent variable data. As Subramony (2009: 756) reports: 'the predictor-outcome ratings stemming from the same source ($\rho = .44$; 95% CI: .39; .50) were significantly larger in magnitude ($Z = 3.43$; $p < .01$) than those in which these ratings came from separate sources', confounding study results.

5.4 Unravelling the mysteries of the 'black box'

As we have seen throughout this chapter, there has been a great deal of research into the HRM–performance relationship, yet many commentators are still intrigued by the challenge of the 'black box' (e.g. Boselie, Dietz, & Boon, 2005; Wright & Gardner, 2003). A black box can be defined as 'an unclear mechanism going on between the input and the output of a relationship' (Boselie, Dietz, & Boon, 2005: 77). HRM is such a

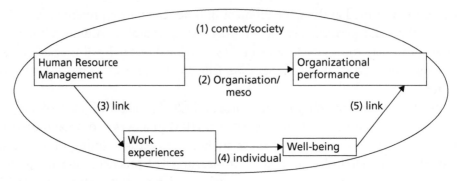

Figure 5.3 The black box and levels of analysis

Source: Paauwe and Blok (2015).

broad concept and is influenced by so many factors, ranging from the organization to the employee and his or her attitudes and behaviours. We therefore need to distinguish between these different levels of analysis in order to incorporate the many layers of factors. In other words, if we want to say something about the HRM–performance relationship and the black box that occurs in-between, we must distinguish between micro, meso, and macro levels of analysis.

The micro level of HRM is closely related to the fields of organizational behaviour and industrial and organizational psychology, and is focused on the individual employee and his or her attitudes and behaviours (Wright & Boswell, 2002). The meso level of HRM examines the impact of HRM practices at the organizational level, whilst the macro level of analysis is concerned with issues outside the organization and the influence of this external context. Different aspects of both HRM and performance operate at these various levels of analysis. We therefore propose that there are a variety of theories that can assist us in analysing and unravelling the mysteries of the black box present at the different levels of analysis. Figure 5.3 depicts these different levels of analysis and their related black boxes (Paauwe & Blok, 2015). We now address each of the five identified 'black boxes' in turn.

5.4.1 BLACK BOX 1: CONTEXT/SOCIETAL LEVEL OF ANALYSIS

Organizations form an integral part of society, and, as such, the HRM decisions taken inside organizations are influenced by events at the (macro) organizational, industry, national, and international level (e.g. through the actions of governments, competitors, and employee and employer representative bodies). In other words, it is important to understand the societal context of the organization when trying to unravel the HRM and performance relationship.

Dominant theories that explain processes at this level of analysis include institutional theory (DiMaggio & Powell, 1983; Meyer & Rowan, 1977; Scott, 1995)—as discussed extensively in Chapter 4; the five-forces theory (Porter, 1985); and the contextually based theory of the firm by Paauwe (2004). Porter (1985) argued that firms should analyse their competitive environment before selecting an appropriate strategy. Based on the five-force factor model that describes the attractiveness of a market, an organization is able to establish the extent to which it is able to be competitive in that market based on the business model adopted. More recently, Paauwe (2004) developed the contextually based human resource theory (CBHRT), which depicts different dimensions and forces, including the product/market/technology dimension, the administrative heritage, and the social/cultural and legal dimension, that influence the shaping of HRM practices. The CBHRT combines both strategic management theories as well as a more institutional perspective (for an extensive treatment, see Chapter 6).

5.4.2 BLACK BOX 2: CONNECTING SOCIETAL AND ORGANIZATIONAL LEVELS OF ANALYSIS

At the organizational (meso) level of analysis, common theories used to explore the HRM–performance relationship include the RBV of the firm (Barney, 1991), AMO theory (Appelbaum et al., 2000), strategic balance theory (Deephouse, 1999), strategic climate theory (Schneider, 1990), and human capital theory (Becker, 1964). It is problematic, however, to specify these theories as operating purely at the organizational level as they often make the connection either between macro and meso level (RBV, strategic balance theory) or between the meso and micro level (strategic climate theory, human capital theory, AMO theory). For example, strategic balance theory analyses competitive forces to achieve competitive positioning, while simultaneously taking into account institutional factors in order to comply with legitimacy requirements. Subsequently, the two forces (competitive and institutional, both operating at macro level) determine the shape of work and employment practices (meso level). In another example based in AMO theory, employee abilities manifest themselves at the individual (micro) level of analysis, but also at the aggregated organization (meso) level in the form of human capital. Similarly, opportunities are provided by management and the organization, but manifest themselves at the individual level by the degree of autonomy the individual is experiencing. Authors like Jiang and colleagues (2012) and Subramony (2009) use the AMO model to differentiate between bundles of HRM practices that are either focused on strengthening abilities, motivation, or opportunity. These bundles operate at the organizational level of analysis, yet impact at the individual level of analysis.

5.4.3 BLACK BOX 3: CONNECTING ORGANIZATIONAL AND INDIVIDUAL LEVELS OF ANALYSIS

At the individual level of analysis, many theories (in addition to those discussed in Subsection 5.4.2)—especially within the domain of organizational behaviour and industrial and organizational psychology—are available to explain the HRM–performance relationship. This level is particularly focused on sending HRM signals towards employees that will affect them in such a way that they are willing to display 'desired' attitudes and behaviours and subsequent HRM outcomes in return. For example, if HRM practices are perceived as being beneficial by employees (e.g. flexible work arrangements), their attitude in the workplace is expected to be positive, and as a result employees may be willing to reciprocate with higher levels of effort or commitment. These processes are based on social exchange theory (Blau, 1964), and are often expressed through other related theories such as leader–member exchange (e.g. Gerstner & Day, 1997), perceived organizational support (e.g. Eisenberger et al., 1986), and equity theory (Adams, 1963).

Similarly, linking to the organization level, for example, strategic climate theory (Schneider, 1990) is built upon the interaction between the strategic climate at the organizational level and the perceptions of the employees at the individual level of analysis. The strategic climate is said to affect employee attitudes and behaviour towards strategic goals, and in so far as these perceptions are shared, they will in turn contribute to strategic climate as a concept at the organizational level.

5.4.4 BLACK BOX 4: INDIVIDUAL LEVEL OF ANALYSIS

At this individual level of analysis, we rely on the field of organizational behaviour as an important source of inspiration for unravelling the underlying mechanisms in the HRM–performance relationship. This black box concerns the processes occurring in the human mind that could be affected by HRM practices. Clues as to how this works can be found in theories such as organizational justice theory (e.g. Colquitt, Conlon, Wesson, Porter, & Ng, 2001), attribution theory (Heider, 1958), psychological contract theory (Rousseau, 1989), the 'broaden and build' theory (Fredrickson, 2001), and social contagion theory (Locher, 2002). These theories help our understanding of this level of analysis because they explain the part of the relationship that occurs between the attitude of an employee and the HRM outcomes.

Appealing in this respect is the research by Nishii, Lepak, and Schneider (2008), who have built on Heider (1958) to develop an application of attribution theory in the domain of HRM and performance. As with Bowen and Ostroff (2004), they focus on employee perceptions of HRM practices, yet they do so to assess what employees attribute to be the underlying reason HRM practices exist. For example, a climate for safety in a refinery or hospital might be perceived by employees as the sincere concern of management for the well-being of employees. However, some employees might perceive this climate as mainly motivated by a need to cut costs. The attributions employees make determine their attitudinal and behavioural response. Nishii, Lepak, and Schneider (2008) found support for a distinction between attributions that are positively related to employee attitudes, that is, *service quality* and *employee well-being*, and attributions that are expected to relate negatively to employee attitudes, that is, *cost reduction* and *employee exploitation*. The combined attributions of reducing costs and exploiting employees were found to be negatively associated with OCB (organizational citizenship behaviour), while the combined attributions of service quality and employee well-being had a strong positive effect on OCB. Attribution theory helps us to understand that the way in which employees interpret the underlying reasoning behind HRM practices will determine to a large degree their subsequent (positive, neutral, or negative) attitudes and behaviours.

There are many employee and organization factors that can ultimately affect the HRM–performance relationship. At the individual level, in addition to employee well-being, such factors include employee knowledge, skills, and ability; and employee relationships and coordination (Peccei, Van de Voorde, & Van Veldhoven, 2013: 19). More transactional models of HRM suggest that employees are also motivated to higher performance by extrinsic rewards (Tsui et al., 1997).

5.4.5 BLACK BOX 5: CONNECTING THE INDIVIDUAL LEVEL TO THE ORGANIZATIONAL LEVEL

This part of the HRM–performance relationship is the least explored to date. The processes that link individual employee outcomes to organizational performance have been subject to little attention from HRM researchers. Twenty years ago, the focus was primarily on micro- and macro-level theories. Nowadays, it is technically possible to test empirically the linkages between these two extremes. One theory that may help explain this particular process is relational coordination (Gittell, 2000).

Gittell's (2000) theory focuses on the coordination that is carried out by front-line workers themselves (and thus not only management), who are aware of their relationship and interdependency with other workers in order to achieve performance. As relational coordination is characterized by 'frequent, timely, problem solving communication, and by helping, shared goals, shared knowledge...' (Gittell, 2000: 517), this bundling—coordinating the work of front-line workers—will benefit both well-being and performance (see also Gittell, 2011). Relational coordination theory can be applied at the micro and meso levels of analysis and at any point in-between. The power of a network construct like relational coordination is its multi-level and nested design. Gittell, Seidner, and Wimbush (2010) demonstrated that relational coordination influences both group processes and performance in an organization. In a more general way, and thus less focused on the impact of strategic HRM, Van Veldhoven (2012) refers to the domain of organizational studies and more specifically coordination theory, as, for example, developed by Malone and Crowston (1994). Agency theory (Jensen & Meckling, 1976) in the field of economic organization theories is another example. Summarizing, we can conclude that the black box between HRM and performance will never be solved by applying any individual theory: It will always depend on the level of analysis and the kind of linkages being explored. We have to rely on a multitude of theories in the fields of HRM, organizational behaviour, and work and organizational psychology.

5.5 HPWSs: Balancing performance and well-being?!

This chapter has reviewed the evidence to date regarding HRM and performance and has concluded that there is some evidence to support the claim that HRM practices contribute to organizational performance (Combs et al., 2006; Jiang et al., 2012). At the same time, we have also raised questions regarding the field of research as a whole, particularly focusing on the challenges of appropriate levels of analysis to conduct HRM–performance research, and questioning the direction of causality: Do HRM practices improve firm performance, or does high firm performance increase the range and use of HRM practices? In answer to the latter question, we discovered that both are true (e.g. Wright et al., 2005). For the different levels of analysis challenge, we have provided a comprehensive overview of relevant theories that can help to explain the various 'black boxes' that occur in the HRM–performance relationship.

One of the challenges we have not yet tackled, however, is how to deal with the performance conundrum. We began by saying that performance could be measured at three levels (Dyer & Reeves, 1995): Financial outcomes, organizational outcomes, and HRM outcomes. What happens though when there is potential conflict between different levels of outcomes (e.g. profit versus employee well-being)? As attention in this field has shifted from its initial simple focus on financial firm performance outcomes, many commentators have called for more attention to employee-centred outcomes as performance indicators (see, for example, Boxall & Macky, 2009; Guest, 1997, 2011; Nishii & Wright, 2008, Paauwe et al., 2013).

We believe that studies that include both the managerial perspective (financial performance) as well as the employee perspective (employee well-being) are particularly interesting. Van de Voorde, Paauwe, and Van Veldhoven (2012) highlight how two different streams have emerged in the literature in this regard. The first stream is the 'mutual gains' approach, in which both employees and employers benefit from HRM (Appelbaum et al., 2000; Guest, 1997), whilst the second stream is the 'conflicting outcomes' approach in which 'HRM pays off in terms of organizational performance, but has no or even a negative, impact on employee well-being (e.g., Legge, 1995; Ramsay et al., 2000)' (Van de Voorde, Paauwe, & Van Veldhoven, 2012: 391). The following subsections explore what we term a 'balanced' approach to performance, investigating whether 'mutual gains' or 'conflicting outcomes' studies are winning the HRM–performance research debate. Related to this issue of balance is the emphasis on HPWSs. Is it only about increasing performance (in its operational or financial meaning) or do the different HPWSs have different foci and different conceptualizations of what performance means?

5.5.1 HPWSs

HPWSs are bundles of HRM practices designed to improve firm performance, and as such hold an important position in the HRM–performance debate. However, there is no single definition or description of what HRM practices constitute such a system. Based on our experience working with a number of organizations, the following are elements that are typically included in an HPWS:

- Challenging targets/customer-oriented units.
- Decentralization/delegation of decision-making.
- Work by semi-autonomous task groups/teamwork.
- Performance management linked to financial performance indicators.
- Business process reengineering → customer focus.
- Benchmarking performance → shareholder value.
- Creating and stimulating learning and development at all organizational levels.
- Information and communication: From top down to flowing in all directions.

To build on this, the characteristics of high performing organizations from an HRM perspective, as identified by Lawler III (2005), are illustrative. During the course of his career, Lawler III undertook a significant amount of research on the 'people' element in high performing organizations. His research resulted in the following common elements:

- Create a value proposition that defines the workplace.
- Hire people that fit the values, core competences, and strategic goals.
- Continuously train employees to do their jobs and offer them opportunities to grow and develop.
- Design work that is meaningful and provides feedback, responsibility, and autonomy.

- Have a mission, strategies, goals, values that employees understand, support, and believe in it.
- Have reward systems that reinforce core values and strategy.
- Hire and develop leaders who create commitment, trust, and a motivating work environment.

Based on their review of numerous academic studies, Boselie, Dietz, and Boon (2005: 72) indicate that the following practices are most often incorporated in an HPWS: Training and development, contingent pay and reward schemes, performance management (including appraisal), and careful recruitment and selection. Boselie, Dietz, and Boon (2005: 73) note that 'these might be seen to reflect the main objectives of most conceptualisations of a "strategic" HRM programme'. Pfeffer (1995) similarly identified thirteen HPWS practices ranging from employment security to incentive-based pay, and from self-managed teams to wage compression. This list in particular highlights how context-specific such a bundle of practices might be (i.e. self-managed teams might work well in one organizational setting but not in another, depending on the nature of the work or the motivation of employees).

Irrespective of context, what HPWSs do have in common is the 'systemic' effect: the fundamental idea underlying the notion of the HPWS is the synergistic effect of the range of HRM practices selected (Boxall & Macky, 2009). The systems are made up of a mix of work practices (i.e. the way the work is organized, e.g. self-managed teams) and employment practices (i.e. how people are managed: 'all the practices used to recruit, deploy, motivate, consult, negotiate with, develop and retain employees, and to terminate the employment relationship' (Boxall & Macky, 2009: 5).

5.5.2 MUTUAL GAINS OR CONFLICTING OUTCOMES PERSPECTIVE

HPWSs are designed to achieve high performance, but what do we mean by 'performance' in this respect? Some bundles of HRM practices are designed to achieve specific organizational outcomes, such as high commitment or high-involvement work systems (aimed at increasing employee commitment or involvement through appropriate HRM practices) (Boxall & Macky, 2009). Other HPWS bundles are more generally aimed at increasing bottom-line firm performance. What happens if an organization wants to develop an HRM system that can deliver bottom-line performance as well as employee and HRM outcomes such as well-being, commitment, and job satisfaction? Do we know whether the HRM–performance relationship is supported in this scenario?

Van de Voorde, Paauwe, and Van Veldhoven (2012) address the question of whether the focus on both well-being and financial performance can be achieved simultaneously (mutual gains) or whether these are conflicting goals. Whilst the mutual gains perspective is described by Peccei (2004) as the optimistic perspective—the HPWS is good for the organization and for employees—the conflicting outcomes perspective is the pessimistic view. This pessimism starts from the premise of organizational performance as a multidimensional concept (Paauwe, 2004): Employee well-being and organizational performance can be considered as parallel outcomes, engendered by different sets of HRM practices (Boxall & Purcell, 2008). This implies the need for a trade-off between the two, or as Van de Voorde, Paauwe, & Van Veldhoven (2012: 393) state: 'Enhancements in organizational performance are achieved at the cost of reduced employee well-being.' Authors such as Godard (2001), Ramsay, Scholarios, and Harley (2000), and Legge (1995) share this view, indicating that in organizations aiming for higher financial performance employees might experience higher stress levels due to increasing levels of work intensification.

In order to establish which perspective receives most empirical support (mutual gains or conflicting outcomes) Van de Voorde, Paauwe, & Van Veldhoven (2012) reviewed thirty-six quantitative studies (published between 1995 and May 2010), all of which encompassed multiple HRM practices, measures of organizational performance (operational, such as labour productivity and financial outcomes), and different indicators of well-being. Specifically, based on Grant, Christianson, and Price (2007), they distinguished between happiness well-being (satisfaction, commitment), relational well-being (trust, quality of relationships), and health well-being (stressors, strain, anxiety, burnout). They found that:

- Happiness well-being: '60% of the data points indicated a positive association between both HRM and happiness well-being and HRM and performance; as such, the results are largely in line with a mutual gains perspective' (Van de Voorde, Paauwe, & Van Veldhoven, 2012: 397).

- Relational well-being: 'The studies show that HRM is predominantly positively associated with relational aspects of employee well-being and with organizational performance. We found that almost 60% of the included data points provided evidence for a mutual gains perspective' (Van de Voorde, Paauwe, & Van Veldhoven, 2012: 399).

- Health well-being: 'the majority of the included data points show a negative relationship between HRM and health-related well-being, and no relationship between HRM and organizational performance. We therefore conclude that the preliminary evidence obtained for health-related well-being is most in line with the conflicting outcomes perspective' (Van de Voorde, Paauwe, & Van Veldhoven, 2012: 399).

In brief, the happiness and relational dimensions of well-being are linked with the mutual gains perspective, whereas the health dimension is not: the use of HPWSs may be associated with a health risk for employees in the form of job strain, stress, and subsequent effects in term of absenteeism and burnout. HRM practices aimed at increasing the level of well-being (happiness and relational/trust aspects), however, may act as a buffer for avoiding or reducing the health-related risks of HPWS (Jensen, Patel, & Messersmith, 2013).

5.6 Conclusions: Towards a multidimensional perspective on performance

In this chapter, we have argued for the development of a more holistic, multidimensional concept of performance, balancing both well-being and financial performance. This involves adopting a broad stakeholder rather than the narrow shareholder perspective. Organizations, individuals, and society at large are all impacted by this balancing act, based on how organizational actors address competitive, legitimacy, and fairness challenges. For individual employees, these decisions ultimately affect their well-being as 'human' resources; for organizations, these decisions impact the financial viability of the firm; and for societies, these decisions play into creating the overall conditions in which we all live and work as citizens.

In Chapter 6, we combine our theorizing thus far (on strategy, fit, institutional theory, and performance) to present the Contextual Strategic HRM Framework. This framework offers a way forward to understand better the strategy, HRM, and performance linkages that promise sustainable competitive advantage to organizations.

6 The Contextual SHRM Framework

6.1 Introduction

Based on our interest in the relationship between strategic human resource management (SHRM) and performance, so far we have presented a range of insights derived predominantly from the fields of strategic management, organizational behaviour, and industrial and organizational psychology, applying theories such as contextual fit, institutional theory, and the resource-based view (RBV) of the firm. These insights are substantiated by a burgeoning field of ongoing research in the area of SHRM and performance, giving rise to various concepts, approaches, and empirical results.

In this chapter, we develop and present our Contextual SHRM Framework. This framework builds on the work of Paauwe (2004), who first introduced the contextually based human resource theory (CBHRT). The framework explains how contextual factors influence HRM systems, which ultimately impact performance outcomes. We will first outline the background to the CBHRT before explaining how we have further developed the thinking behind this theory to present the revised Contextual SHRM Framework.

6.2 Background to the CBHRT

In Chapter 2, we provided an overview of the various approaches to strategic management. The CBHRT was based on various insights from the field of strategic management. Relating this field specifically to the issue of strategic HRM and performance, the CBHRT was based on the following design criteria:

- Both the process and content of strategy are relevant;
- Both the 'outside-in' perspective (Porter-like approaches) and the 'inside-out' perspective (RBV) should be included;
- Alongside (bounded) rationally, planned strategies, politics and related power positions and resources also play a role, which leads to an emergent and interactive approach to strategy development;

- In addition to competitive market forces, it is important to consider the social, legal, and cultural environment;
- Also shareholders are not the only stakeholders interested in the outcomes of strategic HRM. Customers, employees, and their representative bodies are also important parties.

In Chapter 3, we discussed the context of HRM in terms of the various types of fit, as distinguished in the field of strategic HRM modelling and theorizing. The CBHRT was also based on this thinking in its design:

- Apart from the well-known distinction between vertical (or strategic) fit and horizontal (fit), it is also important to take into account organizational and environmental fit.

In Chapter 4, we focused on context again, this time drawing from institutional theory. A closer examination of the field of industrial relations and the kind of models that have been developed since the seminal work of Dunlop (1958) has generated a range of insights with regard to why context should matter to the field of strategic HRM. Neo-institutional theory develops this thinking, focusing on the embeddedness of organizations (including HRM) in their wider institutional environments. The CBHRT drew from the following characteristics of this theorizing:

- The external environment can be subdivided into economic, technological, and political forces.
- Strategic choice and discretion of the actors involved (human agents) counterbalance a point of view with respect to the environment that would otherwise be too deterministic.
- The field of both HRM and industrial relations is characterized by different rationalities (economic and relational).
- Values and ideology play a role in the shaping of HRM policies.
- History and processes of (de)institutionalization play a significant role in the way in which HRM policies emerge.

Finally, in Chapter 5, we presented an overview of the ongoing research in the area of HRM and performance. Discussing and analysing the results, we developed a broad, multidimensional perspective on performance, which was at the heart of the CBHRT:

- Both financial performance and employee well-being are important in achieving organizational effectiveness in the long run.
- Human resources are not just resources designed to contribute to added financial value. Considering moral value, fairness, and legitimacy are also an integral part of the performance construct.
- Human resource management (HRM) is more than just being strategic and (financially) performance-oriented. It also involves the process of delivering services professionally.

- The very essence of the management of human resources expands beyond the boundaries of the organization, and is influenced by stakeholders and institutional arrangements inside and outside the organization.

These premises led to the concept of performance in the CBHRT being defined in three dimensions: Strategic, professional, and societal.

6.3 **An eclectic approach to building the CBHRT**

In the HRM and performance literature, the majority of classic SHRM models are based on open systems theory, which emphasizes that organizations can be described as input, transformation, and output systems involved in transactions in a given environment. This way of conceptualizing places a strong emphasis on functionalism, and results in models that delineate how many 'boxes' there should be between strategic impulses and final outcomes (e.g. Becker et al., 1997; Guest, 1997).

Open systems theory, however, theorizes at a very abstract level, and thus lacks the specific detail required to generate hypotheses in the field of SHRM. Commentators have expressed their concern with this lack of adequate theorizing (including Dyer, 1984; Zedeck & Cascio, 1984). Wright and McMahan (1992) were among the first to tackle this growing feeling of unease and offered a range of potentially useful theoretical perspectives in their widely cited paper, including RBV of the firm, behavioural perspective, cybernetic systems, agency and transaction cost theory, resource dependence/power model, and institutional theory.

Various commentators (e.g. Delery & Shaw, 2001; Paauwe & Boselie, 2003) have since acknowledged the importance of the RBV in SHRM research in particular. Inspired by Barney (1991), authors such as Wright, McMahan, and McWilliams (1994), Paauwe (1994), Kamoche (1996), and Boxall (1996) were among the first to introduce the RBV into SHRM research. They stated explicitly that people par excellence fit the criteria and assumptions of value, rareness, inimitability, and non-substitutability, which, according to Barney (1991), are the necessary conditions for organizational success.

Moving the field forward, in their overview of the field of organization sociology, Lammers, Mijs, and Van Noort (2000) discerned two main approaches to studying and analysing organizations: the 'systems' and the 'actors' perspectives. The 'systems' perspective perceives the organization as a socio-cultural entity, which is being kept together by shared goals, norms, and solidarity (inspired by the functionalist way of analysing organizations). The 'actors' perspective, in contrast, refers to the organization as a conglomerate or coalition of actors/parties. On the one hand, actors are willing to cooperate to benefit their own interests, but on the other, they can compete and block each other due to conflicting interests (building on conflict theory in the sociological tradition).

Lammers (1990) argues, however, that if we observe organizations and organizational phenomena (like SHRM), we cannot simply take one perspective or the other. We will always see goal-oriented systems emphasizing a common purpose, and we will always equally be able to discern power and conflict among competing actors. He labels this the *double character* of organizations: Systems and actors.

In a similar duality argument, the field of strategic management has experienced a paradigm shift from the 'outside-in' perspective of the 1980s (Porter, 1980) to the 'inside-out' and dynamic capabilities perspective of the 1990s (Teece, Pisano, & Shuen, 1997). We have since learned that it is wise to consider both perspectives simultaneously. The combination of market conditions and a firm's resources and capabilities enable a certain strategic positioning of the firm in order to fight competition and to achieve sustainable competitive advantage. This is an ongoing interaction, implying continuous renewal and organizational adaptation.

Lewin and Volberda (1999), discussing a framework for research on strategy and new organizational forms, emphasize the need to consider the joint outcomes of managerial intentionality, adaptation, and environmental selection. They label their approach as 'coevolution', defined as the joint outcome of managerial intentionality, environment, and institutional effects (Lewin & Volberda, 1999: 526): a firm's strategic and organizational adaptations coevolve with changes in the environment. Changes in the environment can be competitive, dynamic, technological, or institutional, for which the outcomes can be traced back to the interaction between managerial intentionality, organizational adaptation, and environmental dynamics (such as market pressures and institutional changes) (Lewin, Long, & Caroll, 1999: 535).

In a similar vein, based on a contrast between the assumptions of the RBV and institutional theory, Oliver (1997: 701) distinguishes two types of rationality: 'resource based theorists assume that managers make rational choices bounded by uncertainty, information limitations and heuristic biases, whereas institutional theorists assume that managers commonly make non-rational choices bounded by social judgment, historical limitations and the inertial force of habit'. As opposed to 'economic' rationality, which is motivated by efficiency and profitability, 'normative' rationality refers to choices induced by historical precedent and social justification.

Based on these theoretical foundations, Paauwe (2004) introduced the CBHRT. The RBV was an important assumption, but this is complemented by adopting perspectives from institutional theory, systems thinking, the actors' perspective, and coevolution. Paauwe (2004) took this eclectic but reasoned approach to building the CBHRT as he realized how highly relevant all of these sources are to achieving a better understanding of the relationship between strategy, HRM, and performance. Building from this starting point, we explore further the conceptual development of the CBHRT, and propose a revised framework that provides a more nuanced framework for analysing the connection between the firm's context, the business strategy, SHRM, and organizational performance.

6.4 **The CBHRT**

Commentators believe that people (human resources) encapsulate the general RBV assumptions of value, rareness, inimitability, and non-substitutability (Barney, 1991). In 1994, Paauwe—inspired by the RBV—developed the human resource-based theory of the firm. In 2004, Paauwe revised this theory to incorporate explicitly both the strategic market context and the institutional context into his theorizing, developing the CBHRT (see also Trompenaars & Coebergh, 2014). This theory (see Figure 6.1) incorporates elements of the contingency and configurational models (Delery & Doty, 1996), new institutional theory (DiMaggio & Powell, 1983), RBV (Barney, 1991), and is inspired by the Harvard approach (Beer et al., 1984).

In the CBHRT, two predominant dimensions in a firm's environment are argued to dominate the crafting of SHRM, albeit moderated by other internal factors. First, SHRM is determined by 'competitive' mechanisms. These mechanisms consist of demands arising

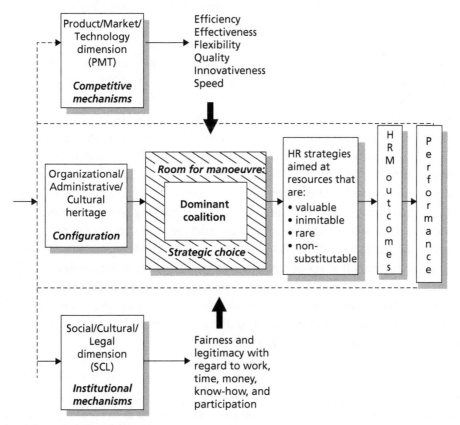

Figure 6.1 The contextually based human resource theory

Source: Paauwe (2004).

from relevant product–market combinations and appropriate technology (PMT), and are aimed at achieving certain desirable organizational capabilities, often expressed in terms such as efficiency, effectiveness, flexibility, quality, innovation, and speed. The RBV argues that a series of organizational capabilities are necessary for firm success, and that these capabilities require a firm's internal processes, systems, and management practices to meet customer needs, and direct both the skills and efforts of employees towards achieving the goals of the organization (Sparrow, Scullion, & Farndale, 2010).

This PMT dimension (competitive mechanisms) represents the tough economic rationality of domestic and international competition, and resembles the concept of competitive isomorphism that, according to DiMaggio and Powell (1983), assumes a system of economic rationality, emphasizing market competition and economic fitness as drivers for similarity. For example, universal best practices emerge when firms benchmark against each other, copying practices that promise to deliver desirable outcomes. However, although firms temporarily benefit by keeping up with competitors, if all organizations within a given field are engaging in the same activities, this does not result in sustained competitive advantage (Barney, 1991). In Weber's (1946) terminology, the prominent kind of rationality in this dimension is 'zweckrationalität' (instrumental rationality), based on criteria of efficiency and effectiveness.

Simultaneously, it is also important to remember that the competitive market is embedded in a system of 'institutional' mechanisms, such as the social, cultural, and legal (SCL) environment. Prevailing values and norms and their institutionalization channel and alter the outcomes of competitive market forces.[1] In this set of mechanisms, we recognize the concept of institutional isomorphism. Neo-institutional theory argues that a SHRM system needs to be legitimate within prevailing conditions in a specific organization field, rejecting the notion of one best way of doing things in all contexts (Delery & Doty, 1996). This institutional isomorphism (DiMaggio & Powell, 1983) identifies three mechanisms that influence decision-making in organizations: Coercive mechanisms that stem from power sources stronger than the organization (e.g. the influence of trade unions, works councils, employment legislation, government); mimetic mechanisms that result from patterns of responses to uncertainty (e.g. benchmarking and the imitation of strategies of successful competitors); and normative mechanisms that are associated with the adoption of standards and routines considered appropriate in a specific environment (e.g. the impact of HRM professional bodies and employers' associations) (Paauwe & Boselie, 2003).

---

[1] Institutionalization is defined by Selznick (1957: 17–22) as 'to be infused with value beyond the technical requirements of the task at hand'. Scott (1992: 117) defines it as 'the process by which actions are repeated and given similar meaning by self and others'. Finally, Scott and Meyer (1994: 10) define it as 'a process by which a given set of units and a pattern of activities come to be normatively and cognitively held in place and practically taken for granted as lawful'.

All three mechanisms have the goal of achieving legitimacy (the acceptance of organizations in the wider society in which they operate) to ensure access to necessary resources from potential exchange partners. For example, there are demands for legislative compliance, as well as compliance with shared societal values of fairness (a fair balance in the workplace exchange relationship between the organization and individual). Institutional isomorphism has a similar effect to that of competitive isomorphism in that organizations look increasingly alike, and hence do not achieve competitive advantage above others in the field, as they are not able to differentiate themselves.

Weber (1946) refers to legitimacy as 'wertrationalität' (value rationality). Paauwe (1994) prefers the concept of 'relational' rationality, which refers to establishing sustainable and trustworthy relationships with both internal and external stakeholders (given the criteria of fairness and legitimacy). The CBHRT highlights the intrinsic tension in the shaping of SHRM systems between 'economic' rationality (competitive mechanisms) on the one hand and 'relational' rationality (institutional mechanisms) on the other.

In addition to these two sets of mechanisms, there is a third, internal dimension to consider: the organizational/administrative/cultural (OAC) heritage of a firm. This configuration may be considered the outcome of past strategic choices interacting with the organizational structure and culture that they engendered. Bartlett and Ghoshal (1989) use the concept of administrative heritage to identify the influence of structures, methods, competencies, and values that originated in the past. They consider this heritage an important influential factor (for better or for worse) in continued organization structuring, including SHRM. The human capital that a firm possesses, in terms of the skills, knowledge, and abilities of the collective of employees, is another aspect of the heritage mechanisms. Barney (1991) outlines the idea that one of the reasons why resources (including human capital) are imperfectly imitable is the unique historical conditions of a firm, elsewhere referred to as 'path dependency' (Barney, 1995). This heritage refers to the unique configuration or 'Gestalt' of the organization. Delery and Doty (1996) distinguish this as taking a configurational approach, emphasizing a unique vertical fit between HRM policies and practices with other organizational characteristics (e.g. organizational structure, technical system, and culture).

As illustrated in the CBHRT (Figure 6.1), the first three competitive, institutional, and heritage mechanism 'boxes' describe the current reality facing an organization. The competitive mechanisms link to outcomes such as efficiency, effectiveness, flexibility, quality, innovativeness, and speed; the institutional mechanisms result in fairness and legitimacy with regard to work, time, money, know-how, and participation. The heritage mechanisms feed into both the competitive and legitimacy-based outcomes for the organization. At first glance, the CBHRT may therefore give the impression of being based on general systems modelling (input–process–output). However, with the introduction of the 'dominant coalition', this impression is corrected, as the modelling also includes an actors' perspective, indicating the leeway available to shape the SHRM system.

In contrast to isomorphic influences, the RBV (Barney, 1991) explains how firms attempt to differentiate themselves by cultivating their resources in a way that is different from their competitors. The RBV focuses on how firms maximize their sustainable competitive advantage from available resources (Morris, Snell, & Wright, 2006). The firm is seen as a bundle of tangible and intangible resources and capabilities required for product/market/technological competition (Kamoche, 1996). As traditional sources of competitive advantage (such as quality, technology, and economies of scale) become more easily imitable, and therefore less of a factor for competitive differentiation, competitive advantage can still be achieved through developing HRM capabilities that are valuable, rare, imperfectly imitable, and non-substitutable (Barney, 1991; Boxall, 1996; Wright, McMahan, & McWilliams, 1994). This approach to differentiation is less about being reactive to the firm's environment as in neo-institutional theory, and is more about exercising strategic choice at the actor level, by building on and cultivating internal resources and capabilities.

In the CBHRT, we therefore see the role of active human agency (through the dominant coalition) in the decision-making process. Examples of members of the dominant coalition in the employment relationship include top management, supervisory board members, middle and lower management teams (dependent upon the unit of analysis), works councils, trade union shop stewards, and, of course, the human resource (HR) department/director. All of these actors have their own values, norms, and attitudes, shared with others to a greater or lesser degree. In this respect, it is important to note that the interaction between the actors involved and their shared ideology vis-à-vis each other's position and role is an important element in creating understanding and credibility. In contrast, a lack of shared ideology may result in tension and conflict.

The three influences on the dominant coalition (competitive mechanisms, institutional mechanisms, and heritage) do not imply that actors only react to market forces, administrative heritage, or the institutional setting. The CBHRT does not adhere to a deterministic contingency perspective. On the contrary, the shaded area in Figure 6.1 represents the leeway (room for manoeuvre) available to the dominant coalition in making their own strategic choices (Child, 1972). Oliver (1991) explored the strategic responses of organizations to the institutional processes that affect them, and suggested a scale of organizational resistance ranging from passive conformity (acquiescence) to proactive manipulation. There are thus limits to the willingness and ability of (members of) organizations to conform to different institutional mechanisms and pressures, and hence room for strategic choice. Conditions that determine room for manoeuvre include, for example, labour–capital ratio, the financial health of the company (solvency), the rate of unionization, and market strategy. In the case of an organization with a market monopoly, for instance, room for manoeuvre is obviously considerable. However, when the number of manufacturers is high, competition keen, and financial resilience low, there will be little room for manoeuvre for structured SHRM activities.

Ultimately, the dominant coalition is involved in shaping and selecting an HRM strategy, based on aligning with different internal and external forces. It is also challenged with enabling an HRM strategy that can make a genuine contribution to sustainable competitive advantage. The unique shaping of the HRM strategy is aimed at generating HRM outcomes, which in turn contribute to the performance of the organization as a whole (see the models of Becker et al., 1997; Delery & Shaw, 2001; Guest, 1997). In Chapter 5, we dealt with this topic extensively, based on multiple frameworks distinguishing the sequence of HRM activities, HRM outcomes, and firm performance. However, most prior conceptual SHRM–performance models take HRM strategies and/or policies and practices as a starting point, ignoring the prior elements that lead to the development of the HRM strategies. The CBHRT emphasizes the importance of these prior elements, as they all affect the shaping of the HRM strategy. This is a process which, in itself, affects the kind of outcomes it generates: Outcomes aimed at achieving both economic rationality (e.g. productivity, increasing shareholder value) as well as relational rationality (e.g. appropriate work–life balance that contributes to fairness, or ecologically sound ways of producing in order to avoid depletion of natural resources, and thus contributing to legitimacy).

6.5 **The Contextual SHRM Framework**

Having described the conceptual model underlying the CBHRT, we continue here to explain how this model has been further developed as our understanding of SHRM

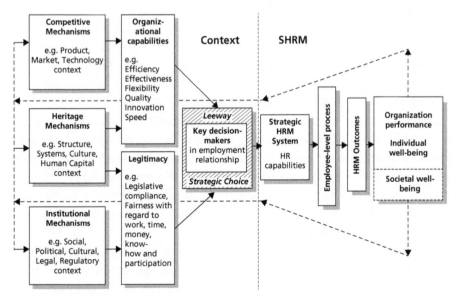

Figure 6.2 The Contextual SHRM Framework

has increased. This development has led us to propose the Contextual SHRM Framework (see Figure 6.2).

The first point to note is that in the Contextual SHRM Framework there are two sides to the framework as depicted in Figure 6.2: the 'context' side and the 'SHRM' side. The context side retains the three dominant factors in an organization's context of the CBHRT: the competitive mechanisms, institutional mechanisms (broadened to include political and regulatory elements in addition to the SCL dimensions), and the organization's heritage mechanisms. The role of agency is also maintained, renamed as the 'key decision-makers' (formerly the 'dominant coalition') in the employment relationship, who have leeway for strategic choice in any given organizational context. The SHRM side of the framework has been expanded somewhat further to include a more detailed depiction of the employee processes, HRM outcomes, and performance outcomes. Our reasoning behind these and other changes is as follows.

The outcomes of the competitive, institutional, and heritage mechanisms have been made more explicit. Specifically, we identify these as 'organizational capabilities' and 'legitimacy' factors. These describe how the firm is dealing with its reality, often describing a desired state. For example, from an institutional mechanisms perspective, there may be legislation in place requiring employee involvement in corporate decision-making (e.g. a system of codetermination). In order to achieve legitimacy, the organization may set up a works council to achieve the required level of employee voice. The legislation is part of the institutional mechanisms affecting the firm, but the means to achieving legitimacy is the firm's response to meeting the demands for legitimacy (defined at the exchange level as between an organization and society, and at the fairness level as between employee and employer).

Similarly, a firm may be competing within a very tight market in which customer demands are constantly changing. This is the competitive reality facing the firm, defining what is required to survive in the marketplace, and, as a result, the firm may choose to focus on developing flexibility as a core organizational capability to deal with the reality. Goals and targets in organizational capabilities and legitimacy are the firm's responses to the experienced competitive and institutional mechanisms. Developing the heritage mechanisms further, we can see that they can affect both organizational capability and legitimacy. For example, the extant human capital present in the firm can contribute to achieving high levels of efficiency and innovation. Equally, the firm's extant SHRM system can present the firm as a fair employer, creating legitimacy within the firm's social context, and, in turn, encouraging people in the labour market to be attracted to work for the firm in the future.

It is also important to highlight the different types of alignment or 'fit' represented in the framework (see Chapter 3). First, there is the alignment between the organization's heritage and its SHRM system. This can best be described as 'organization' fit, that is, creating an appropriate linkage between the HRM system and other relevant systems in the organization including technological, production, and control systems (Wood, 1999). Secondly, there is the 'strategic' (vertical) fit between the competitive mechanisms and the SHRM system. This ensures that the HRM system is aligned with the business strategy, which, in turn, helps the effective implementation of strategy and hence has important performance implications (Boxall & Purcell, 2008). The third type of fit is 'environmental': This entails ensuring an appropriate alignment of the SHRM system with the institutional environment of the organization, including the social, cultural, political, and legal contexts. Finally, 'internal' (horizontal) fit is present in the SHRM system itself, as its various components must fit together to maximize the synergies of the system.

Having explored the context side of the Contextual SHRM Framework, we build on the notion of internal alignment to uncover the SHRM side of the framework. Here, rather than focusing on valuable, inimitable, rare, and non-substitutable HRM strategies (based on RBV theorizing), we explore the key decision-makers who are responsible for devising a strategic HRM system. The aim here is to create HRM capabilities that can support the organizational capabilities arising from the competitive, institutional, and heritage mechanisms. HRM capabilities are defined as 'the routines embedded in the tacit and implicit knowledge of members of an organization functioning to acquire, develop, nurture, deploy, and redeploy human resources in a dynamic, competitive environment' (Park, Gardner, & Wright, 2004: 262). Whereas an HRM strategy focuses on the broad outline of policies and practices the organization will put in place, we propose here that we need to model the whole strategic HRM system, including the activities of the HR department and how it is structured and delivers its services (see also Chapters 10 and 11).

There are also issues regarding levels of analysis that were less developed in the CBHRT, which was largely positioned at the macro level, locating a firm within its broader context. HRM outcomes, however, are the result of employee-level processes in the organization—employee attitudes and behaviours that are reactions to the SHRM system. These attitudes and behaviours result in different levels of employee job satisfaction, turnover, absenteeism, engagement, organizational citizenship behaviours, and commitment, to name but a few HRM outcomes (see Chapter 5 for a discussion of micro-level processes, particularly Van Veldhoven's (2012) 'bath tub' model of HRM). HRM outcomes are a result of the application of a range of HRM practices affected by a variety of moderating and mediating contextual factors. For example, when a performance management system is implemented, how the employees will feel about the organization or change their behaviour as a result is significantly impacted by whether they perceive that the performance management system is fair (i.e. organizational justice as a mediator of the system–outcome relationship: See, for example, Farndale, Hope Hailey, & Kelliher, 2011). Similarly, how employees might respond to the introduction of a new pension or retirement plan could be greatly affected by their age (i.e. age as a moderator of the system–outcome relationship: See, for example, Kooij et al., 2014).

Hence, employees react to HRM systems based on their individual-level perceptions, hopefully in line with what was intended when the system was designed. If a firm introduces a new work–life balance policy, it may do this with the intention of increasing job satisfaction. This policy is implemented by line management (one of the contextual mediators) and the employees experience the new set of practices. There is potential, however, that what was intended is not fully enacted by the line manager, and/or the employee perceives the new policy to be unhelpful in achieving a better work–life balance (irrespective of the policy's intentions). This is the difference between intended, actual, and experienced HRM (Nishii & Wright, 2008). Employees react to the new practices, either by showing higher or lower levels of job satisfaction dependent upon their experience or perception of the practice, not on the intended aim of the practice.

It is not our aim here to describe in depth the organizational behaviour literature that explains how this process works (see, for example, Becker et al., 1997; Den Hartog, Boselie, & Paauwe, 2004), but to note that this micro-level activity (employee-level processes) is part of the macro-level SHRM–performance linkage. Employee behaviours and attitudes are affected by the HRM system they experience, which in turn feed into their productivity, efficiency, timeliness, flexibility, engagement, and so forth (i.e. HRM outcomes), which ultimately contribute to the firm's overall performance.

In the Contextual SHRM Framework, we have also placed greater emphasis on a holistic sense of firm performance, balancing financial performance and employee well-being, both of which affect broader societal well-being. As discussed in depth in Chapter 5, it is important to offset a managerial perspective that focuses on financial performance indicators (organization outcomes) such as productivity, customer satisfaction, sales, and profit, with an employee perspective that pays greater attention to employee well-being, including happiness, health, and relationships (Guest, 2017; Meyers, Van Woerkom, & Bakker, 2013). The ideal scenario is where these two perspectives are mutually reinforcing, although there is evidence that they can also act in conflict with one another (Van de Voorde, Paauwe, & Van Veldhoven, 2012). Societal well-being emphasizes that the performance of a firm (both financial and in terms of employee well-being) consequently impacts on the society in which it is embedded. Firms do not operate in a vacuum; as we have emphasized throughout, firms both react to and help to create the context in which they are embedded. The societal implications of firm performance in turn feed back into the context in which the organization is operating (Watson, 2004), becoming an antecedent to the institutional, competitive, and heritage mechanisms the firm faces.

6.6 Applying the Contextual SHRM Framework

Based upon experience to date, the Contextual SHRM Framework presented in Figure 6.2, as well as the previous version of the framework (the CBHRT), have been used for:

- Teaching
- Academic enquiry/research
- Force-field analysis/consultancy.

6.6.1 TEACHING

Students getting to know the field of SHRM for the first time often think of it as a functional area in which a range of related HRM activities (like staffing, appraisal, reward, training, and development) are meant to control and manage the in-, through-, and out-flow of employees. They do not necessarily relate it to performance, to the process of generating added value, nor do they relate it to the specific context and background of the organization itself. Once they start to develop a feel for strategic HRM, they can consider possible performance effects, but very often in the restricted financial economic meaning of performance. They may start to think about the possible linkage with corporate or business strategy, but probably ignore other possible contextual factors. This is too narrow a perspective, ignoring all the mechanisms in the context that impact on the shaping of the SHRM system. As soon as students start to develop a feel for the uniqueness of the organization in its specific context, the key decision-makers, and their degree of leeway for strategic choice, learning can progress at a deeper and more reflective level. This kind of learning involves an analysis of the various forces that have an impact on the SHRM system, and the opportunities for shaping HRM practices and policies that might result in a unique contribution to sustained competitive advantage. The contextual SHRM framework and subsequent application and analysis in real life situations helps to build context sensitivity, which is an important competence for (future) HR and line managers, as it will help them to avoid the mistake of merely reproducing familiar HRM system when moving from one job or organization to another.

6.6.2 EMPIRICAL RESEARCH

The framework has been used to carry out a range of case studies aimed at generating insights in the forces and actors that have an impact on shaping the SHRM system and the conditions defining leeway. In Chapter 7, we provide an overview of the possibilities and findings in this respect. We raise here the question of whether the Contextual SHRM Framework is capable of being applied to generate a set of hypotheses that can be tested through a quantitative research design, or propositions for exploration in qualitative research. The left side of the framework (context) is descriptive, outlining the mechanisms (competitive, institutional, and heritage) that impact both the key decision-makers and their leeway for shaping the SHRM system. As with Beer and colleagues' (1984) widely cited Harvard model, the Contextual SHRM Framework in this respect focuses more on mapping relevant factors, than a set of related testable hypotheses. Descriptive qualitative research of an explorative nature naturally fits better with this kind of modelling. However, we believe that hypotheses are possible with respect to factors determining leeway. Based on the theorizing in this chapter, supplemented by exploratory research by Paauwe (1991) and Boselie (2002), we propose the following hypotheses with regard to the conditions governing leeway. Of course, each hypothesis requires more detailed theoretical justification, but this provides some examples of the type of tests that could be carried out:

Hypothesis 1: Market growth (in contrast to market decline) is positively related to the extent of leeway the key decision-makers in the employment relationship have in developing the SHRM system.

Hypothesis 2: The number of relevant stakeholders of an organization is negatively related to the extent of leeway the key decision-makers in the employment relationship have in developing the SHRM system.

Hypothesis 3: Rules, procedures, regulations, and legislation (coercive mechanisms) are negatively related to the extent of leeway the key decision-makers in the employment relationship have in developing the SHRM system.

Hypothesis 4: A monopoly market structure offers more leeway to the key decision-makers in the employment relationship in developing the SHRM system than a polypoly (or perfect competition) market structure.

Hypothesis 5: A differentiation strategy (in contrast to a cost-reduction or price strategy) is positively related to the extent of leeway the key decision-makers in the employment relationship have in developing the SHRM system.

Hypothesis 6: The ratio of labour to total costs is negatively related to the extent of leeway the key decision-makers in the employment relationship have in developing the SHRM system.

Hypothesis 7: Financial leeway is positively related to the extent of leeway the key decision-makers in the employment relationship have in developing the SHRM system.

The second part (SHRM) of the Contextual SHRM Framework is more normative or prescriptive, stipulating that in order to achieve sustained competitive advantage (high firm performance) firms should develop a SHRM system that contributes to positive HRM outcomes. Examples have been presented in Chapter 5 of the SHRM–performance models for testing this linkage. In the HRM and organizational behaviour literatures, there are many examples of hypothesis testing for the micro-level relationship between HRM practices and employee-level outcomes, such as performance management's link with employee commitment (e.g. Farndale, Hope Hailey, & Kelliher, 2011), work–family practices' link to absenteeism (Giardini & Kabst, 2008), and HRM practices' link to job satisfaction (e.g. Kooij et al., 2010) to name but a few. It is therefore more straightforward to build hypotheses for testing in quantitative studies to explore what type of HRM system leads to desired HRM outcomes, and in turn to positive firm performance. This involves exploring how organizational-level (macro) practices (e.g. reward plans, performance management systems) affect employee-level (micro) attitudes and behaviours (e.g. engagement, absenteeism), and how, in turn, these attitudes and behaviours affect aggregate-level HRM outcomes (e.g. productivity, employee turnover). Ultimately, these HRM outcomes are then argued to influence bottom-line financial firm performance and degrees of well-being. In other words, levels of productivity or employee turnover have implications for the bottom-line performance of the firm, at the same time as being indicators of levels of employee well-being. This chain of effects is represented in Van Veldhoven's (2012) 'bath tub' model of HRM.

Based on a case-study approach, the Contextual SHRM Framework also allows for broader testing of the full framework by establishing whether companies that have made optimal use of combining both the competitive and institutional mechanisms, alongside the heritage mechanisms, do indeed possess unique competitive advantage or do perform better (in terms of financial and well-being measures). Such case studies may be based in strategic balance theory (Boon et al., 2009; Deephouse, 1999), which has demonstrated how firms that create a balance between the need to differentiate themselves within the competitive marketplace and the need to be legitimate within the broader societal (institutional) context, have higher overall performance. As Wah, Ismail, and Ibrahim (2004: 557) in their empirical application of strategic balance theory note: 'Organizations seeking competitive advantage should be as different as legitimately possible'!

6.6.3 FORCE-FIELD ANALYSIS/CONSULTANCY

During a range of executive education sessions with HR and line managers, we applied the Contextual SHRM Framework to participants' companies. The context side of the framework is used to describe the present situation by outlining both competitive and institutional mechanisms, taking into account the specifics of the organization (including its heritage). This enables the HR manager to identify the specific organizational capabilities that are being sought, at the same time as considering ways in which the firm desires to achieve legitimacy (which may or may not support the identified organizational capabilities). The analysis then continues by considering who the key decision-makers in the employment relationship within the firm might be.

Based on this mental framing and application of the framework as a force-field analysis tool, the participants are able to establish a clear overview of the firm's current situation, including upcoming challenges, required organizational capabilities, and 'legitimacy' issues. During this exercise, the participants work in pairs, each partner fulfilling alternately the role of consultant and client. In the consultant role, they help their client by posing appropriate questions to analyse the different mechanisms (see Appendix 6.1 for an overview). The systematic overview of mechanisms impacting on the firm and relevant actors is used as a stepping-stone for the next stage in which, during a creative process, the contours become visible of the kind of SHRM system that, based on the degree of available leeway, would be possible and would contribute to sustained competitive advantage. It goes without saying that this stage is the most difficult to complete successfully, and can often be too time-consuming for a training event. However, participants appreciate having an in-depth analysis and overview of the current situation with the present challenges and issues. In Figure A6.1 we provide an anonymous example of a force-field analysis of a 'soup and sauce' factory and its subsequent design of the SHRM system.

A number of companies have used, with our help, the Contextual SHRM Framework (or CBHRT) to develop an insight in the specific context and degree of leeway available for their company, in order to generate potential SHRM systems that can help contribute to sustained competitive advantage. This is achieved by creating an appropriate alignment between competitive (formerly PMT), institutional (formerly SCL), and heritage (formerly OAC) mechanisms in order to achieve a unique competitive position embedded in the relevant context, both from a business/market as well as legitimacy/fairness perspective. This provides the sustainable aspect of competitive advantage that organizations desire.

6.7 Summary and conclusions

Based on the building blocks of strategic management, organizational behaviour, industrial and organizational psychology, contextual fit, institutional theory, actor agency, and the RBV, we have outlined the origins of the Contextual SHRM Framework and its predecessor, the CBHRT. These are theoretical frameworks that enable a more complete overview of the factors that influence the shaping of a firm's SHRM system. Moreover, they emphasize different rationalities and resulting outcomes, and take into account the various actors involved and their interaction with strategy and the wider societal context. The Contextual SHRM Framework is primarily representative of a macro view of HRM, but also includes a reference to micro-level HRM outcomes, taking a strategic HRM perspective and using this lens to observe the employment relationship. Our hope is that the Contextual SHRM Framework might be applied in both qualitative and quantitative studies to help progress our understanding of the contextual SHRM–performance relationship.

With this chapter, we conclude the more theoretical part of this book. The second part of the book contains a range of chapters that reflect the empirical reality, emphasizing the importance of putting theory into practice. These chapters demonstrate, at various levels of analysis, insights that can be generated using the theorizing outlined in the previous chapters. We start with Chapter 7, which provides examples of case studies at company level that we have carried out using the Contextual SHRM Framework, and shows how the combination of using both RBV principles and an institutional perspective has resulted in a unique shaping of the SHRM system, contributing to financial, well-being, and professional performance. Chapter 8 applies the framework at the level of the industry sector, exploring a range of sectors, comparing those with high and low degrees of institutionalization and revealing how this affects the shaping of the SHRM system. Chapter 9 takes us one level of analysis higher by considering differences in institutional settings at country level. Case studies of multinational corporations (MNCs) are presented to show how the framework can be applied at this international level of analysis.

Before concluding, the remaining chapters (10 and 11) move on to consider the implications of strategy, HRM, and performance specifically for the HR department. The emphasis here is on the added value of the HR function, that is, how well the HR function can implement and deliver its services. Without this performance measure, many of the desired outcomes of an otherwise well-functioning SHRM system would not be achieved.

■ APPENDIX 6.1: EXAMPLE QUESTIONS

A6.1.1 COMPETITIVE MECHANISMS

Which market/competitive mechanisms have a direct impact on the shaping of your organization?

- Product–market combinations
- Technology (e.g. automation, web-based)

A6.1.2 INSTITUTIONAL MECHANISMS

Which institutional mechanisms have a direct impact on the shaping of your organization?

- Legislation
- Socio-political context
- National culture
- Rules or regulations
- Procedures

- Covenants
- Influence of social partners (trade unions, works councils, and other relevant stakeholders).

A6.1.3 HERITAGE MECHANISMS

What are the key characteristics of the heritage of your organization?

- Organization structure
- Organization systems
- Human capital
- Organization age
- Spirit of the times (zeitgeist) when organization was founded
- Management philosophy, mission, and strategy of the founders
- Current ownership structure
- Critical incidents in the past (e.g. mergers, takeovers, reorganizations)

A6.1.4 ORGANIZATIONAL CAPABILITIES

What are the core organizational capabilities on which your organization prides itself?

- Efficiency
- Effectiveness
- Flexibility
- Quality
- Innovation
- Speed
- Other.

A6.1.5 LEGITIMACY

What are the core legitimacy goals of your organization?

- Legislative compliance
- Fairness towards employees regarding their working conditions/hours of work/reward systems/skill development/participation in the organization
- Other.

A6.1.6 KEY DECISION-MAKERS

Which actors/stakeholders/groups/parties determine the HRM strategy of your organization?

- Board of directors
- HRM director
- Social partners (works council and/or trade unions)
- Line management
- Employees.

A6.1.7 LEEWAY/ROOM FOR MANOEUVRE

What is the leeway or room for manoeuvre available to the key decision-makers with respect to strategic HRM choices in your organization?

- Caused by legislation, collective bargaining agreements (CBAs), or covenants between social partners
- Determined by specific (business) knowledge, experiences, or available resources (e.g. time, financial resources, natural resources)

A6.1.8 STRATEGIC HRM SYSTEM

Which HRM policies and practices can be applied for the benefit of the HRM strategy of your organization? NB be as specific as possible.

- Planning/recruitment/selection/socialization
- Appraisal/rewards
- Training/development
- Participation/decentralization/empowerment/autonomy/teamwork
- Leadership/coaching/mentorship
- Job design/division of labour.

What is the best structure of the HR department for your organization?

- HR employee capabilities and roles
- HRM practice delivery mechanisms
- HR department reporting structure
- HR evaluation processes.

A6.1.9 HRM OUTCOMES

Which HRM outcomes can be used to measure the effects of the HRM strategy in your organization?

- Satisfaction/motivation/commitment/trust/stress/loyalty (subjective data)
- Employee turnover/employee absence/conflicts between management and employees (objective data).

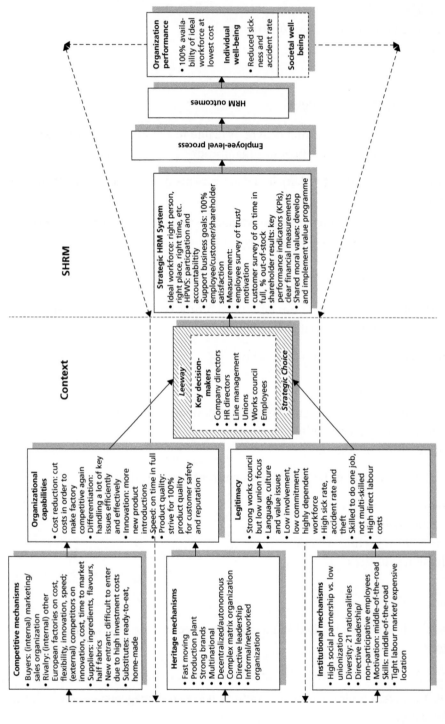

Figure A6.1 Example of a force-field analysis of a 'soup and sauce' factory

A6.1.10 PERFORMANCE

Which performance indicators can be used to measure the effects of the HRM strategy in your organization?

- Financial: e.g. productivity/service and product quality/customer satisfaction/R&D efforts, sales/market share/growth/profits/market value
- Well-being: e.g. employee health, satisfaction, engagement, happiness, stress levels, intention to quit.

7 Contextual SHRM Framework: Organization level

7.1 Introduction

Having outlined the Contextual Strategic Human Resource Management (SHRM) Framework as the culmination of a review of relevant literature and theory related to strategy, human resource management (HRM), and performance, the second part of the book now focuses on applying this framework in practice. In this chapter, we present a range of company case-study vignettes in order to illustrate different aspects of the Contextual SHRM Framework and how organizations are able to apply it to help them achieve long-term viability. By examining the various dimensions of the framework (the competitive, institutional, and heritage mechanisms and the key decision-makers), organizations have been able to understand the extent of leeway and strategic choice for shaping an HRM system that is uniquely their own, which has helped significantly to build a sustainable competitive advantage. The illustrative cases are part of ongoing research projects. Here we present a summary of the main characteristics and findings in order to demonstrate how the Contextual SHRM Framework can be, and has been, applied.

The first case study (Section 7.2) is an example of a company in the socially sensitive industry of temporary work agencies. The company took the lead in demonstrating its responsibility towards society at large by initiating the industry's first collective bargaining agreement (CBA), as well as becoming actively involved in drafting legislation (i.e. creating an institutional setting) to further augment both the legitimacy and security standards of temporary work agencies. The company was able to forge a highly respected reputation among the general public, which, of course, had beneficial consequences for its position in the marketplace.

The second example (Section 7.3) is illustrative of how fostering consistency and longevity in the specific characteristics of an organizational configuration, rather than succumbing to pressures for constant organizational change, can help to establish long-term viability. A highly successful Dutch theme/leisure park has purposefully nurtured its unique heritage mechanisms over the course of many years (i.e. its path dependency) and this has reaped commercial rewards in the face of stiff competition.

The third case (Section 7.4) presents the influential role of key decision-makers in forming an HRM system. The highly dynamic fast-moving consumer goods industry meant that Procter & Gamble (P&G) had to stay ahead of the game, leading the way in innovation and brand identity. Restructuring became a necessity to maintain its competitive position, and, led by a new charismatic CEO, the company shifted their internal labour market focus to one that drew in new talent and ideas from outside. This was a major change, threatening internal legitimacy for external competition needs, but paid off due to the skilful way in which it was handled, aligning corporate and HRM strategies.

In Section 7.5, we highlight the experience of Scania, a truck maker also operating in a highly competitive market. The company balances lean production principles with flexible working practices to meet its competitive needs. Importantly, efficiency is not the only idea behind these principles and practices; the company is also focused on institutional mechanisms of legitimacy and fairness for all workers. Additionally, Scania is focusing on the future with its ageing workforce, aligning the HRM system with the needs of older workers, and ensuring a healthy workforce overall.

In Section 7.6 we present an example from the mail and parcel delivery industry: PostNL. As the market has shifted from regular mail to parcel deliveries being the sustainable business, PostNL has had to change its HRM system to remain competitive. The company has focused on partnering with agencies as well as focusing on its own employees to maintain legitimacy at a time when jobs were being lost and wages lowered.

Finally, in Section 7.7, we present a case that shows how the Contextual SHRM Framework can also be applied to understand an organization during more challenging times. In the office supplies market, SupplierStore (a pseudonym for confidentiality reasons) has faced severe competition from both retail outlets and e-commerce almost since its inception, and its answer has been to adopt a low-cost business strategy. As prices in the market were forced downward, very little flexibility for developing a sustainable HRM system or business emerged. The resultant control-based HRM system led to employee dissatisfaction, questioning the firm's ability to meet legitimacy needs.

7.2 A responsible employer providing economic employment flexibility

In the 1960s and 1970s, the rise of temporary agency work was a sensitive subject across industrialized nations. Operators in the temporary agency sector faced two major obstacles in their struggle for legitimacy in the eyes of the general public and policy-makers: Countering the negative stereotypes surrounding the industry, many of which had arisen from the activities of illegal labour subcontractors; and, relatedly, having to work within constraining legislative frameworks. As the largest temporary work agency in its home market of the Netherlands, and the second largest in the world, Randstad is a noteworthy example of a company that relies upon its ability to manage both these socio-cultural/institutional pressures *and* the product–efficiency pressures demanded by their clients.

Conscious of the social sensitivities surrounding its services, Randstad has been involved in an active search for much-prized legitimacy throughout its history. The firm has been at the forefront of establishing minimum standards for the professional contracting of temporary staff. In the early 1960s, it introduced social security insurance for temporary agency employees and took steps to address concerns over working conditions and training possibilities. A decade later, in the early 1970s, Randstad's management actively engaged with the trade unions in drawing up the first collective agreements for temporary agency workers. Twenty years on, Randstad was one of the main architects of the 1999 'flexibility and security' (flexicurity) legislation, which brought temporary agency workers under normal Dutch labour law.

Some of these efforts to professionalize the business increased the cost of temporary agency workers. For example, the introduction of social security insurance in the 1960s raised the price of a 'temp' by approximately 30 per cent, but demand for agency work boomed as companies, who previously had been wary of having uninsured personnel working on their premises, now saw new possibilities for taking advantage of agency work. The more recent flexicurity legislation, meanwhile, has been criticized for both its complexity and its negative impact on the economic attractiveness of using 'temps' (the new law increased the opportunities for client organizations to hire workers on such contracts directly).

Nevertheless, most agencies now agree that the various institutional constraints have proved beneficial for their business. The flexicurity legislation did a lot to augment the societal acceptance of the industry as a regular (responsible) employer. It also stimulated the market for relatively high-skill temping and increased market possibilities for 'managed services', whereby the agency not only provides the temporary employees, but also takes responsibility for their operational HRM (both markets offering the agencies higher margins), such as coping with redundancies and layoffs. The responsible attitude shown by Randstad has helped it to gain major contracts with other large companies that have set their own similar standards for corporate social responsibility. It has also facilitated cooperation with the national government, opening markets previously restricted to the nationalized Public Employment Service in the Netherlands. In addition, the increasing professionalization of the field and growing standards for consistent trustworthiness and socially responsible behaviour of the agencies themselves also functions—especially for the larger agencies like Randstad—as a form of market protection against the smaller, less organized agencies. It effectively raises the operating standards in the temporary agency workers' market, increasing the benefits to the larger agencies (such as Randstad and Adecco) of being able to offer well-established and sophisticated formalized structures.

In 2015, the company agreed on a new CBA and, fully in line with recent developments, the contract partners not only included the trade unions but also the works council. Preceding the final settlement, there was a survey among all employees; over

50 per cent of all employees completed the survey in order to express their preferences. The next stage involved forty employees from all levels in the organization, who discussed the different topics of the new labour agreement in various themed groups (including 360-degree appraisal feedback, benefits schemes, and job evaluation and classification). This demonstrated how the process of creating the new CBA was all about intensifying participation and emphasizing the importance of co-creation between management, employees, trade union representatives, and works council members.

The conviction that the company can contribute to society through its professional experience in employment issues is deeply ingrained in Randstad. Each consultant can recite the company's mantra, *'knowing, serving, trusting, aiming for perfection'*. The recent inflow of immigrants, refugees, and asylum seekers in Western Europe has resulted in close cooperation between Randstad and the Crisis Centre for Asylum Seekers (COA), in order to help them to find a job once they have been given a permit to stay in the country. Potential candidates can attend workshops about how to apply for a job and about the Dutch labour market. A consultant will help them with job applications and is also actively involved in selecting suitable vacancies. Other topics that demonstrate the involvement and social responsibility of Randstad include the (un) employment situation of young people, and the issue of how to combine flexibility and security. In this area, they undertake research and are strongly involved in the public debate with politicians, employers, trade unions, and academics.

This short case study shows how socially responsible behaviour, in which due attention is paid to the institutional setting, has made good business sense for the Randstad corporation by strengthening its legitimacy and reputation at a global level and not only in the Netherlands. Randstad has developed into the leading Dutch agency for temporary employment, with a national market share of 18 per cent (Randstad, 2015) and a strong international presence. Operating in thirty-nine countries, its main markets are the USA, the Netherlands, France, Germany, Belgium and Luxembourg, Spain, and the UK. The company ranks worldwide among the top five temporary work agencies and is the third largest (after Adecco and Manpower).

7.3 Heritage mechanisms win prizes: Efteling theme park

Competing in the market of leisure/theme parks, one firm based in the Netherlands with an excellent reputation is Efteling. Efteling has won several prestigious international prizes recognizing it as one of the best theme parks in the world, beating competition from its more internationally renowned and better-resourced rivals such as Walibi World and Walt Disney World. On an annual basis, Efteling attracts over four million visitors, and in 2014 attracted more visitors than the Walt Disney Studios in Paris.[1] In 2015, it received the award for the 'best day out' from the Royal Dutch Automobile Association (ANWB), plus the following Diamond Theme Park Awards: Best fun park, most child-friendly park, best events park, most spectacular park of the Netherlands, best attraction, best service, e-award, and most beautiful park. What is the secret behind the success of this park, based in the south of the Netherlands? We demonstrate how the park's origin and administrative heritage are among the dominant forces shaping its policies and contributing to its continuous success.

When it began in the 1930s, Efteling was a playground for local children, but by the early 1950s it had developed into a 'fairy tale' park designed according to the drawings of the famous artist Anton Pieck. Over the years more and more attractions have been added, until today Efteling is a spectacular fully equipped leisure park complete with hotel, residential bungalows, and a golf course. In the Netherlands there is a well-known saying that everybody will visit Efteling at least three times in her or his lifetime: Once as a child, once as a father or mother with their own children, and once as a grandfather or grandmother. Nowadays, its appeal has also spread to overseas visitors. Almost annually, Efteling adds a new attraction in order to stimulate return visitors and prevent a decline in numbers. The park management ensures that all new attractions are also built and shaped in such a way that they fit the general 'Anton Pieck' theme of the park.

The secret of Efteling's success can be traced back to its origins; in particular to the way in which the organization has managed to preserve its administrative heritage to the present day, to such a degree that many people in the Netherlands consider Efteling as part of their national heritage. Visiting other theme parks and comparing them with Efteling, the differences are immediately apparent. Whereas other parks are simply a collection of entertainment toys (such as roller coasters), Efteling is beautifully situated in its natural environment. The uniform layout throughout the grounds ensures that it remains faithful to Anton Pieck's artistic vision. Visitors who might not appreciate all the attractions—which may either make you giddy with excitement or nauseous!—will still want to visit the park to stroll through its beautiful landscape and admire the lovely fairy tale-like scenery. For over sixty years, Efteling has safeguarded the culture of fairy tales and the designs of Anton Pieck. In 2013, the park also organized special symposia devoted to the famous German fairy tale writers the Brothers Grimm, and in 2005, Efteling joined the activities for the global celebration of the Hans Christian Andersen year by giving a central place to his fairy tales in the park.

The secret of the park's success is in part due to the preservation and cultivation of the heritage of its original designer and its focus on fairy tales, which has a huge appeal to families with young children. It also has to do with the fact that the only shareholder

---

[1] Source: Ranking by the USA-based organization Themed Entertainment Association (TEA).

is the Efteling Nature Park Foundation; its main objective is stimulating and maintaining arrangements for recreation and relaxation, with a strong focus on preserving nature and safeguarding the environment. This has resulted in a theme park that has taken utmost care in embedding all the entertainment attractions in a beautiful setting by making sure that the surrounding nature has been preserved as much as possible; this is a unique feature of this theme park, compared to its competitors both abroad as well as in its home market. An expanding company might consider this kind of corporate governance structure a major hindrance to plans for growth in visitor numbers and sales revenue. However, this shareholder is not interested in receiving any kind of dividend on its shares, and so the financial position of Efteling is very strong. More importantly, the park's management team has used this institutional embeddedness as an opportunity for developing and fostering a formula, which has resulted in a unique commercial advantage for this small player facing stiff competition from nearby multinational corporations (MNCs).

People management within Efteling reflects the character and culture of the park, as it can be compared with a family-owned company. In total, the park employs around 2,500 employees, the majority of whom are seasonal and holiday workers; permanent employees only constitute around 10–20 per cent of the workforce. Many employees have a long-standing employment relationship with this company, dating back to parents and even grandparents. Several of the seasonal workers have also been members of staff for over twenty years. During the low season, some are entitled to unemployment benefits based on Dutch social security legislation, and the Efteling organization stays in touch with them by sending them information, newsletters, and Christmas gifts. When the high season starts again, they are simply rehired. All new employees (both permanent and seasonal workers) receive comprehensive training in hospitality. The main slogan of the training and socialization programme is about enchantment: 'You are the one who helps create the best possible fairy tale.' In order to make this happen, the core of the programme is focused on two dimensions: Hospitality and reliability, irrespective of the specific job one holds.

Unsurprisingly, the atmosphere among employees is very much that of a community, characterized by a warm, easy-going attitude alongside a high degree of dedication to Efteling. The advantage of fostering such a family-like culture is a strong sense of loyalty and commitment among employees. In order to stay alert and keep track of the latest developments Efteling has established close relationships with a number of schools and universities. Final-year students can join a talent development programme (the Efteling Academy). In addition, the park has also invested—together with two universities—in a pilot project for knowledge development and research in storytelling and business development. Efteling and educational organizations have thus established a two-way inspirational relationship. In 2011, Efteling won the prize for best learning company of the year in the Netherlands.

Management faces the twin challenges of combining the best of two worlds: On the one hand, preserving the family atmosphere and employee and customer love for Efteling, while, on the other, trying to achieve a higher degree of service quality, become more cost-effective, and pursue continuous innovation. The sound financial situation of the park does not constitute a burning platform in this respect, but due to the competition in the Dutch marketplace coming from more global players (such as Walibi World and nearby Disney World), Efteling will need to remain alert and flexible to stay ahead of competition.

Applying the Contextual SHRM Framework, we can see how the present organizational configuration, including the company's HRM strategy, has been clearly influenced, even shaped, by its administrative heritage (encompassing both the artistic values of the original designer as well as the objectives of the dominant shareholder). More importantly, we can also discern how this heritage has been deliberately used to develop and expand the theme park in a highly consistent way. This has resulted in a very strong competitive position.

7.4 Influential decision-makers impacting HRM systems

P&G is an American MNC providing consumer goods globally, with its origin in Cincinnati, Ohio. Proctor & Gamble Company was founded in 1837 as a soap and candle business at a risky time amidst national financial distress in the USA. Today, P&G is a globally recognized leader in consumer goods, with a wide range of household products including paper-based goods, soaps, detergents, and other health necessities. Of its five main business segments, fabric care and home care (at 29 per cent) and baby, feminine, and family care (at 27 per cent) saw the greatest proportion of net sales in 2015. P&G operates in 80 countries across the globe and employs approximately 140,000 employees. It is recognized as one of the top global innovators in the industry, with a global research and development network. In addition to its organizational capabilities based upon innovation, P&G is home to leading iconic consumer brands such as Dawn, Bounty, Crest, and Pampers.

P&G operates in a continually changing and multifaceted global environment and derives its competitive advantage from its continuous emphasis on innovation and product branding. P&G has constantly been at the forefront of new corporate practices such as branding, diversity advertising, diversity programming, and employee profit sharing. Its innovative work environment is supported by a heritage mechanism sustaining a collaborative culture in which social networks extend across geographical regions and employees are highly mobile across these networks.

In order to maintain its distinctive work culture and uphold its organizational mission, P&G's strategic HRM system operates in synergy with the company's competitive mechanisms. Heavy internal recruiting and training employees for leadership positions is conducted to maintain a collaborative environment and relationship-oriented culture. Employees freely move between geographical regions to fill openings in foreign subsidiaries, resulting in a very high number of expatriates across the company, approximately the third or fourth largest number of expatriates among any organization.

P&G extended its facilities outside of the USA in 1915 when it opened a plant in Hamilton, Canada. Since then, it has steadily expanded to its current position as a global industry leader. In its efforts to build a global brand and global organizational capabilities, P&G has focused on both its culture of collaboration and a centralized system of operation. Collaboration on a global scale is done via webcasts conducted every six months, global conferences, and an HR summit held once every two years. HR leaders within each (regional) group are regularly in touch via monthly phone calls. The head of HR, Dick Antoine, meets with and has phone calls with HR leaders of businesses twice a week. Thus, communication is of high importance to managing an integrated global work environment. With respect to its centralized system of operations, P&G features a single HR database with information on headcounts, salary, promotions, terminations, and so on. This enhances efficiency and reinforces a common organizational culture across the globe. Operational HR processes are globalized so that each regional branch has the same essential practices, standards, and tools. HR practices, such as recruiting, may exhibit slight variations and tailoring to local needs; however, the success drivers such as assessment tools, compensation management, enrolment, and performance scorecards are uniform around the world.

In June 1999, P&G, under the leadership of CEO Durk Jager, announced a massive restructuring effort, Organization 2005. Organization 2005 was designed to boost the company's innovative environment and accelerate global rollout in order to double sales by 2005. The formal chain of command changed from geographical, product, and function to product, geography, and business process. Jager, as one of the key decision-makers, sought to reduce management layers from thirteen to seven in order to streamline operations.

Massive layoffs were predicted as well as the shutting down of underperforming plants across the globe. Large levels of employee transfers and relocations led to negative moral and behavioural changes in a previously collaborative culture. In Europe, 2,000 employees were transferred to the strategic business headquarters in Geneva. Jager's aggressive restructuring efforts soon became key legitimacy issues, threatening the company's culture and employee satisfaction. They were seen as brusque by lower management and employees were not on board with his abrupt attempt to overhaul the company's 163-year-old culture.

A heavy focus on 'promotion from within' practices and employee training have traditionally been the cornerstone of P&G's relationship-oriented work culture. Contrasting this strategic HRM system with the company's organizational capabilities, which featured a heavy focus on innovation, company executives looked towards changing their recruitment practices when faced with an economic setback in March 2000. P&G lost nearly 50 billion dollars in market capitalization following a 50 per cent drop in the price of its stock. In the same time frame, P&G saw a shift in leadership as Jager stepped down after just eighteen months and a new CEO, A. G. Lafley, took over the company. Lafley brought to the company a fresh perspective on innovation. He recognized that a large proportion of P&G businesses were not performing at desired levels, brands were falling short of delivering good consumer value, prices were too high, and the company was lagging in innovative efforts. Lafley acknowledged an excessive focus on internal affairs and management of internal transactions. P&G's research and development productivity was stagnant amidst the proliferation of new technology and intense external competition.

Lafley, presenting a shift in the key decision-makers, likewise brought about a shift in P&G in the form of a new restructuring effort. Emphasis was placed on the four core businesses that made up 54 per cent and 60 per cent of sales and profits respectively, as well as on leading brands, the top ten profitable countries, reducing capital spending, and cutting costs. Underperforming businesses were shut down and nearly ten thousand jobs lost. Brands such as Comet, Crisco, and Jif were sold off, and unprofitable product lines discontinued.

Lafley made a startling announcement with his changing approach to innovation. He announced an insourcing model of R&D in which 50 per cent of innovation would be coming into the company from outside sources. He realized that there was an abundance of knowledge outside of the company that P&G needed to access and innovation was deemed a priority both internally and externally. In this way, the traditional strategic HRM system was complemented by bringing in external sources of knowledge and expanding the innovation integral to P&G's organizational capabilities.

R&D was revived in the form of the Connect and Develop plan. The idea was to restructure the organization to achieve high performing results while maintaining adaptability. Connect and Develop was positioned as a way to bring good ideas into the company, enhance them, and capitalize on P&G's internal capabilities. It was positioned as a way to 'turbocharge' existing capabilities rather than a transformation, as 'transforming' brought with it negative connotations.

Connect and Develop proved to be a successful plan and now over 50 per cent of P&G's innovations come from outside of the company, growing from 15 per cent in 2000. It has brought over two thousand products into the marketplace and generated over a billion dollars in sales. Connect and Develop was a lesson on combining external expertise with internal resources to capitalize on new sources of growth. By initiating a new strategic model focusing on external resources, existing employees are provided with challenges to old concepts and new ideas are brought forward to enhance a culture based upon innovation and competing on a global scale.

7.5 **Scania**

Scania is one of the world's leading manufacturers of heavy trucks and buses, established in Sweden, but currently with subsidiaries in over a hundred countries. Here we focus on Scania Production Zwolle in the Netherlands. This business area of Scania accounts for 60 per cent of production within Europe, and trucks departing from Zwolle are going to over sixty countries worldwide. Since opening in 1964, the workforce in Zwolle has grown to approximately 1,800 employees. In 2013, Scania won the HR Proffie Award (a prize for the best HR policy in the Netherlands). By way of an example, a summary of the contextual scan of Scania can be seen in Figure 7.1.

Scania's objective is to become the best manufacturer of trucks in Europe. To accomplish this, it works with a 'strategic platform' from which its core values originate. These core values (customers first, respect for all employees, fostering a culture of continuous improvement) determine the organizational culture and are the starting point for all business development.

Scania operates in a highly competitive, rapidly changing environment. In order to maintain its competitive advantage, it operates based on the 'lean' principles of the

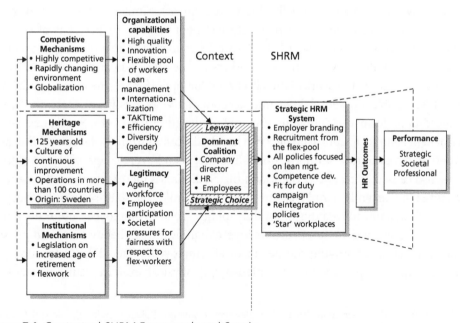

Figure 7.1 Contextual SHRM Framework and Scania

Scania Production System (SPS), which is derived from the famous Toyota lean manu-facturing system. SPS means a continuous focus on improving processes and efficiency. Scania encourages employees to come up with suggestions for improvement to make the company more efficient and able to provide the highest quality, holding twice-daily meetings for this purpose. Once a year Scania employees complete a survey to measure their work satisfaction and allow them to make suggestions for improvement. This survey enables Scania to respond to the needs of its employees and quickly undertake action when necessary.

In addition to lean management, Scania needs a large pool of flexible workers in order to cope with the dynamics in the marketplace, which are closely related to the cyclical nature of the economy. Flexibility allows Scania to react rapidly to market fluctuations or internal developments. What is particularly impressive in Scania is the alignment between the strategic need for flexibility and lean production and their HRM policies. Although the HRM policies are fully aligned with the principles of lean management, they also meet the demands for legitimacy and fairness. This level of balance between competitive and institutional mechanisms is arguably something that helps to make Scania so successful.

Operating in a highly dynamic market requires a flexible workforce alongside those working on a permanent contract. However, these flexible employees also have a need for security, which they can achieve by ensuring they maintain appropriate levels of training and skills. To aid this, Scania offers the pool of flexible workers the same training and develop-ment opportunities as is available to the permanent workers. Moreover, the pool of flexible workers is also the main source of recruitment as soon as core employees with a permanent contract leave the company (usually due to retirement). Similarly, flexible workers are offered a permanent contract when the flexible pool exceeds 30 per cent of the total workforce, based on an agreement with the works council. The role of the works council is essential in monitoring which flexible workers will be offered a permanent contract and when. Every quarter, the works council checks for opportunities to offer a permanent contract to flexible workers, taking into account the work quality of these workers as evidenced in performance appraisals and contract length. In 2014–15, Scania had offered a permanent contract to approximately two hundred workers from the flexible worker pool.

Another development within Scania is the increasing average age of the workforce. This is also caused by recent legislation in the Netherlands increasing the retirement age by two years. Currently, employees need to work until their sixty-seventh birthday. In response, Scania introduced the 'fit for duty' policy. To keep employees 'fit for duty' until they reach the age of sixty-seven, Scania invests significantly in behavioural and physical training, aimed at improving the health of all employees. The BRAVO training pro-gramme,[2] for example, focuses on intensifying physical exercise, quitting smoking,

---

[2] The meaning of the acronym 'BRAVO' is Bewegen (moving), Roken (smoking), Alcohol (alcohol), Voeding (food), and Ontspanning (relaxing).

drinking less alcohol, eating healthy food, and relaxing. Some 40 per cent of Scania's employees participate in this programme. There is a special BRAVO programme for older employees, which focuses more on changing their lifestyle. Participation is on a voluntary basis; however, a supervisor can encourage an employee to follow the programme when he/she thinks it would be beneficial. If an employee wants to focus on just one part of the BRAVO training programme, for example quitting smoking, Scania also offers this. Besides the training programmes, Scania also supports exercising elsewhere by sponsoring a running clinic by paying part of its costs. Scania also tries to stimulate a healthier food pattern at work. In the canteen, a distinction is made between 'green routes', which lead employees to the healthier food, and 'less green routes'. All products are marked with smileys (red, yellow, or green) to indicate the level of calories. All these initiatives are supported and communicated to the workforce via their internal newsletter, ensuring employees are aware of what is going on and can participate.

The HRM policies for absenteeism due to illness have also been changed. An employee who is ill has to ask for permission to stay at home, and at the same time a discussion/consultation takes place to see what kind of work-related activities the employee still can do in order to speed up the process of getting back to work. Within Scania, both the supervisor and employee are responsible for the reintegration process. This dual responsibility helped Scania to reduce its absenteeism rate to less than 4 per cent. However, some employees, mostly older workers, can be ill for a longer period of time, suffering from ailments than can be linked to permanent disabilities. Nevertheless, Scania tries to encourage these employees to reintegrate by sending reintegration-employees to help them identify what kind of work still can be done.

The time it takes to produce one truck, the 'TAKT-time', is a very crucial indicator within an assembly plant. Sometimes employees have difficulties or experience great stress to achieve this TAKT-time. In these cases, employees are able to call an 'Andon'. An 'Andon' is an all-round employee whose job it is to help other employees achieve the TAKT-time. If older or sick employees are frequently unable to keep up with the required TAKT-time, there are a couple of standard remedies available: First, they are offered 'fit for duty' programmes; second (a harsher approach), the company waits until the employee has been sick for two years and then he or she is dismissed. Scania argues that neither approach is beneficial for either the employee or the organization, and has therefore opted for a different approach. They identified this group of workers (80 out of the 1,800 total employees) and created a profile that included all tasks each employee was still able to perform. This profile was then compared to the job description. This comparison showed which workplace was best for a particular employee, and labelled this a 'star-workplace', which means that the company guarantees that this employee can work in that job until retirement. Scania wants to keep the whole of its workforce sustainable by providing them with job rotation, training, international exchanges, and potential-building programmes. By making use of the Scania Ergonomic

Standard (SES) instrument, the workplaces and work processes are continuously screened in order to safeguard the employees against hazardous working conditions and to keep them versatile, agile, and flexible.

7.6 **PostNL**

PostNL is a leading corporation in the Benelux in mail and parcel delivery and e-commerce. PostNL also operates in Germany and Italy, but our focus here is on PostNL in its home country, the Netherlands, where it employs some 50,000 people, both full and part-time. A summary of the contextual scan of PostNL can be seen in Figure 7.2.

Since around 2007, PostNL has been struggling with a shrinking market and a decline in physical mail (due to digitalization and email) and increasing competition (due to liberalization of legislation within Europe). It is therefore forced to focus on cost-saving initiatives, which has caused some employees to be transitioned to alternative work and mail delivery to become increasingly expensive. This has also resulted in full-time mail delivery employees (covered by an extensive CBA with many benefits) being replaced by

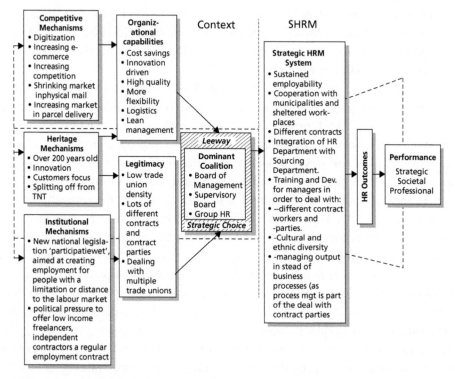

Figure 7.2 Contextual SHRM Framework and PostNL

part-time employees working only a few hours a day and being paid on the basis of a new CBA. This new agreement is more in line with new competitors in the market, who often pay their workers on a piece rate basis. Previously, full-time employees had an extensive range of tasks, including taking care of money orders and cash on delivery. Nowadays this has been removed, making the content of the job much simpler and hence requiring fewer qualifications. Moreover, as the new competitors operate with low-paid part-time employees, PostNL had to react to market dynamics. This change in staffing has caused some unrest in the company, even leading to strikes that generated attention within the community.

More recently, PostNL has managed to compensate partly for the decline in demand for mail delivery by focusing on parcel delivery, due to the increase in e-commerce and online shopping. They have already established eighteen parcel sorting and delivery centres throughout the Netherlands, employing some 1,300 workers.

Given the current market dynamics, the parcel delivery business unit has become very important as it is both profitable and is able to compensate partially for the loss of employment in the regular mail delivery unit. In terms of social responsibility, this unit has also helped to create new job positions. Postal workers working in mail delivery who were employed on a full-time basis and faced the risk of being laid-off, were offered jobs as parcel deliverers. If an employee did not want to accept the offer, there were other work options available, either in or outside the company.

In four out of the eighteen depots, sorting is carried out by PostNL employees, while in all other depots, contract workers are also employed. Among these contract workers are those who work for PostNL on a self-employed basis as subcontractors. Every day, some 2,600 delivery routes are planned in order to deliver an average of 500,000 parcels. In June 2015, PostNL offered the subcontractors a regular labour contract. They could also decide to remain as independent contractors and receive higher compensation. Nevertheless, in July 2015, some subcontractors blocked the sorting centres. The courts decided that these blockades were disproportional and should be stopped immediately. In the end, 15 per cent of the self-employed workers opted to become employees of PostNL.

The second group of contract workers are those who are in some way restricted in terms of access to the labour market. Two intermediaries are used for recruiting these people. First, PostNL works together with agencies that employ people who have physical and mental disabilities. PostNL can meet customer demands while also providing disabled people with an opportunity to do meaningful and rewarding work by engaging them in morning shifts for mail sorting. Secondly, PostNL cooperates with municipality agencies to help people reintegrate into the labour market, recruiting people who have been unemployed for a long period of time to get them used to working again. PostNL pays the agency a fee, which covers managing these workers, which means the agency is the employer rather than PostNL. However, it is a challenge to keep all these workers motivated and ensure they have the same focus, that is, providing a high-quality and punctual service to the final consumer. Both PostNL and society at large benefit from this: By offering work to these people, PostNL is able to deal with work peaks, while the long-term unemployed finally have an opportunity to go back to regular work and contribute to society.

In summary, PostNL works with many different groups of employees or contract workers to cope with peak hours in its sorting processes, responding to these higher demands in a social responsible way by working with people who have restricted access to the labour market. In this way, PostNL also contributes to societal well-being while improving the reputation/legitimacy of the company. Concurrently, PostNL is responding to the very competitive marketplace by creating social complexity within their workforce that is hard for competitors to imitate. To engage both employees and contract workers, PostNL checks the quality of work, employee productivity, and contributions to the environment, emphasizing that everyone can contribute to the company's performance and, if they do well, both employees and contract workers will be rewarded. PostNL aims to retain this healthy mix of workers.

Since PostNL has so many different groups of workers, they also have to deal with several trade unions. Although trade union density within PostNL is not very high, the company tries to ensure that both employees and contract workers are treated fairly and that their interests are properly considered.

Another way in which PostNL has responded to the competitive market is by introducing lean management. It has restructured its work processes, reducing the number of steps required for each process. For example, the central sorting centre has been abandoned because it took longer for employees to deliver the parcels. Currently, all depots run the complete process locally (sorting and delivery), which is much more efficient than the original process.

Increased efficiency was also gained by having more employees able to deliver over a total weight of 500 kg per delivery route. Because of the advent of internet shopping, the total load of parcels for delivery has increased. At the same time, however, there was a risk that the PostNL's parcel delivery process would slow down because not all self-employed deliverers were allowed to drive/carry freight above 500 kg. A driver requires an additional driving permit for this kind of work, so PostNL required all self-employed drivers (employees and contract workers) to qualify for this additional permit. Since all drivers are now allowed to deliver freight above 500 kg, PostNL is able to respond to the new demands of customers and remain competitive in the market.

7.7 Operating in challenging markets

SupplierStore (a pseudonym) was founded in the 1980s in the USA as a pioneering organization in the office supplies discount retail industry. Today, SupplierStore has grown to be a significant player as a wholesaler in the USA, going global in the 1990s.

In the 1980s, warehouse-style discount retailing was a new industrial trend that seemed to be effective in the general merchandising and consumer electronics fields for Price Club and Circuit City respectively. SupplierStore originated with a business strategy and competitive advantage focused upon providing office supplies to small-scale organizations at bulk discount rates in a market where only bigger companies were able to purchase large enough quantities of supplies to warrant such discounted buying. This strategy worked, as buying supplies from manufacturers directly, eliminating wholesalers from the supply chain, and maintaining low overhead costs allowed SupplierStore to offer office products at 20 to 75 per cent off retail prices—giving it a low-cost organizational capability. Costs were kept low, with retail outlets emphasizing functionality—merchandise was stacked on steel shelves in a floor-to-ceiling setup. Customer merchandise was kept on the lower six feet, with additional shelf space used for storage.

SupplierStore's corporate strategy rested not only on low-cost warehouse-style discount retailing, but also on organizational capabilities based upon rapid expansion and garnering market share to block new firms from entering a growing and lucrative industry. Goals for market expansion were set at entering multiple new markets and establishing a range of new retail outlets annually largely through mergers and acquisitions.

Technological expansion, with the availability of personal computers and fax machines, proved to be quite advantageous to SupplierStore's existing organizational capabilities, and allowed their sales to grow at a breakneck pace. Geographic expansion was combined with customer expansion as SupplierStore began to seek out the business of large firms. This was done by acquiring contract stationers and merging them with their retail businesses.

In the late 1990s, federal anti-trust regulations prevented a major merger taking place, and SupplierStore had to hold off expansion activity. Consequently, it arguably made poor choices in opening up stores in locations with a competitor-saturated market share, a strategy that worked against established organizational capabilities, while continuing to expand aggressively globally as well.

A heavy focus on a low-cost business strategy and aggressive market expansion has had direct implications for the company's strategic HRM system. Organizational capabilities and the company's low-cost competitive advantage have pushed for an excessive focus on employees needing to meet sales quotas at all costs. This has led to high employee turnover rates and a less than positive corporate culture. Anecdotally, employees have reported being pressurized to sell supplementary warranties and service plans with electronic goods such as laptops. Employees who fail to meet sales quotas are subject to disciplinary action with a constant threat of termination. Employees who meet sales quotas are rewarded with team commissions.

This type of strategic HRM system leads to employees finding 'loopholes' in order to maintain service quotas. For example, some employees have reported lying to customers about the availability of laptops if no interest is shown in purchasing the complementary warranties or service plans.

With rapid technological expansion and the proliferation of e-commerce, SupplierStore's heritage mechanism of warehouse-style discount retailing, which had previously served to build upon its low-cost competitive advantage, was rapidly becoming a part of a dying industry. E-commerce sites offer convenient selection and purchasing of office supplies at highly competitive prices with extremely low profit margins, and low prices are often coupled with free-shipping benefits. Customers of office supplies have little need to buy such merchandise from store locations as products are uniform and require minimal browsing compared to produce markets or clothing industries.

SupplierStore is facing key legitimacy issues today, including carrying unsustainable debt loads owing to excessive spending in times of insufficient cash flow. Currently, the company is hoping to repeat history with an expectation of different outcomes as it pursues, yet again, a merger with a major competitor. The Federal Trade Commission, however, remains unwavering in its attempts to block such a merger from occurring, as institutional mechanisms aim to prevent the formation of monopoly markets. Adding to this is a protracted decline in the market for store-sold office supplies. There is, therefore, expected to be little change in the strategic HRM system that is in place to support this aggressively competitive, low-cost corporate strategy.

7.8 Conclusions

The selected case studies provide examples of the way in which the theoretical framework of the Contextual SHRM Framework helps to analyse and explain the interaction between the different mechanisms in an organization's context. This includes the importance of taking into account an organization's heritage mechanisms—its organizational configuration and path dependency—and of (re)interpreting it not as a burden from the past but often as an important element to be cultivated and adapted in order to realize consistency between corporate strategy and the related HRM system, as the Efteling case shows. Bringing about legitimacy by taking into account the interests of a variety of stakeholders is also extremely relevant in establishing viability in the long term. The example from Randstad convincingly demonstrates this point. Both the Scania and PostNL cases highlight how to balance what could be considered negative work environments due to competitive needs (e.g. emphasizing efficiency, lean working, downsizing, reducing skill demands) with maintaining a sense of legitimacy and fairness among all workers. In contrast, the SupplierStore case illustrates what can go wrong when this balance between competitive and institutional mechanisms is not maintained. Finally, the P&G case provides evidence of the role of the key decision-makers in the whole process, demonstrating how they are able to shift the direction of the business and yet keep the HRM system aligned.

All of these case-study vignettes are at the level of individual organizations. In Chapter 8, we extend the analysis to the level of whole industries. Based on empirical evidence, we again demonstrate the value of analysis in which the interaction between the various dimensions of the Contextual SHRM Framework helps to explain the shaping of HRM systems, both with respect to content and to process.

8 Contextual SHRM Framework: Sector level

8.1 Introduction

Chapter 7 described how the Contextual Strategic Human Resource Management (SHRM) Framework can inform and explain strategic human resource management (HRM) policy decisions inside organizations. This chapter looks at how the framework can explain the selection of a SHRM system at the sector level: Here, we highlight in particular how competitive, institutional, and organizational constraints interplay to affect employment practices in different organizational settings.

To reiterate, the framework argues that there are key decision-makers in the employment relationship within a firm. These actors should base their judgements and decisions on SHRM matters on careful assessment of three contingent mechanisms: Competitive, heritage, and institutional. The nature of the three dimensions imposes certain constraints on decision-makers' 'degree of leeway'. However, rather than being observed necessarily as constraints, as we shall see throughout this chapter these may also offer opportunities and sources of potential competitive advantage, if applied appropriately.

The chapter presents evidence from four quite different industry sectors: Health-care, call centres, agriculture, and a contrast between the metal industry and the information technology (IT) industry. In the health-care industry, this application of the Contextual SHRM Framework shows how historical heritage mechanisms are being affected by new competition drivers, while remaining constrained by strongly institutionalized regulations and organizational structures. In the second sector-level case, call centres represent a relatively new industry, which is highly technology based, and frequently outsourced and offshored to minimize costs. In this context, we are able to analyse the phenomenon of offshoring—exploring the 'low road' SHRM implications of service-related activities being relocated to lower-cost labour countries. In the third case, the agriculture industry demonstrates how a highly constrained competitive and institutionalized context does not necessarily mean that there is only one HRM solution. We explore how the role of agency ultimately determines the SHRM system adopted. Finally, in contrasting the metal and IT industries (described in full in Schilstra (1998)), we examine how the firms set about achieving a balance between internal and external regulation of their employment relations. Some of the findings are surprising, even counter-intuitive to standard managerial orthodoxy. However, we shall argue that an interpretation of the findings according to the Contextual SHRM Framework offers a compelling explanation for the apparent anomalies.

8.2 **The Dutch hospital sector**

Basing this first sector-level analysis in the health-care sector in the Netherlands (comparable at least to other European health-care organizations),[1] we begin by considering the important heritage mechanisms at play: Hospitals in the Netherlands are configured based on a functional structure of task differentiation with specialized units, such as surgeons in the surgery department, and medical laboratory technicians in the diagnostics department. This silo structure, emphasizing differences between units, has made coordination between departments difficult. More recently, hospitals in the Netherlands have been transitioning towards a more process-oriented and customer-focused structure, in which divisions (rather than departments) focus on the processing of categories of patients, including both inpatient and outpatient services (Maarse, Mur-Veeman, & Spreeuwenberg, 1997). This means in practice that functional boundaries are crossed, and members of different departments are encouraged to collaborate and achieve common goals. However, due to the well-established functional silos, as yet progress in this respect has been limited.

The theme of restricted communication and collaboration is also present in the governance of hospitals in the Netherlands. Governance is based on a two-tier board model: a board of directors, responsible for the day-to-day running of the hospital, and an independent board of supervisors, responsible for checking and approving major decisions made by the board of directors (Hoek, 1999). Medical specialists do not have a full role in the hospital management and governance structure (Scholten & Van der Grinten, 2002). Instead, they are 'self-employed entrepreneurs' working in so-called 'partnerships'. Despite being strongly dependent on hospital management to be able to treat their patients, medical specialists occupy a rather autonomous position in the hospital: Decision-making in hospitals has traditionally been dominated by these physicians who have pursued goals critical to their status as professionals, but which may be incongruent with organizational goals (Lega & DePietro, 2005). Due to the high status of health professionals, hospital management faces the difficult tasks of engaging them in managerial issues and aligning their interests with organizational goals. The well-entrenched status hierarchy in medicine makes it difficult to communicate, share authority, and collaborate in problem solving and quality improvement across professional

---

[1] We would like to acknowledge Monique Veld (Utrecht University, The Netherlands) for her preparation of the data for this hospital sector case. For further details, see Veld (2012).

demarcation lines (Nembhard & Edmondson, 2006). Ultimately, this may adversely affect patient care.

The core of hospital staff is comprised of professionals: Physicians, nurses, allied health practitioners (such as respiratory therapists, occupational therapists, dieticians, and pharmacists), and health administrators (Garman, Leach, & Spector, 2006). Management of professional employees has traditionally involved high levels of employee discretion. As such, professionals often identify primarily with their profession rather than with the wider organizational context (Johnson, Selenta, & Lord, 2006). These professional networks create a shared sense of identity and common norms and values among their members (Golden, Dukerich, & Fabian, 2000). They often also provide training and education, both before and after organizational entry, reinforcing this professional identification.

Given this heritage perspective, we also need to consider how hospitals position themselves in the marketplace. Hospitals exist to deliver care to patients: an existence that has traditionally been based on supply-driven principles. However, the health-care sector in the Netherlands, as in other European countries, is changing from a supply-oriented system towards a more demand- and patient-oriented system. Policy-makers are seeking to combine market incentives with a framework of rules to guide competition, maintaining the ability to intervene in the case of market failures (Ham & Brommels, 1994). In the Netherlands, the government initiated two important elements to stimulate more market competition. In 2005, a new reimbursement system based on output pricing was introduced—forcing hospitals to make prices transparent and increasing competition (Grol, 2006). In 2006, the new Health Insurance Act (HIA) was introduced, under which every person who legally lives or works in the Netherlands is obliged to buy, from a private insurance company, a basic benefit package (Enthoven & Van de Ven, 2007), aimed at achieving a more equitable and cost-efficient health-care market (De Jong & Mosca, 2006).

This increase in market competition has stimulated hospitals to strengthen their customer profile and expand their services (Maarse, Mur-Veeman, & Spreeuwenberg, 1997), by, for example, publishing annual reports and performance indicators on hospital facilities and performance, and measuring patient satisfaction continuously. A more far-reaching intervention introduced was (integrated) care pathways: These are clinical management tools used to develop systematic and multidisciplinary care of patients (Verdú et al., 2009), requiring multidisciplinary cooperation and collaboration—addressing head on the primary challenge of functional silos in hospitals.

The competitive mechanisms are thus impacting on the heritage mechanisms: Increased market orientation is affecting both the internal design of hospitals (more collaboration and teamwork across functional divides), as well as stimulating cooperation with other external health-care providers, resulting in the creation of provider networks.

Turning our attention now to the institutional mechanisms, Dutch hospitals operate in a highly institutionalized context. This is mainly the result of a complex set of rules and procedures (e.g. for safety and quality of care) in combination with the profession-alization of specific employee groups. Despite the introduction of increased market competition, the Dutch government still regulates the health-care system by means of control over doctors' fees, the price determination of a large number of diagnosis-treatment combinations, hospital budgets, and quality and safety issues. Additionally, other stakeholders, such as the Dutch health-care inspectorate and patient organizations, have a major influence on hospitals: Hospitals need to report annually to these different stakeholder groups.

Another significant aspect of institutionalization is the national collective bargaining agreement (CBA) for hospitals, which regulates many aspects of the employment relationship. On behalf of all Dutch general hospitals (i.e. non-teaching hospitals), the Dutch Hospitals' Association (NVZ—Nederlandse Vereniging voor Ziekenhuizen) acts as the employer's federation to negotiate with five trade unions representing hospital employees. With an average unionization rate of 30 per cent, Dutch hospitals are relatively highly unionized, at least compared to other sectors of the Dutch economy. At the time of writing, the most recent CBA had been agreed in 2009, and focused on attracting and retaining employees, paying special attention to equal treatment of employees across different ages/stages in their working life. The regulations were designed to result in a better division of work among younger and older employees, better work–life balance, and an extension of the available workforce for the near future.

An additional aspect of the institutional mechanisms affecting hospitals is the avail-able workforce. The Netherlands' population is aging, which raises two challenges specifically for the health-care sector: (1) attracting and retaining highly qualified medical personnel; and (2) the need to provide additional health-care services as people live longer. The combination of an increasing demand for care and a diminishing available workforce carries the risk of increasing work pressure, which is becoming evident in the sector.

Against this analysis of heritage, competitive, and institutional mechanisms impacting on hospitals in the Netherlands, we also need to consider who are the key decision-makers involved in implementing the SHRM system. The key decision-makers of most Dutch hospitals consist of a board of directors, a supervisory board, members of the works council (in which the unions have a strong representation), the human resource (HR) director, and unit managers. The relatively high degree of unionization and the sector-wide CBA reduce the extent to which hospitals can differentiate themselves from their competitors. Additionally, hospitals have little financial leeway as they are dependent on government subsidies and face budgetary constraints. However, given the changes towards a more market-driven health-care system, hospitals have recently gained the ability to negotiate with health-care insurers at least about pricing.

From an HRM perspective, we now need to consider how the various challenges posed by the interplay between internal and external pressures are being addressed. First, as noted, attracting and retaining employees, especially nurses, are critical challenges. In addition to the aging workforce (institutional perspective), hospitals face a weak competitive position in the labour market (competitive perspective) due to a negative image characterized by high workload, relatively low salaries, limited growth opportunities in terms of personal development and salaries, and a hierarchical structure mainly due to the position of medical specialists (heritage perspective) (Boselie, 2010). One initiative being taken by some hospitals in response is to cooperate with regional training centres and other hospitals: For example, one group of thirteen hospitals have agreed to create more training opportunities for specialized jobs, to not actively recruit personnel from other hospitals which signed the covenant, and to help each other out in the event of short-term labour shortages.

Another initiative is the creation of more attractive personal growth opportunities by extending the role of nursing staff, through clinical nurse specialists, nurse anaesthetists, physician assistants, and nurse practitioners. Nurses with an extended role are involved in direct care, combine care from both nursing and medicine, and reduce costs for hospitals as less time by medical specialists is required (Schut, 1995). At the same time, these more expensive nurses are being substituted for less expensive care assistants and aides in their traditional roles (e.g. nutritionist's assistants). Similarly, to reduce costs, ancillary and support services are being outsourced. However, these cost-containment strategies appear to be at odds with the need to attract and retain qualified personnel, and can contribute to the negative image of the hospital sector.

Employees in hospitals are most likely to be committed to and motivated by their work (professional commitment) and their colleagues (ward or team commitment), but they are not usually primarily committed to the hospital itself (Johnson, Selenta, & Lord, 2006). HR functions therefore have to focus their attention on factors that have been shown to increase organizational commitment in hospitals: Adequate nurse staffing, organizational/managerial support for nursing, reduction of workload, leadership, and adequate time for professional development (Aiken, Clarke, & Sloane, 2002).

A final focal HR challenge is related to the design of the organization and of jobs. As noted earlier in this section, due to increasing pressure from competitive mechanisms, hospitals are shifting from a functional design towards a process-oriented and patient-focused structure. This restructuring is characterized by efforts to replicate private-sector management principles in hospital settings, and has been reflected in the introduction of commercially derived marketing concepts and management principles, like total quality management (TQM), Six Sigma, Investors in People, and the use of balanced scorecards. This refocusing has direct implications for health-care professionals, as the introduction of consumerism and managerial principles can be seen as fundamentally challenging the (long-)established positions of these people in the organizational heritage

(Laing & Hogg, 2002). Traditionally, patients were seen as 'grateful and passive recipients' of the services offered, as they deferred to the expert role and judgement of health-care professionals (Currie, 2009). These health-care professionals were guided by normative logics of medical professionalism. Recently, the role of 'patients' has been recast as the 'customer' (Geiger & Prothero, 2007). Given that customers nowadays are well informed and expect more and better services, health-care professionals are expected to act as service providers. As a result, they have to regard their relationship with patients/customers differently, rethinking their traditional position in society.

Similarly, the introduction of (integrated) care pathways implies that professionals need to cooperate and collaborate with other disciplines more frequently, both inside and outside the organization, resulting in more multidisciplinary teamwork. In terms of HRM, this means that employees are expected to be able and motivated to work together across both functional and organizational boundaries. This is a real challenge for HRM, given the well-entrenched status hierarchy that still exists in hospitals.

In summary, the focal HR challenges arising out of the competitive, institutional, and heritage mechanisms include: Staff attraction and retention, cost reduction, and organization/job redesign. Based on the Contextual SHRM Framework analysis, we can conclude that these themes demand attention in order to create sustained competitive advantage for hospitals in the near future. However, focusing on these themes alone is insufficient: the development and selection of SHRM systems should address the key issues raised by both the competitive and institutional mechanisms simultaneously. Most attention is currently paid to institutional mechanisms, as hospitals struggle with anticipated labour shortages caused by the aging workforce. However, the competitive mechanisms cannot be ignored as a result of the introduction of more market-driven competition and cost-containment programmes. It is not clear how much attention HR managers in hospitals are paying to these market dynamics, but there is a need to ensure that health-care professionals are able and willing to focus on further improving the relationship with their customers.

8.3 Call centres

In contrast to the health-care industry, which is well established within a nation's institutions and regulations, the call centre industry is relatively new, and is defined as a facility to manage service and sales transactions between provider firms and their customers (Holman, Batt, & Holtgrewe, 2007). In recent years there has been an increasing trend towards offshoring these call centres, particularly from high-cost to low-cost labour economies. A significant driver of this trend has been the increased availability and affordability of the necessary technologies to enable call centre services to be located at a distance from the customer base that they serve (Aksin, Armony, & Mehrotra, 2007;

Batt, 2001). The mode of operation most often chosen by large organizations to offshore their call centre activities is to outsource these to third-party suppliers (Lewin & Peeters, 2006). The primary reason for this has been the promise of cheaper costs from these specialist providers, in addition to the relocation of the activities to lower-wage countries. Alongside reducing labour costs, the industry has attempted to automate the process of customer interactions as far as possible, using technology-based help systems to avoid the need for direct contact with a customer representative (Aksin, Armony, & Mehrotra, 2007).

This technology-led industry is highly competitive (Batt, Colvin, & Keefe, 2002; Lewin & Peeters, 2006), leading organizations to continuously push to find ways to minimize their costs. From a 'pull' perspective, certain countries are offering firms the ability to reduce their costs not only through cheap wages, but also by offering tax incentives to relocate activities such as call centres to them: a commonly cited example country is Ireland (Metters & Verma, 2008). Such are the competitive mechanisms operating in the call centre industry, leading to desired core organizational capabilities of reduced costs and increased focus on customer service (Rao, 2004), greater flexibility of operations in terms of shrinking or expanding workforces (Bean, 2003), and access to bigger customer and labour markets (Aspray, 2010).

From an institutional mechanisms perspective, the location of these offshored call centres becomes crucial. The most common locations for English-language call centres are India, Ireland, Mexico, South Africa, and Canada, whilst Hungary is a popular location in the lower-cost Central European labour market, which has a supply of multilingual employees. A critical pre-condition for selecting a suitable location, alongside cost considerations, is thus a combination of language and culture (Holman, Batt, & Holtgrewe, 2007): the call centre staff must be able to speak the necessary language well, and show a degree of cultural fit with the customers they are to serve. In this sense, the spread of offshored call centres has been different to that of manufacturing, which focused less on such issues of fit and more on pure cost factors. So we see Ireland and Canada as popular offshoring sites for call centres; despite being developed and relatively high-cost labour markets compared with other low-cost locations, they have the advantage of a strong cultural affinity with, for example, UK and US customers (two of the major sources of offshoring of call centre activities). From the late 1980s onwards, as companies started to note the availability of talent in overseas locations that was available at a cheaper rate than in the home country, the offshoring trend of call centres began (Rao, 2004).

In the process of offshoring, the characteristics of the labour market are of critical importance, giving the desired organizational capability of reducing costs whilst still delivering a service. As we will see in Chapter 9, which focuses on an international analysis of the context of strategic HRM, countries have different legislation and regulation in place governing the employment relationship. Issues around work–life balance also vary considerably between countries (Holman, Batt, & Holtgrewe, 2007), which is a significant factor when examining call centres as the majority of employees worldwide are women (Ellram, Tate, & Billington, 2007). Similarly, the influence of trade unions on the employment relationship is more prominent in Western European countries than elsewhere, with their influence being minimal in many of the developing economies. We therefore see significant differences in norms for HRM activities, including pay rates, between countries.

The supply of suitably skilled talent for the call centres is a further important consideration when offshoring. In addition to language skills and the ability to display cultural fit, technical skills are also required to use call centre technologies. The ability to apply tacit knowledge and to deal with different types of people constantly are further necessary competencies (Ellram, Tate, & Billington, 2008; Lewin & Peeters, 2006). India is a prime example of a country that is able to offer this range of skills combined with low employment costs, hence its number one status as the offshore location for call centres (Metters & Verma, 2008). In a developing economy such as this, there is the added advantage that people are very keen to be recruited by the call centres, because they are seen to offer more desirable employment opportunities than some traditional industries such as manufacturing, but also because there are only limited opportunities for such workers (Rao, 2004).

A final institutional reason for offshoring is of an even more practical nature: Variation in time zones. By having operations based across the globe, offshoring is a mechanism for expanding the working day, with employees in one country just starting their day when those elsewhere are finishing. This enables the customer service function of call centres to be available around the clock (Aspray, 2010).

From the perspective of creating legitimacy from an institutional perspective for the firm's call centre operations, this can be a hotly contested issue. In general, the offshoring of activities for the primary purpose of cutting costs results in, on average, poorer working conditions for employees across this industry (Davis et al., 2006). These working conditions may be legitimate within the country of operation, but may not be seen as legitimate in the home country of the company that is offshoring these call centre activities, due to different levels of regulation of the employment relationship and expectations of employees.

The heritage of the call centre industry is relatively short, as this has only emerged as a major activity since the advent of suitable technological solutions. Call centres are not always offshored, and many do exist in the home countries of the large companies requiring this work (Holman, Batt, & Holtgrewe, 2007). Regardless of location, however, the nature of call centre work tends to be highly routinized (Metters & Verma, 2008), requiring semi-skilled staff, and is arguably not dissimilar to the routines of the manufacturing industry, which started the offshoring trend some years prior to call centres. The working conditions, particularly with regard to employee safety, may be said to be better than those in manufacturing; however, the daily routines have been found to be equally repetitive (Tybout, 2000). There is said to be some relief from this emerging with the use of multiple channels of customer support, such as telephone, fax, online chat, and email (Batt, Holman, & Holtgrewe, 2009); however, this can also lead to increased work pressure on call centre employees (Aksin, Armony, & Mehrotra, 2007).

In summary, the competitive, heritage, and institutional mechanisms identify the call centre industry as being one which is largely focused on cost-cutting, offshoring, automation, and routinization, giving rise to questions about the working conditions in these facilities. The key decision-makers identified in the Contextual SHRM Framework in this scenario are most often offshore third-party suppliers, which promise to minimize operating costs. (Compare this to the multiple stakeholders described as the key decision-makers within hospitals, noted in Section 8.2.) The contracting company hands over responsibility for the operation of the call centre to these suppliers, and is therefore not involved in day-to-day management issues (Fjeldstad & Ketels, 2006). Trade unions often play a very minor role in this industry, as it is known for its union exclusion strategies in many countries (Taylor & Bain, 2008). Given this background, we can now consider the related consequences for the SHRM system.

There is some debate as to whether the call centre industry can be described as homogenous, particularly in management practices. Although there is evidence of a standardized call centre management model emerging (Holman, Batt, & Holtgrewe, 2007), a variety of models are described, ranging from 'mass production' (Batt & Moynihan, 2002) and 'assembly lines in the head' (Taylor & Bain, 1999), to the 'professional services model' (Batt & Moynihan, 2002) based on 'high commitment service' (Holman, 2003). The former focus on a Taylorist work organization with a strict labour division and standardized tasks, whilst the latter focus on employees constantly enriching their knowledge and skills through training and development on the job, the provision of favourable working conditions, and long-term employment prospects (Gorjup, Valverde, & Ryan, 2009). Here, we focus predominantly on the 'mass production' model, as this has most commonly been adopted in the offshored call centres due to their primary focus on cost cutting.

Offshored call centre operations have predominantly been linked with 'low road' HRM strategies (Youndt et al., 1996). These strategies focus on workers being subject to high specialization in their activities (Aksin, Armony, & Mehrotra, 2007). This has the positive effect of an employee becoming highly skilled and knowledgeable in a particular area of work, but has the disadvantage of removing variety from the daily routine (Batt, 2001). This is particularly important given that many call centre employees must deal with negative interactions with customers on a regular basis—when routinized, this can take a heavy toll on the employee (Aksin, Armony, & Mehrotra, 2007).

A second cost-cutting element of the low road strategy is the use of computer-based training (CBT). Despite there being some evidence that call centre staff training is most effectively carried out in role-play activities in a classroom environment (Murthy et al., 2008), CBT is preferred by many organizations because this is training which an employee can do in their own time sitting at their workstation—it is a highly efficient and cost-effective way of carrying out training, but has not been found to be most effective for call centre staff due to the lack of personal interaction and opportunities to ask questions.

Finally, on the low road, many call centres have incentive-based pay systems—the more work an employee does, the more money they will receive (Batt, Colvin, & Keefe, 2002). This puts great pressure on employees to work harder in order to receive greater pay, and may in some cases lead to employee burnout (Aksin, Armony, & Mehrotra, 2007). Counter to this trend of taking a low road approach to HRM in offshored call centres, one more positive HRM activity has been reported in some developing country settings: Selective recruitment (Holman, Batt, & Holtgrewe, 2007). This approach uses a number of tools, such as psychological and aptitude tests, to ensure the right person is appointed to the call centre position, reducing the chance of quick turnover of employees.

The often cited reality of the working conditions of employees in offshored, outsourced call centres in developing economies is an SHRM system of low pay, low job security, long hours, high utilization rates (Aksin, Armony, & Mehrotra, 2007), few layers of management hierarchy (on average, 7–15 per cent of the workforce in a call centre is management: Batt, Holman, & Holtgrewe, 2009) reducing opportunities for promotion (Batt, Colvin, & Keefe, 2002), and strict behaviour control systems (Holman, Batt, & Holtgrewe, 2007). This appears to be the emergent standard for people management practices in the offshored call centre industry. Workers are allocated to teams yet expected to work largely in isolation from their colleagues with a minimum of social support (Hingst, 2006). These low road strategies are desirable based on the organizational capabilities being sought, namely cost cutting, customer focus, flexibility, and access to larger markets (Bean, 2003; Rao, 2004). These strategies also achieve legitimacy because they meet the employment regulations for the country of operation (although some may dispute this legitimacy under the ethical discussions around workers' rights on a global scale).

The related HR outcomes are largely described in call centre research as negative due to this low road strategy. Burnout and psychological problems due to high-stress workloads, and physical health issues due to repetitive activities in inappropriately set-up office environments, have been reported (Aksin, Armony, & Mehrotra, 2007; Tybout, 2000). As a result of these negative employee experiences, combined with low pay and employee dissatisfaction, there are high levels of absenteeism and turnover reported across the industry (Metters & Verma, 2008). This has a negative impact on the desired outcome of cost saving from offshoring the call centre: High turnover rates mean more is spent on recruiting replacements, as well as new employees being less productive initially due to the learning curve for the job (Aksin, Armony, & Mehrotra, 2007). In India, the turnover issue has also led to staggering increases in wages in order to keep people in the industry (Farrell, 2006). On the flipside, in some developing economies turnover is less of a problem as call centre employees simply value the job too much to leave, despite the working conditions (Rao, 2004): Turnover rates in call centres in the USA are between 50–100 per cent, but are much lower in the less developed economies where fewer alternative opportunities for employment are available (Bean, 2003).

In unionized call centres (predominantly found in Western Europe), 40 per cent lower rates of turnover have also been reported (Holman, Batt, & Holtgrewe, 2007). However, developing economies have a weaker history of trade union activity. The impact of unionization is also not always seen as positive, with some workers reporting harder working conditions after the intervention of a union due to the union being more interested in pushing its own interests than those of the workers (Doellgast, 2008). One explanation for this is that unions might seek to preserve their influence by deliberately negotiating more restrictive work rules and narrower job classifications, whilst others argue that unions had little to gain by working with management on implementing high-involvement work practices, since this could minimize their role in the workplace.

Despite the issue of turnover and absenteeism costs, research suggests that offshoring call centres still achieves the desired organizational capability of reducing costs and increasing profit margins: One study showed up to 40 per cent cost savings for offshoring call centres (Bean, 2003). In summary, this low road SHRM system observed in offshored call centres appears to be successful given the desired organizational capabilities and local legitimacy, leading to positive financial performance outcomes. The broader issue of the appropriateness of such an SHRM system in the context of employee rights on a global scale is, of course, an issue still open to debate.

8.4 **Agriculture**

The labour-intensive element of the agriculture industry is often associated with low-skilled work combined with precarious employment practices in order to minimize costs in a low-margin business. Within this industry, there are nonetheless some agricultural firms that decide to take a more ethical stance, focusing on the value of employees beyond their use as an expendable commodity. The example we present here (discussed in detail in Kroon & Paauwe, 2014) shows how the structure of an industry, in this case the agriculture industry in the Netherlands, in itself does not have to determine the SHRM system, but is affected to a great extent by the key decision-makers in the firm.

Looking first at the competitive constraints, these are substantial for this industry. Agriculture in the Netherlands is a small but not insignificant contributor to gross domestic product (GDP), producing both food (cereals, fruit, vegetables, meat) and non-food (plants) goods. Post-mechanization, there remain many low-skilled jobs, such as planting or fruit picking by hand. Margins for producers have declined steadily, and labour costs in this sector can be as high as 80 per cent of production costs (Kroon & Paauwe, 2014).

From an institutional perspective, the industry as a whole is highly regulated through sector-level collective agreements bargained between trade unions and the agricultural employers' associations. In addition, due to the notoriously precarious nature of the employment situation of low-skilled workers in this sector, the industry is subject to increasing scrutiny from various agencies and inspectorates. In all, there are considerable institutional constraints facing firms operating in this sector in the Netherlands.

Exploring the organizational constraints, traditional family businesses are gradually being taken over by conglomerates, increasing the average size of farms (facilitated also by the advent of mechanization). Nevertheless, we are still talking about firms that are usually employing 250 employees or less. Fewer students are undertaking an agricultural education to enter the industry, and instead labour needs are being addressed through migrant populations from neighbouring Eastern Europe.

Given these considerable constraints, we might expect a similar response in terms of the SHRM system that is adopted (such as the cost cutting, 'low road' HRM strategy we discussed in Section 8.3). Indeed, the firms included in the study by Kroon and Paauwe (2014) also faced other similar challenges such as labour shortages, and a focus on labour costs. However, what is interesting is that the key decision-makers in the firms reacted to these constraints with regard to their overall ethical stance (an element of the competitive and heritage mechanisms of the firm in the Contextual SHRM Framework—see Chapter 6).

Kroon and Paauwe (2014) found a distinct difference in staffing, remuneration, and employee voice practices between firms, dependent on their position with regard to social responsibility. For example, firms that believed in the use of more precarious employment practices were supported in their use of low-cost immigrant labour by the increasing availability of government-led schemes to legitimize the bureaucracy around such practices. In contrast, the more socially responsible firms were focused on trying to find longer-term solutions to the labour shortage problems. Their focus was on working with local educational institutions to bring people into the industry with an eye to improving their longer-term employability, again supported by government-led initiatives.

In summary, both agricultural firms that believed in the adoption of more precarious employment practices, and those focusing on greater social responsibility, found ways to justify and pursue their activities through the structural properties of the sector in the

Netherlands. The choice of which structural approach to adopt was, however, taken inside the firm, depending on how it wished to position itself in the marketplace. As a result of this decision, different SHRM systems emerged in the two types of firm, highlighting the importance of context and agency in the design of these systems.

8.5 Contrasting the IT and metal sectors

This next case also considers the question of managerial leeway in the selection of a SHRM system, this time to support the performance outcome of flexibility. Flexibility is defined in a number of ways: Numerical flexibility—through the use of temporary contracts or outsourcing to reduce the number of employees on permanent contracts; functional flexibility—by introducing multi-skilling to ensure people can take on different roles in the organization as and when needed; and financial flexibility—introducing forms of variable pay, so that the financial outgoings of the firm on wages are in some way linked with how well the firm is performing. This section contrasts case studies of thirteen firms in the Netherlands in the IT and metal industries (based on the doctoral thesis of Schilstra, 1998; and Schilstra, Dietz, & Paauwe, 2004: ch. 7). The cases compare internal and external regulation of the employment relationship, leading to some perhaps counter-intuitive findings if we were only to analyse these cases from an economic rationality perspective. The Contextual SHRM Framework, with its balance of both economic and relational rationality, helps us to interpret the findings more clearly, understanding the implications of the operating context of firms in these two quite different sectors.

Internal regulation focuses on both individual and collective forms of employee representation that are housed in the firm itself, usually carried out through works councils or enterprise unions. External regulation of the employment relationship at sector level occurs through government rules regarding minimum and maximum protection of employee rights, as well as institutionalizing industrial relations processes. Externally, there are also sector-wide employer and employee bodies that enter into CBAs, which cover all firms operating within a sector in the Netherlands (as we saw in the case of the hospitals in Section 8.2). If we take a managerial perspective, the general assumption is that internal regulation of an industry demonstrates leeway for corporate autonomy and strategic choice, whereas external regulation limits the extent to which the firm's managers are able to make strategic decisions regarding the employment relationship.

Before looking at the IT and metal industries in any detail, it is first important to understand a little about the broader employee relations (ER) context in the Netherlands (see also Chapter 4). Dutch ER is built on a system which encourages multiparty consensus, reaching compromises between the different stakeholders, which are seen to be mutually beneficial. External, centralized regulation of the employment relationship across industry sectors is common (although a slight shift towards some decentralization of this process has been noted in recent years—Trampusch, 2006). Against the backdrop of this external regulation, firms are increasingly attempting to gain some leeway over the SHRM system they are able to put in place (to help them be both legitimate and competitive).

The hypothesis tested by Schilstra (1998) focused on the introduction of flexible working practices in two very different sectors in the Netherlands: IT and metal. Schilstra hypothesized that it would be easier to introduce flexible working in the newer, less established IT industry, than in the more established metal industry. Table 8.1 summarizes the differences between these two sectors in the Netherlands.

Table 8.1 Contrasting the Dutch metal and IT industries

Metal industry	IT industry
Employment relationship: – Long established, institutionalized – Both employers as well as employees are well organized	Employment relationship: – Newer, weaker institutionalization
Key decision-makers: – Strong employers' association (against company level agreements) – Four trade unions (28% membership density, evenly spread across firms) – Works council per site and a central works council (with substantial union input)	Key decision-makers: – Weaker employers' association with fewer members (resists collective external regulation and standardized reductions in working hours), though increasing in comparison with the past – Four trade unions (5–10% membership density with low recruitment), aiming to increase CBAs – Works councils at sites exist but are primarily a consultative body with little union input – 'Platforms', which are cross-firm works councils, have separate CBAs for the hardware and software areas of the industry
Leeway: – Collective bargaining tradition at sector level (primary terms of labour covering all employees in the industry) – Collective bargaining tradition at company level (augmenting minimum labour standards requiring union approval)	Leeway: – Sector agreements only apply to the hardware part of the industry as too few software firms are members of the employers' association (in total 18% of IT workers covered) – Large degree of management leeway
SHRM system determination: – Business strategy is linked to trade union goals at sector and company level	SHRM system determination: – Business strategy is linked to works council goals at company level
Flexible working heritage: – High use of temporary employees, overtime, and multiskilling (in firms where business is predictable) – Low use of performance-related pay but some forms of variable pay present (e.g. profit sharing)	Flexible working heritage: – Unpredictable market demand means many short-term contracts – High use of outsourcing – High use of variable pay (although the trade unions resist the link to performance)

Based on the case studies, the outcomes of attempts to increase the implementation of flexible working practices as part of the SHRM system across both sectors were as follows:

- very few firms faced serious constraints (either external or internal) to their plans to introduce more flexible working arrangements;
- works councils enabled employees to have insight in company information, and therefore a joint problem-solving approach was adopted;
- both internal and external regulation can be beneficial from a management perspective (evidence: the IT firms voluntarily accepted sector-wide agreements and involved works councils rather than management deciding unilaterally; and metal firms preferred to use supplementary internal regulation through works councils).

Why were these outcomes observed across both sectors despite their substantial differences in managerial leeway? From an economic rationality perspective, we might have expected to see management assert its right to strategic choice, rather than sharing this with employees through works councils and trade unions. However, the answer appears to lie in legitimacy. Adopting a relational rationality lens to interpret these findings, we can see that trade union involvement in policy decision-making accords greater credibility to the outcomes for employees, leading to less chance of rejection of the new policies. The external process also uses professional negotiators (both from the employers' federations as well as from the trade unions) who are not personally affected by the outcomes, enabling a less personal and more focused discussion to take place. It was also found that trade unions are dominant where collective bargaining exists, otherwise works councils are used for firms seeking to legitimize their decisions. Trade union-negotiated CBAs were also found to give greatest legitimacy due to the legal weight of these agreements, and the fact that they covered all employees rather than only those at a particular site (as with works councils).

In summary, this study found that external regulation creates legitimacy that may be desired by management as part of the process of implementing corporate strategy. This finding would be counter-intuitive if we only adopted an economic rationality perspective, expecting to see that managers would prefer to maintain autonomy over the implementation of flexible working practices. These findings may, however, be very specific to the Dutch context, given its tradition in general of a tripartite employment relationship—involving the government, employee, and employer representatives in the widespread development of CBAs. This only reinforces the importance of the benefits of applying the Contextual SHRM Framework to analyse a firm's context (the competitive, institutional, and heritage mechanisms, as well as who are the key decision-makers) to understand the SRHM system and how this might lead to firm-level performance.

8.6 **Conclusions**

In summary, the four sets of analysis presented here highlight the very different sector contexts in which organizations are operating. The highly institutionalized hospital, agriculture, and metal industries in the Netherlands contrast strongly with the dynamic IT and call centre industries. However, we cannot assume that organizations in the highly institutionalized settings only have to worry about institutional mechanisms: It is correct that they may have to deal with more regulation of their activities, but this must be offset against the competitive demands being placed on the industry. In the case of hospitals, this means attempting to develop competitive advantage through their people, attracting and retaining key staff members at a time when the image of the industry is suffering. In agriculture, this means coming up with creative solutions to labour shortage problems whilst keeping labour costs low—either through low-cost immigrant labour, or through focusing on the education of future employees for the sector. Similarly, the metal industry used its institutionalized system of works councils as a mechanism to garner support for the introduction of flexible work practices. In contrast, the newer industries of IT and call centres are not devoid of institutional considerations—the competitive mechanisms may be dominant, but from a SHRM perspective, an understanding of the regulations surrounding the employment relationship, as well as employee expectations of how they will be treated in the workplace, combine to emphasize the legitimacy requirements for firms operating in these sectors. In short, a balanced approach to considering sector-level competitive and institutional mechanisms, as well as considering the role of key decision-makers, is essential to understanding the SHRM system adopted in any organization operating within these sectors.

9 Contextual SHRM Framework: International level

9.1 Introduction

Throughout this book, we have highlighted the importance of context to the design and implementation of human resource management (HRM) activities: HRM should be sensitive to the institutional environment in which it is embedded. This argumentation culminated in the Contextual Strategic Human Resource Management (SHRM) Framework (see Chapter 6), which, in Chapters 7 and 8, we have applied at the organization and industry sector levels, exploring how these different contexts influence the relationship between SHRM and performance. Here, we expand this analysis and explore another macro-level context: the national-level institutional and cultural influences on the SHRM system in multinational corporations (MNCs).

MNCs are faced with the challenge of operating in multiple competitive and institutional environments simultaneously, so this raises the question of how they deal with this variety. This chapter explores the debate between 'best practice' and 'best fit', considering how drivers at the national and international level affect the SHRM—firm performance linkage in the international context. By applying the Contextual SHRM Framework, examples of SHRM systems in high-performing MNCs are presented as illustrations of the best practice and best fit approaches, and of a balance between the two.

9.2 MNCs: Best practice or best fit?

In Chapter 3, we highlighted the relevance of different types of fit between the SHRM system and the organizational context. However, most of the SHRM literature is quite universal in nature, prescribing what might be described as 'best practices' (rather than best fit) for firms to adopt in terms of achieving the highest rate of return on financial investment.

The international context highlights the dilemma facing all organizations operating as multinationals between adopting a best practice approach as opposed to best fit: To what extent should all activities be controlled or guided from the central headquarters (based

---

TEXTBOX 9.1 BEST PRACTICE VERSUS BEST FIT

Let's consider an example here: Universalistic best practice has often been associated with the Japanese management practices of the 1980s in production manufacturing environments, where cost and quality issues predominated. Companies developed lean or agile manufacturing systems, mirroring practices in the Japanese motor industry (McCurry & McIvor, 2002). The characteristics of these lean manufacturing systems were linked in turn to HRM practices in the form of high-performance work systems, focusing on employee development, employee participation, teamwork, incentive-based pay, and investment in recruitment and selection (Appelbaum et al., 2000; Boxall & Purcell, 2003). These practices became accepted amongst manufacturing companies as the 'best' practices to improve firm performance.

Empirical studies which explored the transfer of these Japanese employment practices found that the US manufacturers that adopted a full system of innovative Japanese HRM practices achieved higher levels of productivity and quality than those manufacturers who only adopted certain individual practices, supporting the universal best practice theory (Ichniowski & Shaw, 1999; Park et al., 2003). *However*, the number of US manufacturers found to be adopting full systems of Japanese HRM practices remained minimal, implying that there are mechanisms other than pure anticipated performance outcomes impacting on the spread of best practice.

---

on best practice), or be adapted at the local level in the different countries in which the organization operates (based on best fit)? The best practice option relies on universal standardization of practices that can be cost-effectively and fairly adopted across the organization worldwide (Pfeffer, 1995). MNCs adopt the practices with which they are most familiar or which appear to promise high returns in performance, regardless of the location of their subsidiary (Gooderham & Nordhaug, 2003). This universality of HRM practices within an MNC creates cross-border equity and comparability, and an alignment of systems internationally to facilitate an internal labour market (Almond, Edwards, & Clark, 2003). However, this standardization can lead to conflict between company practices and local prevailing conditions such as national cultural phenomena, institutions, and business systems (Whitley, 1992). Referring to the Contextual SHRM Framework, this best practice approach is akin to applying *competitive mechanisms* reasoning to achieve organizational capabilities (see Textbox 9.1).

On the other hand, the best fit approach focuses on the need to adapt HRM practices to local conditions, rejecting the notion of one best way of doing things in all contexts (Delery & Doty, 1996): akin to applying *institutional mechanisms* reasoning to achieve organizational legitimacy. MNCs adapt their employment policies to be legitimate in each new setting, including aligning themselves with the social, cultural, political, legal, and competitive aspects of their operating environment (see also Chapter 6).

The best practice approach provides MNCs with economies of scale and consistency across the global system; the best fit approach provides legitimacy in local markets with legislative, trade union and other institutional systems, and cultural norms. But what happens to MNCs aiming simultaneously for efficiency and legitimacy? This is where *strategic choice* comes into play (a fundamental building block of the Contextual SHRM Framework—see Chapter 6).

MNCs hold a unique position, with their cross-border activities creating options on how to operate within the global environment, the primary strategic choice being selecting an appropriate internationalization strategy. The options available are most frequently described in terms of Perlmutter's (1969) and Bartlett and Ghoshal's (1989) classifications: ethnocentric, global strategy in which control is centralized and subsidiaries resemble the parent company (representing the best practice approach); poly-centric, multi-domestic strategy in which control is decentralized and subsidiaries conform to local practices (representing the best fit approach); and the geocentric (or regiocentric as added by Perlmutter & Heenan, 1974), transnational strategy in which subsidiaries and headquarters alike adhere to worldwide (or regional) standards as part of an organizational network (representing a balance between best practice and best fit). In Section 9.4, we present examples of each of these three strategies, explored through the lens of the Contextual SHRM Framework, but first we consider in more depth the specific drivers of SHRM systems in MNCs.

9.3 **Drivers of SHRM systems**

Given these pressures on MNCs regarding how they manage their international oper-ations, here we explore the underlying drivers (from a competitive, institutional, and heritage perspective, in line with the Contextual SHRM Framework) that lead firms to choose between a best practice and best fit approach to maximize firm performance. As a starting point, we can list potential influences on HRM practices in the MNC context: national culture (Schuler & Rogovsky, 1998; Sparrow, Schuler, & Jackson, 1994); nation-ality of ownership, country-of-origin and industry sector (Edwards & Ferner, 2002; Ferner, 1997); and national institutions and business systems (Budhwar & Sparrow, 2002; Whitley, 1992). However, we need a clear understanding of what converts these contextual factors into actual drivers of the SHRM system.

Chapter 6 identified the theoretical building blocks of the Contextual SHRM Frame-work, including neo-institutional theory and the resource-based view (RBV) of the firm. Here, we apply these theories in the context of the international operations of MNCs. Table 9.1 illustrates how we can look at institutional mechanisms (based on neo-institutional theory) and competitive mechanisms (based on RBV) from both inside and outside the MNC.

Quadrant 1 focuses on the *heritage mechanisms* of the Contextual SHRM Framework. Differentiation of practice at the national level between MNCs can be seen due to the historical background of the organization. The power structures and relationships

Table 9.1 Overview of theoretical perspectives influencing SHRM systems in MNCs

	Internal context	External context
Institutional mechanisms	Organisational heritage → institutional differentiation between firms *1*	National level context-dependent best fit → institutional isomorphism of firms *2*
Competitive mechanisms	Strategic choice/ key decision-makers → competitive differentiation between firms *3*	Global level universal best practice benchmarking → competitive isomorphism of firms *4*

between subsidiaries and headquarters are affected by past decisions as much as by external institutional-level influences (Ferner, Almond, & Colling, 2005). Thus, decisions and actions from the past are reproduced in existing organization structures, creating an internal institutionalized environment. For example, Procter & Gamble (P&G) are known as a company that grows its people from within, given its strong tradition (heritage) of developing and promoting people rather than turning to external hires wherever possible.

Focusing on *institutional mechanisms*, quadrant 2 considers how firms take a best fit approach within a particular national level context. This leads to *institutional isomorphism* of MNCs: all firms in a given country adopt the same or very similar practices in a certain area of HRM, for example, collective bargaining rights due to legislative requirements. This is creating legitimacy for the firm to operate in this country. This implies the application of relational rather than economic rationality, as adoption of the practice may not be directly related to the anticipated return on financial investment, but is more due to a sense of obligation for the firm to comply and, as such, will help the firm to achieve legitimacy.

Quadrant 3 brings in the *competitive mechanisms* in MNCs. This quadrant focuses on how the firm chooses to differentiate itself from its competitors by developing an appropriate set of organizational capabilities. If we position this within the best practice versus best fit choice facing MNCs, we see that strategic choice in competitive positioning determines whether a company opts to be more differentiated from or more similar to its competitors and to its environment (Deephouse, 1999). For example, taking an *inclusive* approach to talent management rather than an *exclusive* approach focusing only on high potentials might create competitive advantage in the (labour) marketplace.

Additionally, quadrant 3 highlights the importance of the *key decision-makers*: the role of power and politics can influence organizational actors in deciding whether to extend or limit the extent of global policies to safeguard their own interests (Edwards & Kuruvilla, 2005; Ferner, Almond, & Colling, 2005). Institutional pressures are thus found not to have a deterministic effect, but are moderated by the role of powerful individuals and groups within the organization (Edwards et al., 2005). MNC actors at national or local level can draw on elements from the institutional context in order to prevent the implementation of standardized HRM practices emanating from corporate level (Ferner, Almond, Colling, & Edwards, 2005). For example, a local manufacturing plant that has consistently used a local recruitment agency for all of its hires might reject a corporate mandate to use a different national agency due to the strong relationship the plant has built up with their local agency, as well as the local agency's better knowledge of the local labour market.

Finally, quadrant 4 focuses on the notion of *competitive isomorphism*, as described by neo-institutional theory (DiMaggio & Powell, 1983). Competitive isomorphism explains how, due to competitive pressures, firms across the globe start to look more alike, adopting global-level universal best practice through a process of global strategic decision-making and benchmarking. This form of benchmarking and 'keeping up with the Joneses' provides a certain level of organizational capability, but does not make an MNC stand out as being better than other firms. It is merely a necessary requirement (a form of legitimacy) which prevents the firm from falling behind. Well-known examples of this include the use of balanced scorecards or carrying out employee engagement surveys, as nowadays these are commonplace in many companies. In order to achieve more sustainable and superior levels of performance, the key decision-makers need to develop corporate strategies that differentiate the firm from its competitors (quadrant 3).

In summary, neo-institutional theory assumes that MNCs conform to institutional pressures, adapting their HRM practices in order to achieve legitimacy, which will enable them to acquire the necessary resources to operate successfully within a given context. Conversely, the RBV assumes MNCs are motivated from an economic or competitive perspective to position themselves differently from competitors, creating a set of best HRM practices which only that firm has in place across all of its operations. Thus, in order to understand the link between HRM and performance in the MNC context, the RBV and institutional views need to be combined, distinguishing between rational ('bounded by uncertainty, information limitations and heuristic biases') and non-rational choices ('bounded by social judgment, historical limitations and the inertial force of habit') (Oliver, 1997: 10).

MNCs are, however, faced with maintaining legitimacy as well as remaining competitive not only in a single location, but also in all of the locations in which they operate (Kostova & Roth, 2002). This gives rise to *institutional duality*: the external institutional context can come into conflict with the internal relational context, which depends on the role that subsidiaries play in relation to the headquarters, shaped by levels of dependency and trust between corporate headquarters and subsidiary and the degree to which the subsidiary identifies with the parent company. Kostova and Roth (2002) found that the less dependent a subsidiary is on its local host country, the less likely there will be a need for local legitimacy, and hence more powerful MNC operations will be able to exercise their own strategic choice.

Another related aspect of duality is the distinction between so-called high context and low context perspectives for observing differences and similarities in HRM policies and practices. In high context situations (e.g. coordinated market economies with strict labour legislation and high union presence, such as Germany, Sweden, or the Netherlands), practices are more likely to be customized to fit the local context, but where context is low (as in liberal market economies with much less local regulation and weaker trade unions, such as the USA or UK), universal rationales may be observed (Child, 2000; Whitley, 1992). At the global level, there is very little regulation of HRM (beyond the initiatives of the International Labour Organization (ILO) or the United Nations (UN), for example), and so this could be described as a low context scenario where there is more scope for MNCs to make strategic choices. Hence there is the potential either to adopt universalistic practices by benchmarking the activities of competitors, or to opt for competitive differentiation. However, at the national level, there are more coercive and normative pressures on MNCs to conform to local regulation and culture, and hence, in this high context situation, the leeway for strategic choice is reduced and more local 'best fit' approaches to HRM may be adopted (Farndale, Brewster, & Poutsma, 2008). In this latter scenario, the focus on institutional isomorphism is likely to be stronger.

9.4 **Examples from high-performing MNCs: A methodology**

Applying the Contextual SHRM Framework to the institutional and competitive choices facing MNCs, here we draw on case studies from a major piece of international research known as the Global HR Research Alliance to illustrate how firms are managing this duality. In 2004/5, sixteen well-known MNCs were selected for inclusion in a study based on their superior business performance and reputation as an employer as defined through 2004 *Fortune* listings and equivalent rankings. A series of in-depth case studies in these MNCs was undertaken, exploring what the firms themselves described as human resource (HR) excellence. The study was carried out in collaboration with researchers across the globe.[1] In total, interviews were held with 248 interviewees in the 16 MNCs, based in 19 countries. A multiple respondent approach was adopted, including interviews with 153 HR professionals and 95 non-HR senior executives, line managers, and employee representatives. While 108 of the interviews were carried out at corporate headquarters, 91 were held at either country or divisional head office level, and 55 at unit

---

[1] Philip Stiles and Jonathon Trevor (Cambridge University, UK); Jaap Paauwe and Elaine Farndale (Erasmus University Rotterdam/Tilburg University); Pat Wright (Cornell University, USA); Shad Morris (MIT, USA); Günther Stahl (Insead, Singapore).

level within a specific business division. The hour-and-a-half-long interviews were semi-structured, covering questions about the business context, HRM practices, and the HR function; they were carried out face to face and recorded where possible. In Sections 9.4.1 to 9.4.3, we illustrate different MNCs decisions to adopt a best practice, best fit, or balanced approach to achieve their firm's goal of high performance.

9.4.1 IBM: A BEST PRACTICE APPROACH

IBM,[2] founded in 1911 in the USA, is a major provider of technological innovation for businesses, and today has over 400,000 employees doing business in over 160 countries worldwide. At the time of interviewing in 2004/5, IBM was one of the most centralized firms in the study, alongside another US firm in the technology sector, Oracle. IBM traditionally valued its centralized, top-down system to ensure that everyone was always working from the same page (Morris & Calamai, 2009). Also, from an HRM perspective, IBM had a strong belief that what was developed at headquarters was the best practice for the whole of the corporation, irrespective of location: Some examples are given here of IBMs best practice in performance management, training, and diversity.

First, from a performance management perspective, potential leaders and current executives in IBM were assessed annually against a standard list of eleven competencies as part of the performance management system. This standard approach to performance management was supported by a strong commitment to career development: 'Developing individuals to lead IBM now and for the future is one of our most important corporate responsibilities' (Senior Vice President of Human Resources). 'Learning is truly core to the DNA of IBM. We are a company focused on innovation, and our executives understand that we need to enable IBMers to grow and to foster the practices that produce business transformation,' said IBM Chief Learning Officer. 'Our learning programs are specifically designed to enable IBM to bring increased value to our clients and to provide meaningful learning experiences to all IBMers.' From these quotes, we can see a strong belief from the top of the organization that performance management and development should be standardized in order to add value to the firm.

Secondly, an example of an IBM best practice in training was its Sales Transformation & Learning initiative. The initiative embedded learning into the daily workflow throughout the company's sales teams. Led by global sales transformation managers around the world, the initiative helped IBM manage successful sales teams that understood that a commitment to learning could lead to improved sales results. 'IBM's Sales Transformation & Learning programme has multiple levels to ensure that our sales teams are

---

[2] We would like to acknowledge Dr Shad Morris (BYU, USA) for his preparation of the data for this IBM case.

trained to not only address current client problems, but to anticipate future trends,' said the Vice President for Worldwide High Performance Selling. 'Whether attending the "Software University" to better understand IBM's extensive brand offerings, or using the "Client Business Value" sales aid to identify and address performance gaps and critical issues in the client's business processes, IBM's workforce is dedicated to providing the highest level of client satisfaction and retention.'

Thirdly, IBM is recognized worldwide for having one of the best diversity programmes: It has received several awards of recognition for its leading efforts in this area. Its success is due to the fact that the company made diversity a market-based issue: It was believed that a diverse workforce would better understand today's multicultural and diverse global environment. Linked to this market-based strategic choice, and in response to an external institutional driver (legislation in the USA), was a company-wide effort to make IBM's products and services more accessible to people with disabilities. The company mandated the assessment of accessibility characteristics of all new products and called for the integration of accessibility requirements into IBM's development processes. This measure has also pushed for the importance of recruiting and hiring people with disabilities. From a competitive stance, we can see that IBM has taken a very strong approach to promoting diversity and developing its employees, to enable it to stand out against its competitors and attract the top talent. Market differentiation was stated as a primary driver behind these HRM practices. However, we also see in this last example the importance of local institutions, in that US legislation was also influencing the firm's activities.

Looking more specifically at the Western European operating context and its institutional mechanisms, IBM had recently seen salary reductions and job displacements due to global competition. The firm's approach to dealing with these labour market issues was to work more closely with trade unions, creating trust and flexibility for bargaining among European labour leaders. Some of the main challenges IBM faced in these countries dealt with their labour relations. For example, the pension laws in many Western European countries were quite different to anything IBM had dealt with in the USA. Specifically, the French government had put strong legislative pressure on employers to resolve the problem of underfunding of the state social security system. To restore financial balance to the system, retirement age had increased, as well as employee and employer social security contributions—creating new constraints for IBM in terms of labour costs and benefit plans.

From the perspective of HR managers working in IBM Western Europe, they saw HR as a centralized operation, and believed in across-the-board consistency. If they wanted to customize something, they needed to present a business case to the corporate headquarters. They also recognized the importance of being standardized, operating in a global economy in which their clients were also global. The Vice President of HR in the West Region noted that at the regional level they had to be strategic and consultative: 'corporate can give overarching principles, but they (the regional HR managers) have to apply them locally'—but this is not simply a case of application; it requires insight and innovation on the effects of the local environment and how the principles can be transformed into working practices.

From this case, we can start to see that despite IBM's tradition of a highly centralized SHRM system, since 2004 it has been devolving more autonomy to local business, balancing the best practice/best fit demands, and developing from a global to a transnational organization (to use the terms of Bartlett & Ghoshal, 1989). The demands of the local contexts were being seen as too strong to ignore in order to maintain high firm performance. As the Chairman and CEO Sam Palmisano, stated 'There's always going to be another strategy on the horizon as markets change, as technologies come and go' (Palmisano, Hemp, & Stewart, 2004: 65), so this MNC is dealing with both its competitive and institutional demands. HR leaders need to be able to adapt to local needs and demands, which was described as requiring a strong culture of being client-based and company-focused. As one geographical HR leader put it, 'We do not sit idly at the mountain and wait for the Ten Commandments to come down from Armonk [head office]. We apply the principles [that are found throughout IBM] and have leeway in running the show . . .' In speaking with a variety of global HR leaders, it was clear that this was a difficult issue as IBM was so used to everything being standardized. As one HR manager stated, 'now that managers have more flexibility, they don't want it because they have to justify their decisions'. Yet an impinging need for innovation meant that HR leaders in different environments had to adapt and develop new ideas (practices and processes) that met local needs, and possibly helped other parts of the organization.

In summary, the IBM case presented here shows how a best practice approach can be successful; however, at a certain point in time, elements of the best fit approach have started to creep in as part of the strategic process of the firm's key decision-makers.

9.4.2 IKEA: A BEST FIT APPROACH

In contrast to IBM, from an HRM perspective IKEA stood out amongst our case companies for being one of the more decentralized firms, along with some other MNCs primarily from Asia and Europe. IKEA, founded in 1943 in Sweden, is a global retailer of home furnishing products, today spanning over 40 countries with over 130,000 employees. The firm's vision is 'to create a better everyday life for the many people', seeking the best value way to 'offer a wide range of well-designed, functional home furnishing products at prices so low that as many people as possible will be able to afford them'.[3]

During IKEA's internationalization, which started in the 1970s, various local issues arose across the new countries in which subsidiaries were being established. For example,

---

[3] http://www.ikea.com/ms/en_US/this-is-ikea/company-information/index.html.

in Germany there was a desire for more formalization of rules, in France formal training programmes were requested along with only a limited number of non-French appointments, whilst in the USA there was a need for more customization of products to match the consumer taste. Despite all of these demands for localization, from a *competitive differentiation* perspective the company wanted to keep its 'Swedishness' as it saw this as part of its competitive advantage: It has the social welfare style of Swedish management running through its practices, ensuring employees are treated fairly wherever they may be based in the world. (For example, higher levels of social security insurances are used to retain people in the USA, which is not normal practice for firms in this country.) The way in which this 'Swedish' corporate identity was maintained and developed was through the development of an incredibly strong corporate culture.

As we might expect, IKEA's corporate values are based very much in the Swedish region where the company was founded: Älmhult in Småland, a poorer region whose community had a tradition of hard work. The culture is therefore based around the Swedish social welfare model, and is quite informal, with few layers of hierarchy, but a high level of cost-consciousness. What is remarkable about this case is that rather than having strong hierarchies and systems being controlled from headquarters, the driver behind the development of HRM practices across the whole company is this corporate culture. In terms of the Contextual SHRM Framework, this is an example of the *heritage mechanisms* exerting a strong influence over the shaping of the SHRM system. IKEA depends on its culture being maintained by people growing through the company, with its values reflected in leadership styles, communication methods, ways of working, and reporting hierarchies. Due to a lack of central control of systems and practices, the IKEA corporate culture is key to it retaining its identity: 'Maintaining a strong IKEA culture is one of the most crucial factors behind the continued success of the IKEA concept' (Ingvar Kamprad, Founder).

At the global level, IKEA showed little evidence of global benchmarking of practices, nor was there clear evidence of standard HRM practices being used across the countries in which it was operating. Rather than having standardized HRM systems and policies in place, as in IBM, IKEA focuses on its 'HR idea': 'Giving down to earth, straightforward people the possibility to grow, both as individuals and in their professional roles, so that together we are strongly committed to creating a better everyday life for ourselves and our customers'.[4] In this decentralized HRM approach, the level of global policy-making is very restricted and, as a result, we see more local fit of HRM policies and practices across the company, as presented in the following examples.

From a retail store perspective, there is very little influence on HRM practices perceived to be coming from corporate management. Priorities are seen as being set at the national rather than the international level. The country HR manager meets with the

---

[4] http://www.ikea.com/ms/en_CA/the_ikea_story/working_at_ikea/our_vision.html.

global HR function to learn the global HR priorities, which are translated to national priorities. The national priorities are discussed at an annual meeting of store management teams to determine business plan priorities for stores. Finally, meetings are arranged when all the store HR managers come together to discuss their future priorities. This approach allows best fit HRM practices to emerge, which best serve the local store's needs, but which are still supportive of the overarching corporate strategy.

The strongest aspects of IKEA were described as being the people, the link with the company culture, and the alignment with the business. Everything about IKEA is linked to its culture (see Textbox 9.2) and depends on this culture being maintained by people

---

TEXTBOX 9.2 IKEA KEY VALUES

Togetherness

Togetherness is at the heart of the IKEA culture. We are strong when we trust each other, pull in the same direction and have fun together.

Cost-consciousness

As many people as possible should be able to afford a beautiful and functional home. We constantly challenge ourselves and others to make more from less without compromising on quality.

Renew and improve

We are constantly looking for new and better ways forward. Whatever we are doing today, we can do better tomorrow. Finding solutions to almost impossible challenges is part of our success and a source of inspiration to move on to the next challenge.

Give and take responsibility

We believe in empowering people. Giving and taking responsibility are ways to grow and develop as individuals. Trusting each other, being positive and forward-looking inspire everyone to contribute to development.

Caring for people and planet

We want to be a force for positive change. We have the possibility to make a significant and lasting impact — today and for the generations to come.

Simplicity

A simple, straightforward and down-to-earth way of being is part of our Småland heritage. It is about being ourselves and staying close to reality. We are informal, pragmatic and see bureaucracy as our biggest enemy.

Different with a meaning

IKEA is not like other companies and we don't want to be. We like to question existing solutions, think in unconventional ways, experiment and dare to make mistakes—always good for a reason.

Lead by example

We see leadership as an action, not a position. We look for people's values before competence and experience. People who 'walk the talk' and lead by example. It is about being our best self and bringing out the best in each other.

Source: http://www.ikea.com/gb/en/this-is-ikea/working-at-the-ikea-group/who-we-are/.

growing through the company. People like to stay at IKEA because of the working environment: Although interviewees found it difficult to pinpoint exactly why, it was described as a feeling that people are treated as human beings, and the lack of hierarchy in the company. A number of interviewees, when asked about best practices, always returned to the idea of IKEA's strong, no-nonsense culture and the common values people share within the firm. Because of the strength of this culture, it is easy to return to these shared values at times when tough decisions are required. It also ensures a common language for being able to discuss new ideas. Furthermore, the reliance on culture rather than systems has the advantage of creating flexibility rather than rigidity in the firm; for example, being able to offer people many variations in working times which suit those from all backgrounds and who have different out-of-work responsibilities.

When observing the recruitment and selection processes in IKEA, a strong focus on behaviours and values was noted. For example, during the 1990s IKEA was portrayed as a fun company to work for with no hierarchy in place. Although this was attractive, some people found after a while that it was very difficult to work in an unstructured environment. Such people were then leaving the company, which prompted a shift to recruiting by values. Again, no standard practices were issued by corporate HR, but instead it was highlighted that all recruitment and selection activities should be founded in the corporate culture. This is an example of a way of operating which emerged from a strategic choice from inside the organization that leeway was still required by the local operations, but that corporate culture could provide some structure.

Career development practices also have a very local flavour: There are no strict career progression structures in place, so if someone is interested in a particular project they might make a horizontal rather than a vertical move within the company, which is not perceived as a negative step. The development mind-set at IKEA is based on individuals taking control of their own development through self-managed learning: 'co-workers in charge'. The lack of a standardized system does, however, mean that there is not a strong mechanism in place for identifying high potentials and managing succession planning.

Finally, looking at reward policies, we again see a pattern of local differentiation. Job evaluation is based on a tool that considers the size of the organization in terms of the number of employees (for example, the country manager of Finland would receive less than the country manager for Germany because the size of the IKEA operation in Finland is much smaller). In addition to this, some countries have group bonus systems related to clear performance targets, whilst others choose to have individual performance-related pay.

One interviewee, having worked with IKEA in two different countries, commented on the impact of cultural difference. For example, within the Dutch culture, people are prepared to express opinions within a very democratic environment, but although this seems in line with the IKEA open culture, limits do need to be set so that there is some structure to operations. This structure forms more naturally in the German culture, for example, because Germans prefer to work within a more rule-based environment. Thus, different aspects of the IKEA culture need to be emphasized in both countries in order to achieve the right balance between national and corporate culture.

Reflecting on the earlier observation in IBM in Section 9.4.1 that there had been a reaction to too much centralization and best practice, with increasing autonomy being given to local subsidiaries, we see the opposite happening in IKEA. Corporate HR was, at the time of interviewing, starting to develop some 'top-down' policies for implementation worldwide. People in local subsidiaries valued their autonomy, but at the same time 'wanted guidance from the top'. Some global HR policies had been introduced as part of a '10 Jobs for 10 Years' plan to encourage common ways of working and to avoid reinventing the wheel. This was part of an initiative to increase the firm's ability to benefit from the economies of scale of its operations, but was also linked to the emerging technologies at the time, which would allow international sharing of systems and information. In general, global policies were not mandatory practice, but provided a common platform to which countries could add their own local requirements.

These policies provided a common cross-border language, which was needed as the company continued to expand internationally. They typically made a statement about the link between an HRM practice and the business strategy, and then defined one or two primary directives that all countries had to follow. In addition, a policy had to meet local legislative requirements or standards. For example, in the personnel planning and recruitment policy, the three directives were: In redundancy situations, alternative positions must be sought for people, particularly those with long service; people related closely by family cannot work together closely; and employees must declare any conflicts of interest with the company. Such a directive puts in place common principles, but still allows some leeway for local operations to establish the detail of the HRM policy implemented.

In summary, in direct contrast to the IBM case, the IKEA case presented here shows how a best fit approach can be successful; however, elements of the best practice approach have started to creep in as part of the strategic decision-making process of the firm's key decision-makers. The third case we present here, in Section 9.4.3, shows how an MNC can attempt to develop both a best practice and best fit approach simultaneously.

9.4.3 P&G: A BALANCED APPROACH

P&G is a major consumer products company, today employing some 100,000 people in 80 countries around the world. Like IKEA, it has a strong sense of corporate purpose, values, and principles, but unlike IKEA's decentralized structure, P&G follows a more integrated, transnational strategy, attempting to balance best practice and best fit approaches.

A strong part of the P&G culture develops from its 'build from within' mentality. For example, senior management had largely grown through the company over many years, unless they joined as part of an acquisition. This had created a relationship-orientated culture: People expect to meet each other at different times across the organization. The trust and collaboration created within the informal organization was therefore very important. The success of the firm's integrated network structure was described as only being possible due to this strength of culture. To support this, standardized performance management practices were designed to support the matrix-based structure, with people being assessed for their effectiveness in supporting the interdependency relationships between business units based on: (a) how well they work together; (b) if they have common goals and joint systems to track progress; and (c) their extent of communication and general commitment to the structure.

In general, the HRM practices in P&G are ultimately controlled from the top. Global initiatives are implemented in a very disciplined manner, measuring and monitoring performance using fact-based indicators. Rational reasons for differences in indicators can be discussed but the process must start with a measure, a figure, for which someone is responsible. One interviewee highlighted that the actual globalization of operational HRM processes was considered a best practice in itself, with systems for recruitment, compensation and benefits, and performance management being the same everywhere. P&G also had a single HR database system across the company, making it possible to monitor headcount, salaries, and promotion worldwide. This was described as reducing waste and duplication of effort as well as costs. Some examples of this standardization approach follow.

The training infrastructure that was being developed at the global level and gradually being implemented across the world was an information technology (IT)-based learning management system. The system provided lists of training courses available, as well as their content and schedules, and facilities for employees to register. It also provided tools for trainers to be able to develop their courses. Three forms of training were hosted via this tool: Web-based training (which people follow online); live distance courses (usually in the form of an audio conference); and classroom courses. The training system tracks who has completed what training, and therefore also provides metrics on training and development across the company.

In 2004, a new P&G competency model had been implemented across the globe. Successful behaviours were sourced by research at global level in the corporate functions, resulting in an ideal model. The model was applicable across the globe as it assumed changing priorities in different parts of the organization, and hence it was not essential to be good at everything all of the time. The model in itself was not seen as delivering competitive advantage, but, as part of the whole integrated approach to HRM, it was a contributor. It reappears in all the systems and the corporate language within P&G.

Looking at reward, P&G focuses predominantly on a base salary system, which is in contrast to one of its main competitors, Unilever, which had introduced variable pay at all levels of the organization. P&G had adopted this salary system for the majority of its employees to enable the company to remain flexible to market changes: As targets changed, there were no direct salary implications for individuals so they were more willing to change in line with business needs. The key principles of the reward policy have been in place for many years in P&G; it is only elements of the programme that have changed over time in line with business requirements. This is a clear example of how a firm chooses to differentiate itself from its competitors, rather than policy being a result of external institutional isomorphic mechanisms.

Finally, in the area of employee relations (ER), in an ideal world P&G saw no role for works councils or trade unions as the business was built on principles of mutual respect between employer and employee. However, the firm adjusted this policy as necessary to comply with local legislation, such as that in the Netherlands requiring local works councils to be established where the employees requested this. In contrast to the reward policy, we see here an example of where institutional forces can override strategic choice.

P&G's aim was to create a 'global employment experience': Wherever an employee goes to work, they will be treated the same in terms of employment practices. To achieve this there were multiple global HRM policies in place as described here. However, these policies are not merely dictated from corporate HR, as had been the case in IBM. Some aspects of the global compensation and benefits policy (such as the variable pay scheme for executives as opposed to the salary system for all other employees) were essentially developed at the global level but had the input of business leaders and consultants. The business leaders were asked to comment on which of the approaches suggested by head office would be most appropriate. This was done to ensure that the leaders would be happy to adopt the scheme, and that the best solution for the business was being introduced. Similarly, corporate HR worked with its counterparts across the globe in networks, such as the HR communities of practice (CoP). These CoPs operated as international networks, with a broad range of countries involved, devising global policies on a wide range of HRM activities. For example, the global-level Compensation and Benefits CoP involved subject experts from various internal committees. This global CoP was mirrored at the regional level, where it included more HR generalists, with greater exposure to daily compensation and benefits matters. At the regional level more practical implementation issues were therefore discussed, plus region-specific requirements such as flexible benefits, which were a key component of achieving a flexible organization in this region.

At the time of interviewing, there were many global policies in place covering activities such as open job posting, remuneration systems, and performance management based on a global competency model. However, even with strong control from the centre, there was still an acknowledged need for some adaptation (best fit) of HRM policies and practices to meet local requirements. The starting point for the company, however, is not these differences, but the common practices that it can successfully put in place.

In summary, P&G is balancing best practice and best fit as a transnational firm (in the terms of Bartlett & Ghoshal, 1989), involving regional and local managers in policy development, rather than taking sole control from corporate. This stands in stark contrast to both the traditional, more centralized best practice approach of IBM, and the decentralized, best fit approach adopted in IKEA. However, P&G ultimately shows more evidence of being driven by competitive rather than institutional forces, often adopting standardized practices and reducing local customization of HRM wherever possible. Thus, the more transnational an organization, the more it appears to attempt to coordinate HRM practices from the global level, implying greater perceived value to the firm of standardization and economies of scale and scope above local legitimacy.

9.5 **Summary and conclusions**

This chapter has reviewed the best practice/best fit debate that large multinational firms are facing as they expand their operations to new territories worldwide. We have seen how these MNCs need to decide on an appropriate balance between having a standardized approach to HRM, issuing best practices from corporate to all subsidiary locations in order to maximize efficiency and consistency, and having a customized approach, allowing subsidiaries to develop HRM practices which are perceived as most legitimate in the local context, giving the best access for the firm to local resources and talent.

To illustrate these dual competitive and institutional pressures, case studies from the Global HR Research Alliance Study were presented. First, IBM's best practice approach was described, highlighting its standard HRM policies on core competencies, training, and diversity, which were being implemented in all locations across the globe to maximize the firm's performance. However, when exploring IBM operations in Western Europe, the extent to which operations, including pension regulations and dealing with trade unions, were being affected by local institutions became clear. Over time, IBM has started to relinquish some of the control from the centre, acknowledging the added value of local legitimacy alongside standardization.

IKEA, in contrast, starts from the opposite position to IBM, having a highly decentralized approach to SHRM in all of its stores across the world. We can see how the national context (country of origin) of the firm is impacting on how this MNC chooses to operate: It holds on to its corporate culture, which is strongly based on its Swedish roots. Rather than putting standard policies in practices in place, IKEA gives its store managers leeway to adopt local HRM practices, provided they are in line with the corporate culture and any guiding principles. This allows the best fit approach to flourish, creating high local legitimacy, and hence good access to local talent, for example. Such an approach has led to high performance for IKEA, although the company is now starting to see the value of having a certain amount of control from corporate HR to help support its subsidiaries worldwide, making better use of economies of scale and available technologies.

The final case, P&G, shows how a firm attempts to achieve balance between the best practice and best fit approaches to maximize firm performance. This firm described how it has a range of standard 'best practices' in place across the whole of its operations, but that these 'best practices' had been developed by taking into account the importance of 'best fit' principles: Corporate policy was being developed with the input of regional and local managers through, for example, HR CoP structures. Ultimately, however, the aim of the firm is competitive differentiation (and, of course, high performance), and so it uses the strategic choice leeway of the key decision-makers to develop policies which make it stand out from competitors locally and globally as much as possible.

In summary, when we look at all of the elements of the Contextual SHRM Framework, we have seen, through theoretical and empirical examples, that all of the factors leading to the design of the corporate SHRM system entail different strategic choices for MNCs: Balancing the need for competitive and institutional differentiation against the forces of institutional and competitive isomorphism (see Table 9.1). There is no single best solution to this balancing act, as we have seen high performing firms emerge from both the best practice and best fit approach, and ultimately from an attempt to achieve a balance between these two seemingly conflicting approaches.

In this chapter we have focused on the drivers of SHRM systems of globally operating firms. The next part of the book (Chapters 10 and 11) combines theory and empirical evidence to develop a more practical and implementation-oriented approach. Different HR department roles are identified to support the notion of added value, as well as consideration of the different delivery channels available to HR to implement its activities as effectively as possible. Finally, we explore HR metrics, which aid in the development, monitoring, and measurement of HRM policies and practices: Policies and practices aimed at contributing to sustainable competitive advantage.

10 HR professionals
Roles and performance

10.1 Introduction

In this chapter, we discuss the relationship between the roles performed by human resource (HR) professionals and how these relate to performance. We outline the way in which HR roles have evolved from welfare to strategic business partner, describing the many models and typologies of HR roles that have emerged over time (Section 10.2). We also question the universality of these typologies given that most research in this field has been conducted in the USA and the UK (Section 10.3). We then (in Section 10.4) consider the relevance of one well-known HR typology to a different country context: the Netherlands. Survey research shows that country context is highly influential in understanding HR professional roles in organizations today. In an exploration of multinational corporations (MNCs), we also highlight the relevance of organizational structure across country boundaries to the corporate HR role, based on research covering the USA, Europe, and Asia. Finally, we conclude with thoughts on how this reflection on HR roles and performance fits in the Contextual Strategic Human Resource Management (SHRM) Framework.

10.2 HR professionals: Changing roles and expectations

A review of the literature identifies many frameworks for considering the evolution and development of HR activities, competencies, and roles. Some of these frameworks are merely a list of things that HR professionals do, while others provide a more in-depth consideration of HR activities from an ideal type perspective (spanning from Tyson and Fell (1986) to Ulrich and colleagues (2008) as you will see in Section 10.2). Increasingly, companies are beginning to recognize the importance of people (human resources) to the corporation's success. Business challenges are frequently people-related because it is individual employees who influence the essence of the business: Its profitability, survival, competitiveness, adaptability, and flexibility. The relentless assignment of people management activities to line managers, plus the increasing centralization occurring in many large organizations today, standardizing their approach to human resource management (HRM) through single-source hubs of HR services, imply that the roles and position of HR professional functions need to be reconsidered. To understand how the HR profession has developed over time, we explore here how roles and competencies have changed in line with organizational priorities.

When tracing the history of the HR profession, we can see clear linkages with the organizational contexts in which it has developed. The division of labour through task specialization, using Taylorist concepts such as 'scientific management', was one of the early techniques used to increase corporate efficiency (Watson, 1977). Such a technique allowed the employer to control more rigidly the behaviour of employees, but, consequently, caused a lowering of employee commitment and, in turn, a lowering of compliance to managerial needs. Organizations thus sought to maximize efficiency but simultaneously to maintain the consent of employees to prevent disruptive behaviour. It was out of this challenge of industrialization that the HR profession was born (Watson, 1977). HR was seen as a means to mediate between the need to achieve 'both the control and the consent of employees' (Legge, 2005: 56). The welfare movement (which ultimately evolved into the personnel, and later HR, function) was welcomed during the late nineteenth century, as employers came to realize the self-defeating nature of extreme formal rationality (Niven, 1967). Here we see the first evidence of a need to balance the competitive mechanisms of the firm, advocating efficiency and cost-effectiveness, alongside institutional mechanisms, supporting legitimacy of people management practices, as argued in the Contextual SHRM Framework (Chapter 6).

Working chronologically, Tyson and Fell's work (1986) provides a good starting point for exploring HR role typologies. Struck by the increased fragmentation of the personnel (later called 'HR') function, which they describe as its 'Balkanization', Tyson and Fell made the first attempt at identifying different Weberian ideal types or models of the activities being carried out:

1. *The clerk of works*: In this role, personnel management is an administrative support activity with no involvement in business planning. All authority in personnel management issues is vested in line managers. The principal activities for these personnel staff would be recruitment, record keeping, and welfare.

2. *The contracts manager*: This role is concerned with dealing with trade unions as part of a comprehensive network of corporate policies. Acting on behalf of line managers, personnel staff are the experts in trade union agreements, in fixing day-to-day issues with the unions, and in reacting to problems as they arise.

3. *The architect*: Here, personnel managers seek to be involved in the creation and construction of the organization as a whole. This creative vision of personnel means contributing to the success of the business through explicit policies that seek to

influence corporate strategy, with an integrated system of control between personnel and line management. The personnel function is thus represented within the 'key decision-makers' of the organization (in the Contextual SHRM Framework).

Moving forward a few years, Schuler (1990) discerns an increasing shift from the traditional personnel role as a specialist staff function, to a new breed of HR manager as part of the management team. He claims that the roles of businessperson, shaper of change, organizational consultant, strategy formulator and implementer, talent manager, asset manager, and cost controller were becoming more prominent (Schuler, 1990: 58).

Carroll (1991) also observed a shift in HR roles as a consequence of the more pronounced links to business performance needs, and thus a greater requirement to contribute to organizational effectiveness. In addition to the traditional roles of 'policy formulator' and 'provider of personnel services', Carroll (1991) expected certain roles to take on greater importance:

- *Delegator*: This role enables line management to serve as primary implementers of HRM systems.

- *Technical expert*: This function encompasses a number of highly specific HRM-related skills in, for example, areas such as remuneration and management development.

- *Innovator*: As innovators, HR managers recommend new approaches to solving HRM-related problems, such as productivity affected by a sudden increase in absenteeism due to illness.

Storey (1992: 168) took the HR roles debate further by suggesting a typology based on two dimensions: Action-oriented (interventional) versus non-action oriented (non-interventional) roles, and strategic versus tactical roles (see Figure 10.1):

Figure 10.1 Types of personnel management

Source: Storey (1992).

- *Advisors*: Act as internal consultants in tune with current business issues, leaving the actual running of HRM matters to line and senior management.
- *Handmaidens*: Primarily customer-led in the services they offer, based on a subservient, support-based relationship towards line management.
- *Regulators*: More interventional, formulating, promulgating, and monitoring observance of employment regulations ranging from HRM procedure manuals to joint agreements with trade unions.
- *Change makers*: Seek to put relationships with employees on a new footing—one that is in line with the needs of the business.

Moving forward in time once more, perhaps the most well known and widely applied typology of HR roles was developed by Ulrich (1997). Ulrich also uses two dimensions (people v. process and strategic v. operational) to highlight the roles that enable HR managers to add value to the business:

- *Administrative expert* (process/operational focus): Designing and delivering efficient HRM processes for staffing, training, appraising, rewarding, promotion, and so on, to manage the flow of employees through the organization. The deliverable from this role is administrative efficiency.
- *Employee champion* (people/operational focus): Dealing with the day-to-day problems, concerns, and needs of employees. The deliverables are increased employee commitment and competence.
- *Change agent* (people/strategic focus): Managing transformation and change across the organization. The deliverable is capacity for change, facilitating corporate culture transition by ensuring employees support the process.
- *Strategic partner* (process/strategic focus): Aligning HRM strategies and practices with corporate strategy. The deliverable from this role is strategy execution: HRM practices help accomplish business objectives.

Revising Schuler's (1990) original model, Schuler and Jackson (2001) described in further detail some of the strategic and support roles carried out by HR professionals, suggesting that the following roles would be most prominent in delivering business results:

- *Linking role*: Linking HRM issues and challenges to the business context.
- *Strategic role*: Involvement in the strategic direction of the company.
- *Monitoring role*: Reviewing the actual situation against the strategic plan and deciding on corrective action.
- *Innovator role*: Developing innovative approaches and solutions to improve productivity and the quality of work, while simultaneously complying with legislation in a

dynamic environment of high uncertainty, increasing conservation issues and intense international competition.

- *Change and knowledge facilitator role*: Managing change processes, both at the individual and the organizational level, frequently related to strategy implementation.

- *Enabler role*: Providing services to line management in the traditional areas of recruitment, selection, rewarding, counselling, promoting, and dismissal, enabling line management to make things happen. This role demands a high degree of customer orientation towards line management.

Ulrich (1997), working with colleagues, revised his highly successful typology of HR roles in line with changes being observed in corporate settings. Ulrich and Brockbank (2005) first refined the 1997 model, suggesting the employee champion role could be divided into two aspects: Human capital developer and employee advocate. The former is a future-focused role, supporting the development of employees to increase the value of the human capital (the sum of the knowledge, skills, and abilities of all employees) of the firm. The employee advocate role was more set in current-day issues, dealing with employee relations (ER), workforce diversity, and responding to employee concerns. The Ulrich and Brockbank (2005) model absorbs the Ulrich (1997) change agent role into a revised strategic partner role, which now includes HR as a business expert, change agent, knowledge manager, and consultant to the business. The previous administrative expert is also rebranded as a functional expert, still in charge of HRM administration, but also responsible for developing HRM policies, interventions, and systems. Finally, the Ulrich and Brockbank (2005) model introduces a new role labelled 'HR leader': This role is seen as a sum of the performance of all the other roles, and results in competent leadership of the HR function, involving a focus on corporate governance, as well as those undertaking this role having the personal credibility to act as a leader in the organization.

The Ulrich and Brockbank (2005) model was revised further in 2008 by Ulrich and colleagues. This model, as with the previous iterations, was based on research carried out by the Human Resource Competency Study (HRCS: http://hrcs.rbl.net/) based out of the University of Michigan, which has assessed the state of the HR profession every five years since its inception in the late 1980s. This 2007 round of the survey elected to describe the results in terms of HR roles rather than HR competencies, as had been the case for previous rounds (the argument being that HR roles are what the HR professional carries out through the use of his or her competencies). This resulted in a newly developed typology of HR roles emerging directly from the survey data (see Figure 10.2).

In this model, if we start at the systems and processes level, we can see the operational executor and the business ally. The first of these roles overlaps substantially with the functional expert role, dealing with day-to-day administration and HR policies. Alongside this, the business ally is responsible for understanding the business and its context. These two roles, side by side, represent the basic requirements for operating as an HR

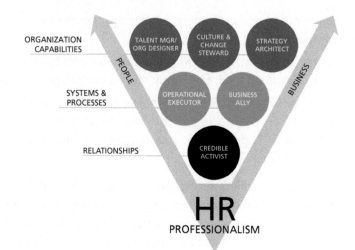

Figure 10.2 Typology of HR roles

Source: Ulrich and colleagues (2008: 226).

professional in organizations today. When expanding into the realms of how HR can help to develop organizational capability, three roles emerge: Talent manager/organization designer, culture and change steward, and strategy architect. The talent manager focuses on ensuring an effective flow of human capital through the organization, whilst the organization designer considers how to embed human capital capability into the firm's structure, processes, and policies. The culture and change steward role is akin to the Ulrich (1997) change agent role, whilst the strategy architect is actively involved in establishing corporate strategy and delivering on it (similar to the Ulrich (1997) strategic partner role). Finally, all of these roles are supported by a relationship-focused role: Credible activist. This requires the HR professional to be: 'credible (respected, admired, listened to) and active (offers a point of view, takes a position, challenges assumptions)' (Ulrich et al., 2008: 34). The HRCS (Ulrich et al., 2008) also observed the linkage between HR roles and performance. The results showed that the credible activist role explained the most variance in individual performance (ibid: 46), and in business performance (ibid: 52).

Most recently, Ulrich and colleagues (2012) provided further new insights into HR roles based on the 2012 HRCS (see Figure 10.3). Again, common themes with previous models can be observed. Ulrich and colleagues (2012) identified the *strategic positioner*, similar to the previous *strategic partner* (1997) and *strategy architect* (2008) roles. There is again the *credible activist* akin to the 2005 *HR leader* role. The *change champion* reflects the importance in previous models too of HR's ability to develop and implement organizations' capacity for change. The 2012 *capability builder* creates perhaps a new emphasis, developing further the *human capital developer* (2005) and *talent manager/*

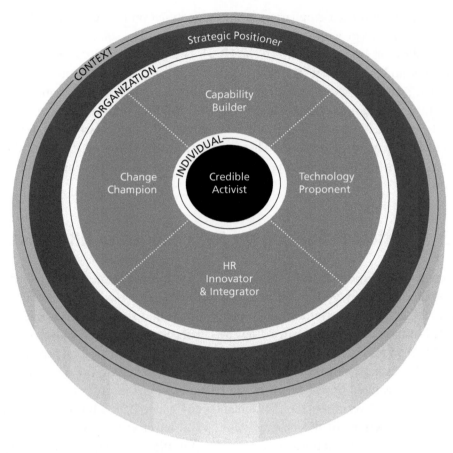

Figure 10.3 HR competency model
Source: Ulrich and colleagues (2012: 52).

organization designer (2008) roles, to include building broader organizational capabilities, including innovation, speed, customer focus, efficiency, and the creation of meaning and purpose at work. This appears to be, in part, supported by the new role of *human resource innovator and integrator*, which emphasizes the importance of supporting organization capabilities with appropriate HRM practices, processes, structures, and procedures. Finally, replacing the *administrative/functional expert* roles of previous models, Ulrich and colleagues (2012) introduced the *technology proponent* role. They claimed that routine administrative HRM activities are now carried out through technology to achieve cost and time efficiencies, and therefore: 'it would not be surprising to see that some of the traditional administrative work of HR no longer regards HR as a functional home' (Ulrich et al., 2012: 256). Overall, the 2012 model places greater emphasis on the use of HRM to assess and respond to external business conditions.

This outside-in approach emphasizes strategic and environmental fit (see Chapter 3), aligning HRM strategy with the business environment and its stakeholders.

Similarities can be drawn between the Ulrich and colleagues (2012) model and the competitive and institutional mechanisms of the Contextual SHRM Framework, leading to desired goals of organizational capabilities and legitimacy of operations. In other words, there are requirements to achieve business goals, but, at the same time, attention needs to be paid to the needs of individual employees, particularly with respect to fair and legitimate work practices. These can lead to conflicting goals facing the HR professional when carrying out the different roles required, as we consider further in Section 10.3.

10.3 **A critical reflection on the changes in HR roles**

Reflecting on the various models, typologies, and commentaries, the change in HR roles may be summarized by the observation that HR professionals have had to become more business-oriented, more strategic, and more in tune with organizational change. This is reflected in the HRCS rounds carried out by Ulrich, Brockbank, and colleagues (2005, 2007, 2012), in which, in addition to HR functional (or technological) expertise, knowledge of the business and the management of change are among the most prominent competences required by the clients of the HR professional in order to add value to a business. The 2007 version of the HRCS highlighted the need for a business perspective, but having knowledge of the business alone as a 'business ally' is insufficient: This knowledge needs to be applied in strategic organization capability-building roles, as highlighted in the 2012 model (Ulrich et al., 2008, 2012).

How HR professionals can actually deliver value to the organization is, however, somewhat less clear. First, where does HR sit in terms of its responsibilities for HRM compared to the role assigned to line management? Involving line managers in the implementation of HRM is commonplace, and can result in a more comprehensive approach to HRM and speed up decision-making since line managers are closer to employees (Renwick, 2003). It can also reduce costs and lead to smaller HR teams, who may then focus on strategic and business issues (Francis & Keegan, 2006; Larsen & Brewster, 2003). The involvement of line managers in the implementation of HRM practices therefore means that they have a role to play in the HRM–performance chain and are crucial to successful implementation (Purcell & Hutchinson, 2007). However, the roles which line managers play are often unclear (Bos-Nehles, Van Riemsdijk, & Looise, 2013), resulting by definition in the HR professional's role as the counterpart to line management also being ambiguous.

This is the first of a number of ambiguities facing the HR professional (Legge, 1978, 2005). Similarly, Caldwell (2003) talks of ambiguities and uncertainties, describing instances of competing role demands and increasing managerial expectations of performance. In his re-examination of the HR role typology developed by Storey (1992), Caldwell (2003) notes that some changes in roles have occurred; however, perhaps most importantly, he highlights that none of the role typologies capture the real complexities of the activities carried out by HR. Again, although acknowledging some changes in roles, Guest and King (2004) nevertheless confirm that HR professionals have been unable to overcome many of the ambiguities and related problems inherent in their organizational position. Caldwell (2008) is also critical of the prescriptive competency models, concluding that they are ineffective at predicting performance in a business partner role and need to include more consideration of the context in which roles are being enacted.

Most recently, the issue of paradox and a need for balance within the HRM field in general has been highlighted by Boselie, Brewster, and Paauwe (2009). They argue that HR activities constitute a balancing act between HRM and industrial relations (IR), soft versus hard HRM, control versus commitment HRM systems, pluralist versus unitarist HRM, with all of these being supported by competing underlying theoretical frameworks (e.g. resource-based view (RBV) versus institutional theory, as discussed in Chapter 6). The HR professional thus finds him or herself in a difficult position from which to operate effectively within the organization.

In general, the role prescriptions presented in Section 10.2 imply that HR professionals acquire a power base by reacting to business needs: Supporting the dominant strategy, culture, and priorities of line management. Legge (1978) refers to this as a 'conformist innovator' approach, accepting the dominant utilitarian values and bureaucratic relationships within the organization, and trying to demonstrate added value (contribution to the bottom line) within this framework. This is an attitude and approach that holds a number of evident risks, such as the eventual inability to differentiate HR professionals from regular line managers in terms of contribution or expertise. This gives rise to the scenario of HRM without the presence of HR professionals (Flood, Gannon, & Paauwe, 1996).

An alternative way of acquiring power, or rather influence, is the 'deviant innovator' approach, whereby the HR professional identifies with a set of norms that are distinct from, but not necessarily in conflict with, the norms of organizational success (Legge, 1978: 79–85). Inspired by this notion, Shipton and McAuley (1994: 9), based on Kets de Vries (1990), refer to the need for an:

Organizational fool, who without danger to himself can take non-consensual stances . . . personnel people are perhaps uniquely fitted for this role because they frequently have the key responsibility for exploring, with members of the organization in which they work, the issues surrounding the management of change and the factors that make it work.

As highlighted in Chapter 5, this epitomizes the belief that HR professionals cannot focus solely on performance criteria such as efficiency, effectiveness, and flexibility.

Ward Lilley, as long ago as 1991, remarked that HR professionals must be prepared to risk unpopularity by questioning the short-termism rife in much of the UK economy—a remark that, nearly three decades later, has lost nothing of its relevance on both sides of the Atlantic. In 2011, Farndale, Paauwe, and Boselie found, in a series of case studies, a corporate crisis (e.g. being found guilty of cartel operations in the pharmaceutical or chemicals industry, or of mis-selling in the financial services industry, both requiring a fundamental shift in the mode of operation to regain customer support and ensure the survival of the firm) created momentum and a sense of urgency for organizational change. As a result, firms increased substantially their focus on compliance and risk management to deal with the fallout of the changes happening, with compliance playing a more substantial role throughout the firm, including as part of the HR function. The related new organizational culture focused on compliance, ethics, and transparency, with HR playing a significant role in developing this culture through communication and education. However, the ultimate accountability rested with line management. The responsibility for compliant behaviour was also being delegated to the individual employee level, with the importance of self-control and shared values being emphasized (Gençtürk & Aulakh, 2007; Jiang, 2009).

Exploring HR's response to this changing context, which demanded a higher level of incorporation of compliance-related activities to achieve business goals of legitimacy amongst customers as well as financial success, we observe that the HR agenda is still today being led by business priorities (Guest & King, 2004; Ulrich, 1998). Business-related competencies are increasingly being sought amongst HR professionals, with a key task being the provision of clear tools and information for line management to carry out HRM activities. This, alongside the inability to evaluate HR's direct contribution, supports the idea that line management involvement, to an extent, dilutes the HR profession (Purcell & Ahlstrand, 1994), almost removing its need for existence. The case studies described (Farndale, Paauwe, & Boselie, 2011) showed that there was a whole range of activities in which HR was now involved in order to support the compliance function and broader compliance initiatives (e.g. a new code of conduct, risk awareness). Although the day-to-day roles of the HR function had changed, the 'strategic partner' role (Ulrich, 1997; Ulrich & Brockbank, 2005) was still prevalent, as business priorities had also shifted towards compliance. The compliance function was perceived to be the 'conscience' of the firm, and HR has not stepped in to adopt this role for itself.

Farndale, Paauwe and Boselie (2011) interpreted these results, commenting that a new role for HR focusing on attitudinal change through a climate for compliance was emerging. However, although this role was evident, it does not appear that it was being pursued from a moral position of HR professionals. It appears that the profession is still focused on supporting business priorities as a conformist innovator (Legge, 1978), with HR professionals seemingly reluctant to take on additional governance and compliance responsibilities.

Looking to the future, we might therefore consider that more appropriate perform-ance criteria for HR than efficiency, effectiveness, and flexibility might be fairness (in the exchange relationship between the individual and the organization) and legitimacy (the relationship between society and the organization). Referring to the Contextual SHRM Framework, this means a stronger focus on the impact of institutional and heritage mechanisms for creating legitimacy, alongside the competitive mechanisms for creating organizational capability. A specialist or manager in the area of HRM would be the right person to counter or correct extreme economic rationality, ensuring the long-term interests of multiple organizational members are considered, and the outcomes of organizational effectiveness will benefit the various stakeholders (and not necessarily just the shareholders) of the firm.

In this respect, Kamoche (1994) underlines the inherent paradoxes of strategic HRM as a concept encompassing both the issues of 'strategy' and 'human' (see also Chapter 1). On the one hand, strategic HRM is characterized by the dominant organizational imperative for performance and productivity, which, according to Kamoche (1994), draws from an industry-based view of the firm and is informed by a rationalist view of human action. On the other hand, HRM is concerned with meeting the complex and often ambiguous needs and expectations of employees, the humanizing of work, and a concern with 'equitable' or 'fair' practices, labelled by Hendry and Pettigrew (1990) as 'developmental-humanism'. In this respect, Gowler and Legge (1986) refer to the contrast between human *resources* and resourceful *humans*. In the same critical vein, Lefebvre (2001) rightly notes, 'Humans may be called "resources", but they should be treated as "sources" of their own creativity and be allowed to be self-led, not only being led.'

Competing with other functional areas like marketing and finance, the HR function is apparently in search of mechanisms to legitimatize its actions (see Figure 10.4). This is a quest in which the organizational imperative has been the dominant criterion. However, such a criterion does not do justice to the intrinsic complexities of the concept of strategic HRM, which is not simply a matter of integrating the HR dimension into the business strategic planning process (Kamoche, 1994: 40).

Figure 10.4 Legitimacy through acceptance

Source: Kamoche (1994).

Perhaps a better way of reconciling both strategic and human aspects is to take the RBV perspective as a starting point (see Kamoche, 1994; Paauwe, 1994; Wright, McMahan, & McWilliams, 1994) because it takes into account the competencies and capabilities of the 'human' resources, rather than focusing exclusively on dominant business-like criteria such as those dictated by a specific product/market combination. Kamoche (1994: 41) makes a strong plea for this view to enable consideration of the specific nature and complexities of human resources:

This paradigm emphasises that the skills of employees are conceived of as a vital resource, which the firm is able to build upon rather than simply to exploit rationally and ideologically. Therefore, the full potential of HRM can be realized and can be a key determinant in a firm's performance, without the *a priori* imposition of the organizational imperative.

For HR professionals, this paradigm implies focusing on using multidimensional/multi-faceted approaches in their development and rendering of specialist HR services. Taking this view, a simple one-sided approach, exclusively based on the strategic demands of the marketplace, is inappropriate.

10.4 **HR roles in context**

In addition to considering the *content* of the HR roles as we have done so far, we have to remember that all HR professionals are operating within a certain organizational (and national) context. If we refer back to the Contextual SHRM Framework, we can see that this context is made up of the competitive, institutional, and heritage mechanisms which constitute the organization, as well as the impact of the key decision-makers in the employment relationship. It is suggested that this context alters the importance or relevance of the various HR roles as part of the SHRM system, irrespective of the typology adopted. For example, Monks (1992) argues that in stable environments a simple model of HRM practice will suffice; it is only in complex organizations, particularly undergoing substantial change, where a more sophisticated approach to practice is required. Other commentators support this linkage between the HR roles and the needs of the organizational context (Carroll, 1991; Guest, 1991). This may lead in some instances to a mismatch between the higher strategic goals of the HR professional and the actual organizational goals that require a much simpler approach to HRM. It is also difficult to combine both the operational and strategic roles in a single department, due largely to the more pressing requirements of service delivery above strategy formulation (Beer, 1997).

Against this plethora of observations on HR roles, it is noteworthy that the vast majority of this work has been carried out either in the USA or the UK. Given the importance of organizational context, alongside further evidence from the international

HRM literature (see, for example, Farndale & Paauwe, 2007), we should consider whether these typologies can be applied in different country contexts. Here, we explore the example of the Netherlands, which shows considerable differences, culturally and institutionally, compared to the USA and the UK. The Netherlands is a typical example of the so-called 'Rhineland' model of IR as a coordinated market economy, while both the UK and USA are representative of the more liberal, Anglo-American model of IR (Paauwe, 1998, 2004).

Starting with the external variables (the institutional mechanisms identified in the Contextual SHRM Framework), there has been little research carried out into these contextual variables when considering HR function roles, with a few exceptions (see, for example, Farndale et al., 2010). Budhwar and Sparrow (2002) suggest that further research is therefore needed with both a cross-national and comparative dimension to take this field further forward. Flood and colleagues (1996) suggest a number of factors which have an impact on the shaping of the HR function in general: These include organizational heritage characteristics (structure, culture, development phase, history, workforce profile, and salary bill), and institutional characteristics (trade union activity, labour market conditions). As the Contextual SHRM Framework shows, the impact of each of these sets of characteristics is moderated by the decisions made by the key decision-makers (e.g. senior management, and the works council in the case of the Dutch organizations), leading to crucial decisions being made on the form and structure of the HR department.

From an institutional mechanisms perspective, national-level regulations, standards, and traditions can affect the way in which HR professionals carry out their tasks. Macro institutions are argued to systematically influence organizational structures, resulting in organizational practices that reflect national patterns (Schuler & Rogovsky, 1998). As we saw in Chapter 5, neo-institutional theory suggests that there are coercive, normative, and mimetic influences present within a given context that restrict the freedom of organizations within which they operate (DiMaggio & Powell, 1983). Employment legislation may mean mandatory approaches to employing certain groups of individuals, to rewarding these employees, and to having them participate in organizational decisions. Standards across an industry or region or within HR professional bodies may have a normative effect on the way the HR is structured and its organizational tasks. Likewise, mimetic forces such as benchmarking against competitors and other successful companies may lead to the introduction of new ways of carrying out the HR function (for a more extensive treatment of the relationship between HR and institutional context see Paauwe & Boselie, 2003).

The more complex the employment legislation in a country, the more HR professionals may be forced into spending the majority of their time on administrative tasks to the detriment of more strategic activities (Brewster et al., 2006; Sparrow & Hiltrop, 1997). In a highly institutionalized setting (such as the Netherlands), the influence of the coercive, normative, and mimetic mechanisms is larger, which limits the degree of leeway of the HR function (Paauwe & Boselie, 2003). Likewise, where there is strong interdependence between employer and employee, more attention may be paid to involvement and participation systems than in other contexts. In addition to legislative and other institutional arguments, national culture can also play a role in influencing organizational activity. Cultural differences can be seen as variations in quality-of-life issues, subordinate–boss relationships, and the degree of individualization; all factors that can influence the roles HR professionals play within organizations (Farndale, 2010).

In many respects with regard to national culture, the USA, the UK, and the Netherlands are rated as possessing similar characteristics. Referring to Hofstede's (1980) framework of national culture, all three countries are predominantly individualistic (giving priority to individual rather than group goals), low on power distance (not accepting an unequal distribution of power in organizations), and low on uncertainty avoidance (prepared to take risks). However, on one dimension, masculinity versus femininity, the Netherlands scores considerably higher than the USA and UK. The main effect that we see from this difference is the way in which employee voice is apparent in organizations (Hofstede, 1980): More feminine countries emphasis more consensus, consultation, and discussion between employees, employers, and other stakeholders, often reinforced by local legislation (Hickson, 1993). This is manifested in Dutch society through a stronger focus on welfare issues and a consensual, partnership approach to ER.

From an institutional mechanisms perspective, the Netherlands has a more regulated employment environment than that of the UK or USA (Looise & Paauwe, 2001). This can be seen in issues such as the regulation of employment relationships, the employment contract, working conditions, the rights of works councils and trade unions, and legislation around diversity management and flexible work arrangements (Paauwe & Richardson, 2001). In this context, employees in the Netherlands are seen as full partners in the enterprise, whereas in the USA, for example, the enterprise is seen as under the control of management (Pot & Paauwe, 2004).

This last finding came from a study in which Pot and Paauwe (2004) compared two companies headquartered in the Netherlands with two companies headquartered in the USA, with all four companies having business units operating in both countries. The study showed that the Dutch organizations' decision-making process took significantly longer than that of the USA organizations, but this extended duration facilitated easier implementation of the decisions reached. Based on a review of HRM practices in the Netherlands and the USA, the same study found that, compared to the USA, in the Netherlands job design is broader, there is more focus on group rather than individual goals and tasks, vocational education is more common, and broad skill sets are more desirable. Performance management in the USA often focuses on the very high or very low performers, whereas in the Netherlands there is more attention paid to the middle performing group. Reward systems also vary, with more emphasis in the USA on tangible incentives such as pay, whilst there is a preference in the Netherlands for more intrinsic rewards such as job satisfaction and work environment. In terms of IR, the Dutch system reduces status differences and encourages industrial democracy, whilst the USA system relies more on authoritarian power structures and management prerogative.

The Dutch IR scene is characterized by what has been termed the 'Polder' model (Paauwe & Richardson, 2001). This model is a system of IR characterized by a socio-economic agreement of tripartite consultation with the aim of reaching consensus between the parties involved. This form of industrial democracy is a key aspect of the Rhineland model of IR, which the Netherlands represents. Legislation, institutions, and stakeholders play a significant role in the development of HRM policies and practices (Boselie, Paauwe, & Richardson, 2003). Rather than being shareholder-focused, as epitomized in the Anglo-Saxon models of organizing, the Rhineland model has a broader stakeholder focus. In the case of the Netherlands, this has resulted in, for example, a highly regulated salary policy, which limits opportunities for performance-related pay (Boselie, Paauwe, & Richardson, 2003).

Due to these differences between the national institutional and cultural context of the Netherlands and that of the UK and the USA, we might expect to observe a different model of HR roles than that presented in the universalist literature. Paauwe and Farndale (2008) carried out a study to explore this hypothesis. A total of 427 HR professionals in the Netherlands were surveyed in 2005/6. The questionnaire included items designed to uncover details about the HR roles being carried out, largely based on elements of the Ulrich (1997) typology described in Section 10.2. Statements were developed which focused on strategic involvement, functional impact, reactive policing, risk management, employee support, management support, trade union relations, and change management.

Based on a factor analysis, the findings show that four HR roles emerged as identifiable in organizations in the Netherlands: Strategic partner, trade union partner, employee partner, and administration deliverer (see Figure 10.5). The strategic and

Figure 10.5 HR roles in the Netherlands

Source: Paauwe & Farndale (2008: 351).

change partner role, including change management, strategy development, management partnership, and culture management, emerged as statistically most reliable. Interestingly, in this Dutch context, the role of building employee commitment belongs to this strategic dimension rather than an employee support role. The ER role has two dimensions—trade union partnership and employee partnership. Trade union negotiation and consultation play a significant role in the Dutch employment arena, and this trade union partnership role emerges as statistically the most reliable factor between these two roles. Finally, there is an administration delivery role. This role includes risk management, which is interesting, as we might assume this would be part of the strategic approach to HRM.

Although we can observe that in the Netherlands four HR roles did emerge, these four roles are not identical to the typology presented by Ulrich (1997). First, we can see that in the Netherlands there is a single, combined strategic HR role labelled 'strategic & change partner'. The elements of this role combine the two separate roles presented by Ulrich (1997) as strategic partner and change partner. In the Dutch context, these roles merge into one, which is in line with the later HR model development presented by Ulrich and Brockbank (2005), so apparently the Dutch were ahead in this respect.

Secondly, Ulrich's (1997) employee champion role is very specifically focused on trade union partnership. Given the importance of industrial democracy within the Netherlands (Paauwe & Richardson, 2001), this perhaps is not surprising, but has been overlooked in the universalistic literature. The HR professional is working proactively with trade unions to ensure a partnership approach to IR. This also provides evidence of the consultation characteristics of the feminine culture of the Dutch context (Hickson, 1993). Finally, the Dutch typology of HR roles and that of Ulrich (1997) do overlap on one dimension—HR administration. Ulrich's (1997) administrative expert has been labelled here as 'administration deliverer', emphasizing the importance of delivering efficient and effective HR administration across the organization, based on Ulrich's (1997) original definition of the role being focused on building an efficient firm infrastructure.

In summary, at the national level there is overlap between the universal typology suggested in this case by Ulrich (1997). However, there are also nuanced differences in the points of focus and emphasis in the HR roles. Only the more traditional administrative role within the HR function appears to be universally applicable.

Looking beyond an international comparative perspective on HR roles that contrasts activities in different countries, we can also see patterns of HR roles emerging in MNCs operating across these country borders. Farndale and colleagues (2010) identified configurations of the corporate HR function based on international HRM structures (see also Chapter 9 on the international application of the Contextual SHRM Framework), exploring how issues of interdependency shape corporate HR roles. They found that in a structure which is more centralized, with strong dependency of subsidiary operations on HQ, this formal dependency, in which corporate HR must focus on implementing and monitoring standard HRM practices, emphasizes a champion of processes role (Evans, Pucik, & Barsoux, 2002). At the other end of the scale, in highly decentralized operations, the subsidiary can act independently of headquarters, so there is little requirement for a centralized HR function to monitor local HRM activities. Instead, in this independent structure, the only roles that the corporate HR function at headquarters can fulfil are more informal ones, being a guardian of corporate culture (Brewster, Sparrow, & Harris, 2005) where possible, and relying on their own personal credibility as influencers to persuade subsidiary operations to cooperate with central HR demands when necessary. In a highly integrated structure, where headquarters and subsidiaries operate interdependently, a dominant role here is as knowledge management champion (Brewster, Sparrow, & Harris, 2005)—ensuring that appropriate linkages exist between all parts of the MNC, allowing knowledge to flow around the firm to enhance its organizational capabilities. Hence, we can see how the formal organizational structure (part of the organizational heritage) impacts the HR roles carried out as part of the SHRM system.

10.5 Summary and conclusions

This chapter has explored how HR roles and competencies have changed over the last half-century in line with organizational priorities. Starting with the welfare movement in organizations born out of the human challenges of industrialization, HR roles have continued to develop, first with a focus on administrative efficiency (e.g. Tyson & Fell, 1986), gradually adding the importance of a business perspective (e.g. Carroll, 1991; Schuler, 1990), later emphasizing the balance required between strategy/operational and process/employee needs (e.g. Ulrich, 1997; Ulrich & Brockbank, 2005), and ultimately emphasizing a need to be integrally involved in building organizational capability (e.g. Schuler & Jackson, 2001; Ulrich et al., 2012).

However, we have argued that it can be dangerous to adopt these HR typologies on face value alone due to the many inherent ambiguities (Caldwell, 2003). First, these typologies assume a 'conformist innovator' role (Legge, 1978) for HR professionals—toeing the business line, reactively responding to organizational needs as they occur. Conversely, a 'deviant innovator' role (Legge, 1978) would mean HR taking on a new role that might question the underlying motives of the business. Farndale, Paauwe, and Boselie's (2011) study of large firms experiencing significant crises highlights the value of this latter approach: Taking the financial services industry as an example, would the same crisis as occurred in 2008 have hit if HR had taken a stronger stance in upholding the moral values of the corporation perhaps in conflict with the economic interests of shareholders? We will, of course, never know the answer to this question, but it presents a good example of why we should at least cast a critical eye over the HR typology literature.

Finally, this chapter has taken an international perspective, exploring how appropriate some of these universally accepted HR role typologies are when applied in a country that is culturally and institutionally different to the place where they were developed. In a study of the applicability of Ulrich's (1997) HR role typology, developed in the USA, in a new context—the Netherlands—we observed how the more feminine culture and stronger regulatory context resulted in a different pattern of HR roles emerging. Although built on similar sets of activities, the HR 'employee champion' role took on a much more nuanced definition in the Dutch context due to the predominance of employee involvement in organizations through, for example, trade unions and works councils. We also described how some of these HR roles are being played out in MNCs, again concluding that organizational structure, in terms of dependencies between headquarters and subsidiaries, is a crucial contextual heritage factor influencing how HR professionals can operate.

In summary, this chapter has highlighted how HR roles fit into the Contextual SHRM Framework by explaining the different contextual settings of HR professionals, operating in organizations affected by local, national, and international factors, which can either enhance or impede performance outcomes. Chapter 11 continues this theme by looking at the HR function as a whole and how it delivers its services.

11 HR delivery and metrics

11.1 Introduction

In Chapter 10, we focused on relating how the roles of human resource (HR) professionals could be linked to performance. This chapter continues the focus on the HR function (department) as part of the strategic human resource management (SHRM) system in the Contextual SHRM Framework (Chapter 6), but rather than looking at the HR professionals and their daily activities and competencies, it explores how human resource management (HRM) activities are delivered in the organization and how this impacts on performance. We consider such issues as balancing delivering HRM through the HR function, versus the use of shared service or self-service facilities (Section 11.2), as well as considering the option of outsourcing to a third-party vendor (Section 11.3). These various delivery models can have different performance outcomes, but also lead to important issues regarding how the HR function is governed within an organization (addressed in Section 11.4). Ultimately, we are also interested in how the HR function is able to show its added value to the organization. This is where HR metrics (Section 11.5), and the more recent focus on HR analytics (Section 11.6), become important points of attention for organizations.

11.2 Centralization versus decentralization: Shared service centres

The HR function within an organization takes on a certain structure in order to deliver its services to its internal clients. This structure has traditionally included three primary delivery channels: a corporate head office HR department, various functional HR offices at business or organizational unit level, plus HR professionals based within these units working closely with managers as business partners. This is what is commonly termed the '3-legged stool' structure in which HRM activities are filtered from the head office through the functional HR offices out to HR professionals operating 'in the field'. When HRM is delivered in this way, however, there is the potential that the intended activities designed at head office may look quite different by the time they are being implemented by an HR professional in an office somewhere potentially on the other side of the country or globe, leading to unanticipated performance outcomes. This is where the challenge of centralization versus decentralization arises in the delivery of HRM.

There are three key drivers of centralization of HRM delivery in organizations: (1) a mechanism to maintain control over the policies and practices being implemented; (2) the advent of advanced technologies enabling the introduction of tools that facilitate organization-wide roll-out of standardized HRM systems; and (3) the effect of mimetic isomorphism (as we discussed in Chapter 4), that is, firms copying the practices of other successful organizations as they aim to reduce costs and standardize their HRM activities. Each of these drivers has contributed to the rise of the phenomenon of shared-service centres (SSCs). An SSC is a business unit designed to provide services, in this case HRM services, to a range of in-house clients in place of separate functions (Sparrow & Braun, 2008). The centre employs advanced technologies to support this structure, with clients deciding what services they require, rather than the HR department deciding what services to deliver. This places more emphasis on the line managers and employees requesting HRM services and having access to self-service facilities (Farndale, Paauwe, & Hoeksma, 2009). The related eHRM systems have been able to deliver timesavings for the HR department and employees, improved HR service quality and productivity, wider dispersion of information and communication, and cost reductions (Ruël, Bondarouk, & Looise, 2004). As a result, when other firms see the benefits of implementing such systems, they are more likely to introduce them themselves (Boglind, Hällstén, & Thilander, 2011).

To understand how HR SSCs come about, we first need to consider the range of HRM activities performed by the HR function. HRM practices are often categorized as being transactional, traditional, or transformational (see Figure 11.1). Essentially, this categorization relates to the relative complexity of the task at hand (Lepak, Bartol, & Erhardt, 2005). For example, record keeping is a relatively routine transactional activity that can be automated quite easily, whilst strategic planning is a transformational activity that involves many people and rarely has a simple process or outcome. SSCs therefore typically start by consolidating transactional activities such as benefits management and employee records (Adler, 2003). Firms are particularly likely to take this first step if

Figure 11.1 Categorization of HRM practices

Source: Lepak, Bartol, and Erhardt (2005: 143).

similar activities have already been housed in an SSC for another function within the firm, such as finance (Boglind, Hällstén, & Thilander, 2011). As experience improves, more advanced SSCs become centres of expertise for activities such as performance management or training, or even more advanced transformational activities such as organization development (also known as change management) or knowledge management.

An argument in favour of this shift towards using SSCs, particularly for the transactional activities, is the advantages of centralization: Internal control, standardization of processes, consolidation of systems, and the potential to deliver a more consistent, customer-focused, and cost-effective HR service (Baldwin, Irani, & Love, 2001; Farndale, Paauwe, and Hoeksma, 2009). In contrast, delivering these activities through the decentralized model of individual HR offices is inherently associated with inefficiencies and inconsistencies (Schulman et al., 1999). A decentralized delivery model does, however, mean that local HR departments are more responsive to local needs, are able to act quicker, and are more in tune with the local operating environment. There is also a greater sense of local ownership of HRM activities.

What a well-functioning SSC attempts to achieve simultaneously is the advantages of both centralization and decentralization: Centralized decision-making but decentralized delivery. Transactional activities and policy decisions are carried out at the centre. This frees up space in the local HR offices for more strategic or transformational activities, that is, the HR professionals working as business partners can focus on the latest change initiative rather than having to manage an appraisal scheme. Therefore, one of the anticipated performance outcomes of introducing an HR SSC is the impact on the role of the HR professionals: 'a shared-services centre is not an end in itself; it is a means to transforming the whole function of HR, to make it more strategic' (Whitehead, 2005).

Based on a study of thirty-nine organizations in the Netherlands operating HR SSCs, Farndale et al. (2009) developed a framework that links the different factors in designing the SSC to the various performance outcomes (see Figure 11.2). Organizations were found

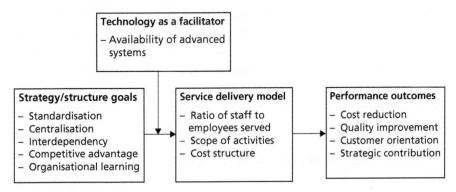

Figure 11.2 Conceptual framework of HR SSCs

Source: Adapted from Farndale, Paauwe, and Hoeksma (2009: 556).

to set up SSCs primarily with the aims of reducing costs and improving the customer focus, rather than being concerned about standardization and control issues per se (although such aims may ultimately lead to these desired outcomes). Interestingly, however, few firms actually collected data on the cost savings that the SSC was able to deliver, although they did confirm that the largest cost of the running the centre lay in the labour.

The strategy and structure goals combined with the availability of advanced technology systems was found to determine the service delivery model adopted in these firms in terms of the number of staff employed to employees served, the scope of their activities (e.g. front-office employees or call agents, HR advisors, or more senior HR experts: Reilly & Williams, 2003), and the cost structure (most commonly either as part of the headquarters or as a separate business unit). The reported performance outcomes of the SSC delivery model included cost reduction, quality improvement, increased customer orientation, and a greater opportunity for the HR function to deliver a strategic contribution to the organization. However, on this last point, there is as yet a lack of evidence to establish whether or not this strategic added value can actually be achieved. In Boglind, Hällstén, and Thilander's (2011) study of a small sample of HR SSCs in Sweden, they found no evidence of HR gaining greater influence. Instead, they found signs of the HR SSC staff actually declining in professional status and compensation.

In summary, the introduction of SSCs is a response to a decision facing large organizations in particular: How to achieve an appropriate balance between centralizing and decentralizing their support functions, attempting to maintain control from the centre yet retain local responsiveness (Farndale & Paauwe, 2007). Decentralization means the function can be faster and more flexible when responding to local demands, such as adapting to new employment legislation. In addition, decentralization transfers ownership of HRM to local units, maintaining local buy-in. However, this mode of operation also runs the risk of missing opportunities for synergies across the function as a whole, as well as producing cost inefficiencies and variable levels of service quality (Schulman et al., 1999). In contrast, centralization has the advantages of control and efficiency directed from the centre, leading to the avoidance of redundancy and duplication of work (Ulrich, 1995). Centralized models focus on economies of scale and scope and creating clarity in strategic alignment. However, ensuring buy-in to the services by local departments can be more problematic due to the geographical separation of units, and response times to clients can be slow due to great distances (Janssen & Joha, 2006). The SSC model attempts to balance these two sets of needs as far as possible.

11.3 **Insourcing versus outsourcing**

The issue of insourcing versus outsourcing of HRM activities brings us back to our '3-legged stool' delivery structure, but now adds a potential fourth leg—third-party vendors. Insourcing is when HRM activities are carried out in-house, whilst outsourcing is when the organization pays another external party to provide a particular service. To a large extent, technology has opened the door to increasing possibilities for outsourcing HRM activities. However, it has also created opportunities for further insourcing, that is, establishing SSCs and self-service systems for line managers and employees (Lepak, Bartol, & Erhardt, 2005).

Deciding whether or not to outsource a particular aspect of the HRM domain is dependent upon the extent to which that activity is related to other corporate activities, and on an assessment of the risks involved and trust in third-party vendors (Adler, 2003). Lepak, Bartol, & Erhardt (2005) developed a detailed contingency framework that explored the various moderating variables which influence the insourcing/outsourcing decision (see Figure 11.3). As we saw with deciding which activities to house in an HR SSC, the first decision relates to whether the activities in question are more transactional, traditional, or transformational. As for the SSC, it becomes increasingly complex to outsource more transformational activities compared to transactional activities. For example, it is relatively straight forward to give instructions to a third party on how you would like a recruitment process to run, but much more complex to describe how you would like a cross-cultural change management programme to be put in place. Lepak, Bartol, & Erhardt (2005) also highlight the importance of deciding—if you are going to outsource—whether this is going to be a one-off contractual agreement or you are building a long-term partnership with a supplier. Different levels of trust will need to be established in the working relationship dependent upon the anticipated ongoing engagement (Adler, 2003).

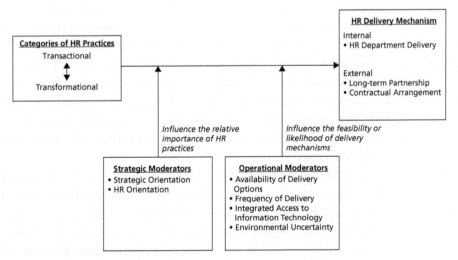

Figure 11.3 Contingency framework for the delivery of HR practices

Source: Lepak, Bartol, and Erhardt (2005: 146).

Regarding the moderating variables, Lepak, Bartol, & Erhardt (2005) highlight both strategic and operational moderators. From a strategic perspective, they highlight the difference between HRM practices that might be considered either core or peripheral to the organization. For example, a firm that follows a cost-oriented strategy might focus on having efficient, core, internal, transactional activities, and due to its minimal use of costly, peripheral, transformational activities, would set up contractual arrangements with external vendors for such activities on a 'need only' basis.

Lepak, Bartol, & Erhardt (2005) suggest that the operational moderators are factors in the organization's context that affect the feasibility of either insourcing or outsourcing a particular HRM practice. These include the following considerations:

- whether there are suitable third-party vendors available offering the required services;
- how frequently the service is required (i.e. a one-off activity might best be set up through an external vendor to save having to establish a process in-house, whereas a more frequent activity may be worth the internal investment);
- the extent to which information technology systems are available to integrate the service being provided externally to the internal systems; and
- the extent of environmental uncertainty faced by the organization, that is, how much planned or unplanned change is taking place, affecting the ability to predict the services required from external vendors.

The insourcing/outsourcing challenge is largely a question of 'make or buy' decisions. Whereas outsourcing is often driven by decisions about capability and resources, and is thus considered from a resource-based view (RBV) of the firm (Barney, 1991), in-sourcing is particularly subject to arguments from transaction cost economics, with decisions being made between whether to 'make' or 'buy' these services (Hesketh, 2006). Adams (1991) uses both agency theory and transaction cost economics in order to highlight various degrees of internalization (make) or externalization (buy). Transaction cost economics suggests that the choice between allocating practices to the external market or to the internal organization is a matter of cost minimization. The focus of agency theory is to determine the most effective contract to control the relationship between the principal and the agent (as we will discuss further when addressing the issue of governance in Section 11.4).

Flood, Gannon, and Paauwe (1996) discussed a number of benefits and drawbacks of the 'make' and 'buy' alternatives. They noted that the option to keep HRM activities in-house results in the opportunity to develop internal know-how, and is especially important when the activities require knowledge of the organizational culture (e.g. implementing a change programme). It also reduces the internal costs of coordination and avoids problems of external agencies perhaps lacking the required qualities. The outsourcing option is beneficial when the organization itself does not possess the necessary expertise or headcount in-house for the activities required, or when an impartial third party may be a useful partner (e.g. when dealing with a difficult down-sizing exercise when an external agent may be easier to work with). Outsourcing allows more focus on core activities, more flexibility, and increased control and monitoring of costs associated with particular activities.

In a study entitled the 'Global HR Research Alliance', we explored this issue of insourcing versus outsourcing. The study was a collaborative research project with partners spanning the globe, designed to explore what multinational corporations described as 'HR excellence'. Companies were selected for inclusion based on superior business performance and reputation as an employer, and included such names as: ABB, BAe Systems, BT, EDF, IBM, IKEA, Infosys, Matsushita, Oracle, Procter & Gamble (P&G), Rolls Royce, Samsung Electronics, Shell, Siemens, TCL, and Unilever. Based on 263 survey responses gathered in 2004/5, the data was analysed by geographic region. Outsourcing was found to be particularly common in Japan and the Americas, whilst it was used less in Europe. However, the practice of outsourcing in general was uniformly seen as only as moderately effective in achieving the organization's goals, irrespective of country or region. Very similar results were also noted for the use of HR SSCs. North American firms had made the most use of outsourcing HRM activities to low-cost locations, with China being a primary recipient of such work.

In brief, based on the findings on this and other studies, although outsourcing is certainly a viable option for organizations, and sometimes either the only or possibly the best option for certain activities (i.e. non-core programmes), it is not necessarily the best solution overall. In-sourcing maintains many advantages in terms of control, cost-containment, and in-house expertise building. Firms therefore need to take into consideration the range of desired performance goals for an activity in choosing the 'make' or 'buy' decision.

11.4 **Governance of the HR function**

So far we have discussed how the HR function might be structured in terms of creating a centralized SSC model, and the decision processes involved in determining whether to keep HRM activities in-house or to outsource them to third-party vendors. The issue that we have not yet raised is the effect that each of these decisions has on the way in which the HR function is governed within the organization. In other words, by changing the structure and delivery methods of the function, there are implications for how HRM flows from one part of the organization to another, from the HR department to line managers and to employees. In this section, we explore these governance implications further.

Drawing from a study exploring the HR intra-firm supply chain in seven large organizations headquartered in Europe and the USA (Farndale, Paauwe, & Boselie, 2010), we can see how the HR function can learn from the principles of supply chain management. The HR function operates through multiple delivery channels implementing a vast range of HRM policies and practices, and, as such, is vulnerable to many sources of risk inherent in this structural complexity. As we noted in Section 11.2, the 3-legged stool is a typical structure in large organizations, often incorporating a corporate head office, some form of centralized HR SSC structure at the organizational or business-unit level, and HR business partners out in the field. This 3-legged structure was replicated in the study's organizations. Most of the firms also preferred to adopt a standardized model of HR delivery where possible, relying on technology to facilitate this, especially through self-service systems.

If we look to agency theory (Jensen & Meckling, 1976), this can highlight some of the issues that this HR delivery structure poses to organizations. In a traditional agency theory relationship, an external principal owns the organization, and internal senior managers control the organization. Principal–agent problems can arise when there is a difference between the interests of the owner (principal) and controllers of the organization. Translating this to the HR function's situation, the corporate HR is the equivalent of the 'owner' of the HRM activities in the firm, whereas the multiple delivery channels (e.g. the HR SSC and business partners) are the 'agents' of the HRM activities, controlling how they are implemented across the organization. The agents have a responsibility to the owner to perform to certain standards, although they may also have their own ideas of how they would prefer to implement certain activities.

However, there is also an additional complication: There is a second body setting standards to which these agents must perform—the business units. Business units are accountable for delivering results and can, at least to some extent, decide which services they will use from the agents. This can again lead to a misalignment between owners and agents' interests. This complex set of relationships needs to be managed to avoid the risk of non-performance. Corporate governance is therefore applied to minimize agency problems, aligning principal and agent interests more closely through principles of good stewardship rather than self-interest (Lubatkin et al., 2007).

In the study (Farndale et al., 2010), some of these corporate governance mechanisms were explored. The findings uncovered the way in which the monitoring of how well the different delivery systems were working was achieved through a range of tools. The first set of tools included surveys of employees and line managers, and the gathering of HRM metrics (see also Section 11.5). Some firms had implemented HR scorecards including key performance indicators (KPIs) that related to delivery methods, whilst others had sophisticated project management analyses and customer-driven service plans in place, all designed to ensure that the HR function was delivering what it had promised. Most of the firms also gathered a range of metrics on how well their SSC was performing. All of these formal mechanisms were outcome-focused, that is, providing data against which performance could be benchmarked or checked against targets previously set.

The second set of monitoring tools in place was more behaviour-focused, that is, they looked at the process rather than the outcome of a particular activity. It is argued that as relationships in a supply chain become more complex, the ability to rely on formal, outcome-based metrics to measure performance decreases, and instead more relational indicators become increasingly important (Morris et al., 2009). In other words, for a sustainable, long-term relationship to develop between the HR function and its myriad of clients across the organization, more than just hitting KPIs is required: the development of trusting relationships is key. In this latter type of governance system, the behaviour-based governance mechanisms take on increased significance (Vachon, 2007). The type of behaviour-based governance mechanisms found in the study (Farndale et al., 2010) included reflection meetings, joint feedback sessions, and explicitly trusting line management to take on responsibilities that used to lie with the HR department. Such mechanisms were, however, much less frequently employed than the outcome-focused metrics.

Putting in place tools to monitor the HR delivery model is, however, only one aspect of the overall governance of the HR function. Monitoring tools provide performance indicators, but they do not provide a structure that enables an organization to be confident that its HR function is operating in an effective manner that reduces uncertainty and minimizes risks. This is where a range of other formal and informal governance mechanisms comes into play. Based on the study's findings (Farndale et al., 2010), one such typical mechanism is that there is an HR leadership team in place, and that this leadership team either has a seat on or reports directly into the firm's executive board. This way, there is a clear line of sight from the top of the organization into the operation of the function. Hierarchy and structure was generally found in the study to be an important factor in a number of other ways too: Restricting levels of access to HR delivery channels (i.e. only certain levels of employee or management were entitled to use certain services offered by HR); centralized control of HR policy development by the headquarters staff only; and in one firm, HR business partners were given independent status from the business, that is, so that they could operate as 'impartial outsiders' in dealing with HRM issues as they arose.

When delivering HRM practices, formal governance mechanisms need to be in place to ensure that appropriate practices are being implemented. In the study (Farndale et al., 2010) this was being monitored at a number of levels: Formal audits, employee hotlines to report non-compliance, standardization to help support compliance, and multiple-person sign-offs for policy documents. Ultimately, the HR professionals were being held accountable for the compliance of the HRM policies and practices, so it was in their interest to ensure that necessary governance mechanisms and monitoring tools were in place to ensure appropriate implementation.

11.5 **Measuring HR effectiveness**

As we have seen, a trend of academic articles started to appear in the 1990s addressing the issue of the relationship between HRM and its proclaimed contribution to the performance of the firm (see Chapter 5). The forerunner to this literature is to be found in the approach to human resource accounting (HRA) as promoted in the seventies and eighties by people like Bulte (1975) and Flamholtz (1985). This approach was later developed by Fitz-Enz (1990) as the concept of human value management. HRA itself was, at least as an academic sub-discipline, quite popular during this period. However, in 1989, after reviewing over 140 articles and several books, Scarpello and Theeke (1989: 275) concluded:

At the theoretical level, HRA is an interesting concept. If human resource value could be measured, the knowledge of that value could be used for internal management and external investor decision-making. However, until HRA advocates demonstrate a valid and generalizable means for measuring human resource value in monetary terms, we are compelled to recommend that researchers abandon further consideration of possible benefits from HRA.

HRA barely appeared as an academic discipline of enquiry in the nineties, but the interest in measuring HR effectiveness has grown enormously since then. Approaches include cost–benefit analysis based on utility analysis, which attempts to estimate the financial impact of employee behaviours. In its ultimate form this results in being able to calculate the return on investment (ROI) for every HRM programme or practice (Phillips, Stone, & Phillips, 2001). Examples include labour turnover costs, gains from selection programmes, financial costs, and gains from training programmes (see, for example, Cascio, 1991; Noe et al., 2000).

Phillips, Stone, and Phillips (2001) present an overview of approaches to HR measurement and accountability (see Figure 11.4). They distinguish, first, a set of 'early approaches', including the well-known 'management by objectives', which dates back to the 1960s. Secondly, the 'solid value-added approaches' include the use of approaches that became popular throughout the 1980s and 1990s, such as key indicators, monitoring, and benchmarking. Their third category includes more composite approaches like HR profit centre and the whole ROI process as outlined in their own book, which focuses on comparing benefits versus costs. The authors also foresee a resurgence of HRA under the new heading of 'human capital valuation'. Proponents of this human capital approach have been, for example, the former Watson Wyatt Human Capital index, Sveiby's intangible assets monitor (1997), and Mayo's human capital monitor (2001).

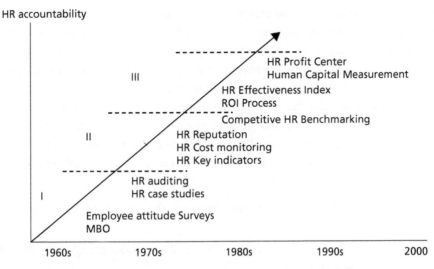

HR accountability

III

HR Profit Center
Human Capital Measurement
HR Effectiveness Index
ROI Process
Competitive HR Benchmarking

II

HR Reputation
HR Cost monitoring
HR Key indicators

HR auditing
HR case studies

I

Employee attitude Surveys
MBO

1960s   1970s   1980s   1990s   2000

Figure 11.4 Overview of approaches to HR measurement and accountability

Source: Phillips, Stone, and Phillips (2001).

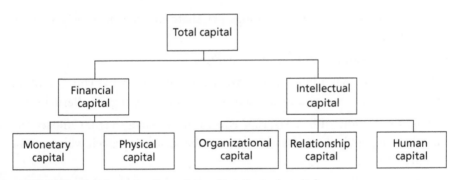

Figure 11.5 Distinction between financial and intellectual capital

Source: Peppard and Rylander (2001).

Based on a distinction between financial and intellectual capital, Peppard and Rylander (2001) present an overview (Figure 11.5).

Although the definition of intellectual capital differs per author, the distinction made by Peppard and Rylander (2001) gives a good overview of the constituent resources:

- Human capital: Comprising the competencies, skills, and intellectual agility of the individual employees.

- Relationship (social) capital: Represents all the valuable relationships (networks) with customers, suppliers, and other relevant stakeholders.

- Organizational capital: Includes processes, systems and structures, brands, intellectual property, and other intangibles that support value creation.

Based on the fact that, from the perspective of financial analysts around this time, the intangibles were starting to be considered crucial in assessing the value of a company (referring, for example, to the Ernst and Young (2001) report on 'Measures that Matter'), one can easily understand the increased interest in trying to measure, monitor, and evaluate the value or potential value creation of human capital.

The overview of approaches and numerous articles and books dealing with adapted versions of the balanced scorecard (Kaplan and Norton, 1992) demonstrate the enormous importance academics, consultants, and practitioners alike attach to the whole issue of measuring HR effectiveness. In brief, here is why measuring HR effectiveness has been and remains so popular today:

- Growing evidence to support the link between the quality of HRM practices and business performance.
- Increased competitive pressure as a consequence of rapidly changing technology and increasingly global markets.
- Drive for cost-effectiveness; pressure on all specialist staff functions to justify their use of resources.
- Pressure to increase constantly earnings per share in order to satisfy shareholders/capital markets.
- General trend towards increased benchmarking.
- Belief in organizational myths such as, you cannot manage what you cannot measure (Ulrich, 1997), and what you measure is what you get (Yeung and Berman, 1997).
- USA-based obsession with measuring effectiveness, which has an impact (through publications in popular business journals) in other countries, albeit with a certain time lag (Pfeffer, 1997).
- Low status of the HRM function, however much it wants to be at the table as a business partner together with accounting, finance, and marketing. For this reason HRM concepts need to be replaced by evidence, preferably quantifiable data (see Pfeffer (1997) criticizing Ulrich (1997)).

The following potential benefits are associated with paying more attention to HR measurement (based on Daniels, 2002; Noe et al., 2000, and the almost classic and still very valuable paper by Tsui & Gomez-Mejia, 1988):

- Strengthening the profile of the HRM function (marketing, PR): Demonstrating added value enhances image and visibility.
- Providing accountability: Measurement and evaluation serve as important accountability tools to determine if the HRM function is effectively utilizing its resources and meeting immediate and longer-term goals.

- Promoting change: the power of data, perceived as objective, is excellent for gaining attention, concern (from the HR function and other stakeholders), and ultimately action.
- Assessing financial impact: HR measurement encourages the HRM function to act 'like entrepreneurs whose business happens to be people' (Fitz-Enz, 1980: 41).

Putting significant emphasis on measurement can, however, also involve risks and unforeseen consequences. For example, Pfeffer (1997: 360) rightly highlights that measurement is easiest if you relate it to the expenditure of resources, such as the number of people working in the HR department and their salary costs, or the costs associated with training. Staffing ratios and measures of resources expended do not, however, inform us about effectiveness, nor do they inform us of the value added as a consequence of HRM activities. Hence, spending fewer resources and having fewer people becomes an end in itself and is easily mistaken for efficiency.

Another problem is the time span of HRM activities before they become manifest in their intended consequences. For example, a range of training sessions across different management layers aimed at strengthening organizational culture in the direction of a new entity after a merger, might take three to four years before its effects become manifest. Another warning put forward by Pfeffer (1997) relates to the abundance of HRM indicators and the risk of losing sight of the 'forest for the trees'. For example, the book by Phillips, Stone, and Phillips (2001) gives an enormous overview of possible indicators, which should all culminate in one figure, that is, ROI. However, it is more important, just as Kaplan and Norton emphasize, to use only a few meaningful indicators per perspective, which are most successful for the attainment of their related objectives.

Measuring HR effectiveness presupposes that the HR function is able to influence firm-level outcomes. Pfeffer (1997) rightly warns that HR as a staff specialist function might, however, only have limited influence. For example, it might design an HRM tool in the area of appraisal, but line management enacts that tool in a work setting that is being created by a combination of the style of leadership, the organizational climate, and team composition, to name but a few. Line management have an enormous influence over people management practices such as appraisal (Farndale & Kelliher, 2013), which can lead to both intended and unintended consequences of HR function activities.

The reasons for measuring HR effectiveness and its potential associated benefits are highly convincing in stimulating academics and practitioners to pursue approaches that are both academically sound and useful for practitioners. The level of sophistication of measurement has been the primary change that we have witnessed in this area, with the emergence of the relatively new field of HR analytics.

11.6 **HR analytics**

Recent surveys of HR managers and trend studies all point to the prominent role of HR analytics as a priority for years to come, alongside topics like leadership development, organizational change, strategic workforce planning, and talent management[1]. The business community has uncovered the power of advanced analytics and statistics, especially for linking HRM practices and interventions to HR outcomes (e.g. turnover, commitment) and other business performance indicators (e.g. sales, productivity and profit). Rather than just signalling certain outcomes on the basis of employee engagement surveys and comparing/contrasting these figures to those of last year, or benchmarking among business units, subsidiaries, or different staff categories, now business community and consultancy firms alike can relate HR interventions and practices (such as a leadership development or sales training programme) to hard business indicators.

This new approach allows firms to assess the effectiveness of these HR interventions. What is more, it might even enable us to *predict* the outcomes of these interventions. An enabling factor is, of course, the availability of electronic data that can easily be collected and analysed. This data comes from both employee surveys and from performance management systems, workforce planning overviews, and productivity and sales figures. Once this kind of data is available and standardized to such a degree that comparisons across units, departments, and countries are possible, powerful statistics and appropriate analytical tools (e.g. regression analysis, structural equation modelling) will result in insights that facilitate an appropriate evaluation (with hindsight) and assessment (future oriented) of the (in)effectiveness of HR interventions/practices.

11.6.1 DEFINING HR ANALYTICS

The common denominator in defining HR analytics is the link between HR data and business performance data. Mondore, Douthitt, and Carson (2011) define the essence of HR analytics as demonstrating the direct impact of people data on important business outcomes. Lawler, Levenson, and Boudreau (2004) highlight its interactive nature by defining HR analytics as the ability to measure how human capital decisions affect the business, and how business decisions affect human capital. Cascio and Boudreau (2010: 21)

---

[1] Sources: BCG/EAPM analysis: The Future of HR in Europe; BCG/WFPMA (https://www.bcgperspectives.com/content/articles/people_management_human_resources_future_of_hr_in_europe/); Creating People Advantage: 2012-Worldwide Survey (https://www.bcgperspectives.com/content/articles/people_management_human_resources_leadership_creating_people_advantage_2012/); DDI Global Leadership Forecast, 2011 (http://www.ddiworld.com/resources/library/trend-research/global-leadership-forecast-2011).

simply refer to fact-based decision-making in the area of HR or people management. All of these definitions demonstrate the importance of HR analytics to business decisions.

Boudreau and Ramstad (2007) present a human capital bridge framework to highlight the evolution of HR analytics. Whereas in the past HR was able to provide data in order to assess the efficiency of HRM practices (for example, how many days are needed to fill a vacancy), HR analytics is about effectiveness and, additionally, about forecasting/predicting the impact of HR interventions. Questions about effectiveness focus on the relationship between the implementation of HRM and management practices and the resultant changes in shared perceptions (e.g. organizational climate), individual perceptions (e.g. psychological climate), and the behaviour and capabilities of employees. For example, typical questions might be: Do HRM practices make employees behave more productively, or does a specific training programme influence sales (see also Textboxes 11.1 and 11.2)? In the future, we can expect more impactful questions to emerge, such as: Suppose we consider investing in strengthening our service climate, will that lead to more engaged employees and subsequently higher productivity/sales?

HRM is following the evolutionary footsteps of other corporate functions that successfully made the transition from professional practice to decision science; for example, from 'Accounting' to 'Finance and Control', from 'Sales' to 'Marketing' and from 'HR' to 'Organizational Effectiveness'. In Textboxes 11.1 and 11.2 we provide illustrations of the power of HR analytics from our own research, which demonstrate the insightful link between an HRM intervention and business outcomes.

TEXTBOX 11.1 PREDICTING BUSINESS UNIT OUTCOMES: MONITORING HRM-RELATED CHANGES VIA EMPLOYEE SURVEYS

A large bank corporation with some 300 local independent branches was introducing a renewed HRM policy:

- stronger articulation of values such as cost-effectiveness, customer quality, and information sharing, also resulting in changes in the performance management system;
- more focus on employee development, training and opportunities to learn; and
- changes in job functions, pay policies, and job security.

The background to these new initiatives was to speed up productivity, improve cost-effectiveness, and offer more specialized financial services to customers. All of these changes were necessary due to increased competition. As the bank was organized on the basis of cooperative principles, the local branches were largely self-governed and could adopt and adapt the principles and policies initiated by corporate head office. This meant the branches differed in their degree of adoption of the new HR policies. Employee perceptions were measured through the annual employee survey. This was done twice—once before and once after the introduction of the new HRM policies. Both times approximately 15,000 employees participated (response rates of 78 per cent and 85 per cent respectively), which can be considered representative for the total organization. The survey measured employee perceptions of performance orientation, employee development, pay satisfaction, and job security. Business performance was measured by annual branch profit per full-time equivalent (FTE). The time interval between the first and second survey was, on average, 2.1 years.

(continued)

TEXTBOX 11.1 CONTINUED

Using HR analytics, the firm was able to determine how much (calculated in euros) of the annual financial performance could be predicted by survey scores. Based on extrapolation to all branches of this organization, the changes in employee survey scores (and thus the related HRM interventions) predict higher annual profits of 178 million euros (approximately USD 240 million), which was 17.9 per cent of the total annual profits across the entire company!

Source: Van de Voorde, Paauwe, & Van Veldhoven, 2010.

TEXTBOX 11.2 EFFECTS OF AN UP-SELLING TRAINING PROGRAMME IN TIMES OF RECESSION

A large retail organization faced intensified competition, which threatened its dominant market position. Moreover, sales in the market as a whole were stagnating due to the 2008/9 global financial economic crisis. In 2011, the organization decided to develop a large-scale training programme to improve the sales skills of the staff working in the stores. The training programme was characterized by a 'trickle-down' effect: First, regional and store managers were trained in the principles and practices of up-selling, and subsequently they themselves acted as trainers and coaches for their own sales staff operating in the stores ('coaching on the job'). The company operated in total 300 stores and had about 3,000 employees. The sales training took place in 2012–13. Both before, during, and after, objective business data were available for every period (four weeks) with respect to KPIs such as number of transactions, revenues per employee per hour, revenues per customer, and number of products per customer per transaction. Data was also collected from store managers and staff to measure perceptions of HRM, levels of engagement, satisfaction of the store managers, and the degree of customer-oriented work climate. A number of stores had not yet been trained, so there was also a control group available for the analytics.

Applying advanced HR analytics to the available data, the following key results emerged:

- The training neutralized the recession effect. The downward trend in the market was a 3 per cent annual decrease. As a result of the up-selling training, the company managed to neutralize this trend.

- The training was associated with an increase in customer satisfaction: Among the trained stores the increase was 29 per cent, whereas the non-trained stores (control group) had an increase of 10.5 per cent.

- Stores were less affected by the recession if they received the up-selling training, but the effect was even stronger when there was a higher degree of implementation and positive evaluation of related HRM practices (e.g. performance feedback, learning and development, participation and involvement, recruitment and selection, and rewards and benefits); when there was an engaged and satisfied store manager; and when there was a customer-oriented work climate present.

Translated into key business performance indicators, the training programme resulted in an extra revenue of Euro 1,068.00 (approx. USD 1,430.00) per four-week period per store. This effect lasted for about seven periods. The increase in revenue per employee per hour is about Euro 3.20 (approx. USD 4.30) during eight periods. So the training had a strong positive effect on performance and was able to act as a buffer against the downward trend in the market. However, the effect seemed to be temporary (covering about seven to eight periods each of four weeks), so a follow-up intervention (e.g. repeating the essence of the training by means of a large-scale event) was apparently needed. In addition to the effect of the training, the store environment in terms of the embeddedness of the training was also found to be important, that is, the accompanying HRM practices, a customer-oriented work climate, and an engaged store manager.

Source: Internal research memorandum, HR Studies Department, Tilburg University.

11.7 **Summary and conclusions**

The HR function is a service function embedded within an organization, and, as such, takes on a complex structure in order to deliver its services to all of its clients housed in the many business and organizational units. In this chapter, we have explored the different options that the senior management team of the organization faces in terms of structuring the HR function, and deciding on an appropriate HR delivery model. This involves weighing up the advantages and disadvantages of centralization versus decentralization, and of insourcing versus outsourcing. In particular, we have focused on the scenario of establishing an HR SSC and looked at the evidence to date of how such structures have been implemented.

We have highlighted how these decisions have multiple implications for how the function should be governed to ensure the effective delivery of HRM to the end clients. This entails the implementation of numerous monitoring tools, as well as ensuring appropriate hierarchies and structures are in place to avoid 'principal–agent' non-performance issues. In turn, these challenges have highlighted a number of potential ways in which HR delivery impacts performance. Finally, we explored how performance, in terms of HR effectiveness, can be measured, taking both an historical perspective as well as exploring the more recent trend towards HR analytics and demonstrating the evidence-based approach of analysing HRM interventions and their impact on business performance indicators.

In the final chapter of this book, we conclude by reflecting on the integration of the relationship between strategy, HRM, and performance, suggesting directions for future research and practice in this fascinating field.

12 Reflections for the future

12.1 Introduction

The broad aims of this book have been to elucidate the macro-level relationship between strategy, human resource management (HRM), and performance, exploring important boundary conditions that have constrained research and practice in the field to date. Adopting a critical perspective, the first boundary condition we have identified is the narrow definition of 'performance' to date, which has been largely driven by a managerialist, profit motive, with little regard for the human element. The second boundary condition is that HRM takes place 'in context', that is, the outcomes of HRM are not universalistic but need to be understood against the setting in which an organization is operating.

We argue that these two boundary conditions have, to date, received too little attention in HRM and performance research, which also in part explains why extant empirical evidence has shown mixed results regarding HRM's strategic contribution. We have therefore proposed adopting a more balanced approach towards measuring performance (between organizational financial performance and employee well-being) and a context-centric perspective on the origins and outcomes of strategic HRM systems, culminating in the development of the Contextual Strategic Human Resource Management (SHRM) Framework.

Whereas some research has suggested a strong link between strategic HRM activities and performance outcomes, other studies have argued that such a link is spurious and cannot be replicated across organizations, sectors, or countries. Overall, extant research findings have nevertheless consistently demonstrated that there is some (if perhaps only weak) association between adopting appropriate HRM practices that align with business strategy, and achieving desired organizational outcomes. The challenge, as successive chapters have indicated, lies in how we define and measure the different variables in this relationship, our research or practice models adopted, the methods we use to analyse our data, and how we apply appropriate theorizing to understand our observations. Here, we reflect further on the balanced approach to studying strategy, HRM, and performance, highlighting priorities for future research as well as implications for practice.

12.2 Core themes

In Chapter 1, we proposed four precepts that formed the basis of our thinking behind a balanced relationship between strategy, HRM, and performance: Human resources are more than just resources; the human resources (HR) function is not solely concerned with financial performance; HRM focuses on the exchange relationship between employee and employer; and the shaping of the employment relationship takes place in an arena of continuous tension between added value and moral value. These precepts have led to three core recurring themes throughout the book that we discuss further here: *Context, actors,* and *balance.*

12.2.1 CONTEXT

The first core theme, most notably addressed in Chapter 4 through the lens of institutional theory, is the importance of understanding the context of organizations in order to make a connection between strategy, HRM, and performance.

It has already been noted in Chapter 2 that the role of strategy is fundamental in creating a clear link between the direction of the organization and its workforce. This role is not, however, straightforward, but involves many complex factors related to the context of the organization, including the role of the organization's founder/owner/key decision-makers in setting the direction; the power and politics that enable or constrain access to resources to develop or implement the SHRM system; and the vast range of institutional forces external to the organization that impact on its functioning.

Such factors highlight the relevance of 'fit' or alignment to the strategic HRM field (as discussed in Chapter 3), emphasizing that the effectiveness of HRM practices is context-specific. Strategic, organizational, internal, environmental, and macro–micro fit combine to produce the overall fit of the SHRM system to its context. Research has, to date, had difficulty in capturing these multiple dimensions of fit, leading to mixed empirical evidence regarding HRM effectiveness. Related to this, we highlighted in Chapter 5 the notion of the 'black box' in HRM and performance research. The black box can be opened at least in part by applying contextual thinking: Why does this relationship occur within this particular setting? What do we know about the external and internal environments of the organization and about the managers and employees that can help to explain whether an HRM practice is considered to deliver effective performance outcomes? Such understanding requires multi-level thinking about the relevance of context.

Context was also an important theme when we discussed HR professional roles in Chapter 9 and the delivery of HRM through the HR function in Chapter 10. The role of HR professionals aligns with the needs of the organization, which in turn are dependent on the operating context. For example, we explained how the employee champion role identified in US research became much more complex in the Dutch context in which employee representation through trade unions is prevalent. Related competencies of HR professionals therefore differ across national contexts, as well as across organizations with different structures and strategies.

What is common across many chapters on this theme of context is the notion of coevolution. Organizations do not exist in a vacuum, but evolve with and influence their context. For example, legislation might require organizations to adopt practices for bringing unemployed people back into the workforce. As a result (all things being equal), unemployment would, over time, be expected to subside, and hence societal pressures for such practices would reduce. Similarly, if firms by choice decide to adopt extensive programmes focused on employee health, we might expect citizens' needs for doctors and hospital services to decline, reducing societal health-care spending. These are merely illustrative examples, but emphasize how organizations are embedded in society and should not be considered as independent entities.

The Contextual SHRM Framework incorporates all of these contextual elements, acting as a template for future research and practice to ensure a holistic picture of SHRM in its context. This can create understanding of how the SHRM system comes about and its consequent outcomes. The cases at organization, sector, and international levels presented in Chapters 7, 8, and 9 provide examples of this process. The Chapter 7 case of Randstad shows how high firm performance can be achieved on the back of a business model that promotes social legitimacy, whereas that of 'SupplierStore' reveals the subsequent impact adopting an alternative low-cost business model in an extremely competitive market has on employees. Each case demonstrates the strong alignment between the context, strategy, HRM system, and financial and well-being performance outcomes.

12.2.2 ACTORS

Whereas context might be considered deterministic, actors in organizations explain the dynamism in organizations. For example, globalization is increasingly leading us to question the universalistic approach to HRM and performance, highlighting the merits of a best fit perspective (although still with its own limitations—see Chapter 3). As firms cross national borders, we learn more about how HRM is practised in different countries around the world, and we either try to learn from what appears to be effective practice, or replace apparently ineffective practice with HRM that has been known to be successful in achieving performance outcomes in another context. Examples of such approaches were presented in Chapter 9. One piece that is missing from this approach, however, is the role of actors in organizations in making strategic decisions.

Organizational actors (here referring to senior, middle, and line managers) can choose which HRM practices to adopt and implement in different parts of the business. Such decisions rely on finding a balance between internal business strategy and external institutional legitimacy. The Procter & Gamble (P&G) scenario presented in Chapter 7 demonstrates a case in point, where an influential CEO changed the direction of the organization, moving the HRM strategy so that it remained aligned with new organizational goals. The health-care sector case presented in Chapter 8 demonstrates the balancing act that actors perform between dealing with new competitive drivers while, at the same time, remaining constrained by strongly institutionalized regulations and organizational structures. Similarly, the agricultural sector case demonstrates how key decision-makers ultimately determine the choice of SHRM system in an industry that is dominated by cost-cutting pressures: Such pressures do not always lead to 'low road' HRM when the firm's management has a more socially responsible outlook. Finally, Chapter 9 illustrates at the international level how IBM changed its global approach to recognizing more local diversity based on the learning and input from key SHRM decision-makers across the organization.

HR professionals working in the HR function are, of course, critical actors in the design and delivery of SHRM systems. The Contextual SHRM Framework can be used as a tool by HR to analyse the organizational context and the potential outcomes that the SHRM system can deliver. Chapter 6 provided the example of the force-field analysis that can be carried out on this basis. By taking this analytical approach, HR can maintain its position as a 'key decision-maker' in the process of developing appropriate SHRM systems to deliver high performance.

12.2.3 BALANCE

As will have become apparent, the theme of balance runs through the notions of context and actors, as well as across the broad topic of strategy, HRM, and performance. The argument we have presented emphasizes both economic and relational rationality, focusing on HRM policies and practices that meet the criteria both of added value (in its economic sense) and moral values (such as fairness, legitimacy, and sustainability).

Strategy research has highlighted the need for balance between leaving strategic decision-making to a select few versus adopting a more bottom-up approach. Chapter 2 highlighted the inherent tensions between strategic perspectives (outside-in versus inside-out; shareholder value versus stakeholder values), concluding that it is important to consider both content and process when linking strategy and HRM, acknowledging the incremental, emergent, and interactive nature of strategy development.

High performance work systems (HPWSs) have, to date, had a clear focus on organizational financial performance (Chapter 5), largely relying on the premises of the resource-based view (RBV) of the firm. Recent research has, however, questioned the assumption of mutual gains of HPWSs for employees and employers, balancing this with an argument of potentially conflicting outcomes for the two parties. In brief, what is good for the organization might not always be good for the employee. For example, performance-related pay systems may balance organizational output with salary bills, but is this at the expense of employee well-being (with the promise of higher pay pushing some employees to burn out)?

Further examples of the importance of balance can be found in the various case studies presented. The sector-level comparison of the metal and information technology (IT) industries in Chapter 8 emphasizes the need to achieve a balance between internal and external regulation of employment relations. Both sectors in the Netherlands prefer external regulation to provide legitimacy to employee representation mechanisms, balancing this against a desire for corporate autonomy to pursue more individualistic approaches. Chapter 9 provides the example of P&G, which, in integrating its activities globally, balanced the need for global standardization of HRM with that for local adaptation. Legitimacy (e.g. the requirements of national legislation) and financial (e.g. economies of scale and scope achieved through standardization) priorities were balanced against each other to produce an effective and sustainable business operating model.

Balance also lies at the heart of the HR department: HR professionals, over time, have been expected to balance welfare and strategic roles to deliver value to the organization (Chapter 9). This balancing act involves developing HRM systems that address critical choices between the economic rationality of hard, control-based HRM systems and the relational rationality of soft, commitment-based approaches to managing the workforce. Similarly, HR professionals have to strike an appropriate balance between a more strategic or operational role in the organization, often with the former only being possible if the latter has been achieved successfully.

The HR function as a whole (Chapter 10) then also has to decide between centralization versus decentralization, and insourcing versus outsourcing, for its delivery of services to achieve the highest performance outcomes. These decisions usually take into account an organization's context, balancing an ability to maintain control from the centre yet be locally responsive. Metrics on the performance of the HR function also require a balanced perspective: What gets measured, gets managed! In other words, whatever we focus on gathering data on in organizations is likely to be subject to scrutiny and change. If we only measure financial performance, this will be the focus of organizational activities. If we also measure employee well-being, this can then become an organizational priority for action too.

Why do we want to achieve balance? Why do we attach value to a balanced approach? Ultimately, we argue, balance is essential for 'healthy' performance. We believe that the primary advantages of a balanced approach to HRM and performance include employees having a higher willingness to trust management; more willingness to change, even when personal risk might be involved; a 'they will treat me fairly' feeling; and more room for manoeuvre for management. The Contextual SHRM Framework demonstrates how actors balance competitive, heritage, and institutional factors to create an appropriate

SHRM system capable of delivering organizational outcomes that balance financial and well-being outcomes, which in the long run have a positive impact on societal well-being. This balance emanates from a humanistic, values perspective, in turn creating sustainability for organizations, employees, and the broader society.

12.3 **Looking to the future**

Having reflected on our observations throughout this book, it is now time to look to the future. In so doing, we distinguish challenges related, first, to the future of HRM, and, secondly, to the future of the HR function in organizations.

12.3.1 FUTURE OF HRM

HRM as a field is largely based on principles of managing the employment relationship in order to achieve organizational goals. We question here whether this is still an appropriate definition of the field? Nowadays, collaborative workforces are arising for the creation and delivery of products and services; workforces not merely limited to the involvement of 'traditional' employees (i.e. individuals having a formal labour contract with one organization). Instead, a range of supplementary workers beyond the traditional employee (e.g. self-employed individuals working for a myriad of organizations) are involved. This is leading to what might be described as the 'fragmented organization', with increasing blurring of organizational boundaries. Combined with high expectations from customers who perceive that products/services are still delivered by one organization, this has the potential to create several challenges. For example, there is the risk of a rise in precarious employment conditions due to suppliers prioritizing short-termism, intensifying work arrangements, and increasingly relying on temporary and/or contract workers.

Given this fragmentation, and a related increase in diversity in organizations, we might want to consider adopting a more 'inclusive' approach to HRM to achieve performance outcomes that include societal well-being. For example, across the world, nations are dealing with the consequences of inequality, drought, war, ethnic and religious conflicts, increasing numbers of immigrants or refugees. Adopting a more inclusive HRM approach not only includes taking into account employee diversity (e.g. by gender, ethnicity, religion, or age), but also implies creating an organizational climate in which all types of employee feel free to express themselves and are respected by their colleagues and management. This will contribute to feelings of fairness and legitimacy.

On a final note here, an area that has perhaps been underplayed in this book concerns how the nature of work itself might be changing before our very eyes. There is a proposed new revolution following on from technological developments: Artificial intelligence and the robotization of work. As the cognitive capability of machines increases, they become capable not only of following programmed instructions, but also of analysing data, generating ideas, and learning. Although it is purported that the HR function itself is in the top ten jobs least likely to be replaced by robots/automation, this does not mean that we can ignore this development as the nature of the workforce is likely to change, hence requiring a new contextual SHRM system.

12.3.2 FUTURE OF THE HR FUNCTION

HRM is becoming established as an industry in its own right with ever-increasing offerings of payroll, recruitment, global mobility, and training services to name but a few, readily available on the market for organizations to buy in rather than manage in-house. The HR function inside an organization therefore takes on a purchasing role, managing a broad infrastructure of HRM services provided through third parties. Much of this trend has been facilitated by the availability of appropriate technologies. The technological revolution has also led to a greater focus on the use of social media for recruitment, performance management, and training activities, as well as for increasing connectivity across organizations. The connected workforce means HR is working across what were traditionally organizational borders, needing increased expertise to operate in this technologically driven context, often at the same time as being reduced in numbers as organizations become leaner and smarter.

The competencies of HR professionals are thus expected to change. As big data and metrics are becoming kings, practitioners need to be able to understand the business through HR metrics and key performance indicators. Analytical skills are required to analyse individual performance and forecast future talent needs. Similarly, with the rise of external HRM service providers, in-house HR functions are increasingly likely to need purchasing skills and an ability to manage relationships with vendors. The technological developments also require HR to be social media experts, if not at least to be aware of (potential) employee activities within (and perhaps outside) the organization. Social media can also be an important employer-branding tool that HR can use to its advantage for recruitment activities.

As we noted in Chapter 11, however, all of these developments in how HRM work and the HR function are changing will likely have significant implications for governance and risk management. Existing organizational structures and monitoring procedures will need to be updated to ensure compliance with legal requirements, as well as ensuring fairness for employees.

12.4 **Final remarks**

In their different ways, all of the core themes and the chapters of this book have explored how strategic HRM has implications for performance. This has been presented in terms of underlying theory, research evidence, examples from practice, and tools for practitioner application. By combining academic rigor with a practical focus, this book presents not only details of how a SHRM system might be effective in an organization, but also why it might be effective. This is important as we cannot learn from evidence without the explanations provided by theory, nor can theory alone, without evidence, give us examples on how to improve performance.

In drawing to a conclusion, we have two final important remarks to make. First, in exploring the relationship between strategy, HRM, and performance, we have found that although this relationship can deliver positive organizational outcomes, HRM alone is not the 'silver bullet'. The proclaimed effectiveness of the SHRM system vis-à-vis strategy implementation and subsequent performance is highly dependent on how embedded the system is in the organization. By this, we mean that effective HRM is dependent on building an organizational climate of trust, and on the quality and acceptance of leadership to champion HRM initiatives.

Secondly, HRM is a vulnerable domain. As we have argued throughout, HRM is highly dependent on developments in the organization's context, including whether operating in a tight or slack labour market, or in a declining or growing product market, under conditions of profit or loss, under a stable or turbulent political system, in an environment where trade unions are powerful or not, and whether line managers are willing and able or not to implement HRM. This latter point is absolutely critical, as without the support of line management, HRM does not exist. We have suggested through this book ways in which the connection between strategy, HRM, and performance can be enhanced, providing a solid basis on which to present to line managers why HRM matters. Following the Contextual SHRM Framework can demonstrate that the HR function/manager is really making an effort to understand and contribute to competitive, heritage, and institutional mechanisms operating in the organization. Moreover, the framework enables a customized and thus unique approach for building SHRM systems that fit with the nature of the business.

In conclusion, we have offered a number of suggestions for advancing the HRM and performance relationship. We have emphasized the importance of strategy, alignment, context, the role of actors, and a holistic conceptualization of performance. Embedded in all chapters is a focus on achieving an appropriate balance between options, rather than providing a universalistic solution to all HRM challenges. The Contextual SHRM Framework, with its emphasis on achieving a unique combination of both economic and relational rationality, of both added value and moral values, is able to generate an agile, sustainable organization that creates room for manoeuvre for the key decision-makers, and that enables the pursuit of different strategic options.

■ REFERENCES

Ackerman, K. F. (1983). A contingency model of HRM strategy. *Management Forum*, 6: 65–83.

Adams, J. S. (1963). Toward an understanding of inequity. *Journal of Abnormal and Social Psychology*, 67(5): 422.

Adams, K. (1991). Externalisation vs. specialisation: what is happening to personnel? *Human Resource Management Journal*, 4(1): 40–54.

Adler, P. S. (2003). Making the HR outsourcing decision. *Sloan Management Review*, 45: 53–60.

Aiken, L., Clarke, S. P., & Sloane, D. M. (2002). Hospital staffing, organization, and quality of care: cross-national findings. *International Journal for Quality in Health Care*, 14: 5–13.

Aksin, Z., Armony, M., & Mehrotra, V. (2007). The modern call center: a multi-disciplinary perspective on operations management research. *Production and Operations Management*, 16(6): 665–88.

Aldrich, H. (1999). *Organizations Evolving*. Thousand Oaks, CA: Sage.

Almond, P., Edwards, T., & Clark, I. (2003). Multinationals and changing national business systems in Europe: towards the 'shareholder value' model? *Industrial Relations Journal*, 34(5): 430–45.

Appelbaum, E., Bailey, T., Berg, P., & Kalleberg, A. (2000). *Manufacturing Competitive Advantage: The Effects of High Performance Work Systems on Plant Performance and Company Outcomes*. Ithaca, NY: Cornell University Press.

Argyris, C., & Schön, D. A. (1978). *Organizational Learning: A Theory of Action Perspective*, vol. 173. Reading, MA: Addison-Wesley.

Arthur, J. B. (1994). Effects of human resource systems on manufacturing performance and turnover. *Academy of Management Journal*, 37: 670–87.

Arthur, J. B., & Boyles, T. (2007). Validating the human resource system structure: a levels-based strategic HRM approach. *Human Resource Management Review*, 17(1): 77–92.

Aspray, W. (2010). IT offshoring and American labor. *American Behavioral Scientist*, 53(7): 962–82.

Atkinson, J. (1984). Manpower strategies for flexible organisations. *Personnel Management*, 16(8): 28–31.

Bach, S., & Kessler, I. (2007). HRM and the new public management. In P. Boxall, J. Purcell, & P. Wright (eds.), *The Oxford Handbook of Human Resource Management*: 469–88. Oxford: Oxford University Press.

Baden-Fuller, C., & Stopford, J. (1994). *Rejuvenating the Mature Business*. Boston, MA: Harvard Business.

Bain, G. S., & Clegg, H. A. (1974). A strategy for industrial relations research in Great Britain. *British Journal of Industrial Relations*, 12(1): 91–113.

Baldwin, L. P., Irani, Z., & Love, P. E. D. (2001). Outsourcing information systems: drawing lessons from a banking case study. *European Journal of Information Systems*, 10: 15–24.

Barney, J. B. (1991). Firm resources and sustained competitive advantage. *Journal of Management*, 17(1): 99–120.

Barney, J. B. (1995). Looking inside for competitive advantage. *Academy of Management Executive*, 9(1): 49–67.

Barney, J. B. (2001). Is the resource-based 'view' a useful perspective for strategic management research? Yes. *Academy of Management Review*, 26(1): 41–56.

Baron, J. N. & Kreps, D. M. (1999). *Strategic Human Resources: Frameworks for General Managers*. Danvers, MA: John Wiley & Sons, Inc.

Bartlett, C. A., & Ghoshal, S. (1989). *Managing across Borders: The Transnational Solution*. Boston, MA: Harvard Business School Press.

Batt, R. (2001). Explaining wage inequality in telecommunications services: customer segmentation, human resource practices, and union decline. *Industrial and Labor Relations Review*, 54(2A): 425–49.

Batt, R. (2002). Managing customer services: human resource practices, quit rates, and sales growth. *Academy of Management Journal*, 45: 587–97.

Batt, R., & Moynihan, L. M. (2002). The viability of alternative call centre production models. *Human Resource Management Journal*, 12(4): 14–34.

Batt, R., Colvin, A., & Keefe, J. (2002). Employee voice, human resource practices, and quit rates: evidence from the telecommunications industry. *Industrial and Labor Relations Review*, 55(4): 573–95.

Batt, R., Holman, D., & Holtgrewe, U. (2009). The globalization of service work: comparative institutional perspectives on call centers. *Industrial and Labor Relations Review*, 62(4): 453–89.

Baum, J. A., & Singh, J. V. (1994). Organization–Environment Coevolution. In J. A. C. Baum, & J. V. Singh (eds.), *Evolutionary Dynamics of Organizations*: 379–402. Oxford: Oxford University Press.

Bean, L. (2003). The profits and perils of international outsourcing. *Journal of Corporate Accounting & Finance*, 14(6): 3–10.

Becker, B., & Gerhart, B. (1996). The impact of human resource management on organizational performance: progress and prospects. *Academy of Management Journal*, 39(4): 779–801.

Becker, B. E., & Huselid, M. A. (1998). High performance work systems and firm performance: a synthesis of research and managerial implications. *Research in Personnel and Human Resource Management*, 16: 53–102.

Becker, B. E., & Huselid, M. A. (2006). Strategic human resources management: where do we go from here? *Journal of Management*, 32(6): 898–925.

Becker, B. E., Huselid, M. A., & Ulrich, D. (2001). *The HRD Scorecard: Linking People, Strategy, and Performance*. Boston: Harvard Business School Press.

Becker, B. E., Huselid, M. A., Pickus, P. S., & Spratt, M. F. (1997). HR as a source of shareholder value: research and recommendations. *Human Resource Management*, 36: 39–47.

Becker, G. (1964). *Human Capital*, 2nd edn. New York: Columbia University Press (for NBER).

Beer, M. (1997). The transformation of the human resource function: resolving the tension between a traditional administrative and a new strategic role. *Human Resource Management*, 36(1): 49–56.

Beer, M., Boselie, P., & Brewster, C. (2015). Back to the future: implications for the field of HRM of the multi stakeholder perspective proposed 30 years ago. *Human Resource Management*, 54(3): 427–38.

Beer, M., Spector, P., Lawrence, P., Mills, D. Q., & Walton, R. (1984). *Human Resource Management: A General Manager's Perspective*. New York: Free Press.

Beijer, S. E. (2014). HR practices at work: their conceptualization and measurement in HR research. PhD dissertation, Tilburg University.

Beltrán-Martín, I., Roca-Puig, V., Escrig-Tena, A., & Bou-Llusar, J. C. (2008). Human resource flexibility as a mediating variable between high performance work systems and performance. *Journal of Management*, 34(5): 1009–44.

Bhattacharya, M., Gibson, D. E., & Doty, D. H. (2005). The effects of flexibility in employee skills, employee behaviors, and human resource practices on firm performance. *Journal of Management*, 31(4): 622–40.

Biron, M., Farndale, E., & Paauwe, J. (2011). Performance management effectiveness: lessons from world-leading firms. *International Journal of Human Resource Management*, 22(6): 1294–311.

Blain, A. N. J., & Gennard, J. (1970). Industrial relations theory: a critical review. *British Journal of Industrial Relations*, 8(3): 389–407.

Blau, P. M. (1964). *Exchange and Power in Social Life*. New York: Wiley.

Boglind, A., Hällstén, F., & Thilander, P. (2011). HR transformation and shared services: adoption and adaptation in Swedish organisations. *Personnel Review*, 40(5): 570–88.

Boon, C., Den Hartog, D. N., Boselie, P., & Paauwe, J. (2011). The relationship between perceptions of HR practices and employee outcomes: examining the role of person–organisation and person–job fit. *International Journal of Human Resource Management*, 22(1): 138–62.

Boon, C., Paauwe, J., Boselie, P., & Den Hartog, D. (2009). Institutional pressures and HRM: developing institutional fit. *Personnel Review*, 38(5): 492–508.

Bos-Nehles, A. C., Van Riemsdijk, M. J., & Looise, J. K. (2013). Employee perceptions of line management performance: applying the AMO theory to explain the effectiveness of line managers' HRM implementation. *Human Resource Management*, 52(6): 861–77.

Boselie, P. (2002). *Human Resource Management, Work Systems and Performance: A Theoretical-Empirical Approach*, Tinbergen Institute Research Series, no. 274. Amsterdam: Thela Thesis.

Boselie, P. (2010). *Strategic Human Resource Management: A Balanced Approach*. Maidenhead: McGraw-Hill.

Boselie, P., & Paauwe, J. (2010). The HR value chain. Internal report, Department of HR-Studies, Tilburg University, Tilburg.

Boselie, P., Paauwe, J., & Jansen, P. (2001). Human resource management and performance: lessons from the Netherlands. *International Journal of Human Resource Management*, 12(7), 1107–25.

Boselie, P., Brewster, C. J., & Paauwe, J. (2009). In search of balance: managing the dualities of HRM: an overview of the issues. *Personnel Review*, 38(5): 461–71.

Boselie, P., Dietz, G., & Boon, C. (2005). Commonalities and contradictions in HRM and performance research. *Human Resource Management Journal*, 15(3): 67–94.

Boselie, P., Paauwe, J., & Richardson, R. (2003). Human resource management, institutionalization and organizational performance: a comparison of hospitals, hotels and local government. *International Journal of Human Resource Management*, 14(8): 1407–29.

Boswell, W. R., & Boudreau, J. W. (2001). How leading companies create, measure and achieve strategic results through 'line of sight'. *Management Decision*, 39(10): 851–60.

Boudreau, J. W., & Ramstad, P. M. (2007). *Beyond HR: The New Science of Human Capital*. Boston, MA: Harvard Business School Press.

Bowen, D. E. (1986). Managing customers as human resources in service organizations. *Human Resource Management*, 25: 372–84.

Bowen, D. E., & Ostroff, C. (2004). Understanding HRM-firm performance linkages: the role of the 'strength' of the HRM system. *Academy of Management Review*, 29(2): 203–21.

Boxall, P. (1996). The strategic human resource debate and the resource-based view of the firm. *Human Resource Management Journal*, 6(3): 59–75.

Boxall, P., & Purcell. J. (2003). *Strategy and Human Resource Management*. Basingstoke: Palgrave Macmillan.

Boxall, P., & Purcell, J. (2008). *Strategy and Human Resource Management*, 2nd edn. Basingstoke: Palgrave Macmillan.

Boxall, P., & Purcell, J. (2011). *Strategy and Human Resource Management*, 3rd edn. Basingstoke: Palgrave Macmillan.

Boxall, P., & Purcell, J. (2015). *Strategy and Human Resource Management*, 4th edn. Basingstoke: Palgrave Macmillan.

Boxall, P., & Macky, K. (2009). Research and theory on high-performance work systems: progressing the high-involvement stream. *Human Resource Management Journal*, 19(1): 3–23.

Bracker, J. (1980). The historical development of the strategic management concept. *Academy of Management Review*, 5(2): 219–24.

Bretz, R. D., & Judge, T. A. (1994). The role of human resource systems in job applicant decision processes. *Journal of Management*, 20(3): 531–51.

Brewster, C. (1993). Developing a 'European' model of human resource management. *International Journal of Human Resource Management*, 4(4): 765–84.

Brewster, C., Sparrow, P. R., & Harris, H. (2005). Towards a new model of globalizing human resource management. *International Journal of Human Resource Management*, 16: 953–74.

Brewster, C., Wood, G., Brookes, M., & Van Ommeren, J. (2006). What determines the size of the HR function? A cross-national analysis. *Human Resource Management*, 45(1): 3–21.

Buckingham, M., & Goodall, A. (2015). Reinventing performance management. *Harvard Business Review*, 93(4): 40–50.

Budhwar, P. S., & Sparrow, P. (2002). An integrative framework for understanding cross-national human resource management practices. *Human Resource Management Review*, 12(3): 377–403.

Bulte, J. (1975). *Human Resource Accounting*. Leiden: Stenfert Kroese.

Caldwell, R. (2003). The changing roles of personnel managers: old ambiguities, new uncertainties. *Journal of Management Studies*, 40(4): 983–1004.

Caldwell, R. (2008). HR business partner competency models: re-contextualising effectiveness. *Human Resource Management Journal*, 18(3): 275–94.

Carroll, S. J. (1991). The new HRM roles, responsibilities, and structures. In R. S. Schuler (ed.), *Managing Human Resources in the Information Age*: 204–26. Washington, DC: Bureau of National Affairs.

Cascio, W. F. (1991). *Costing Human Resources*. Boston, MA: PWS-Kent.

Cascio, W. F., & Boudreau, J. W. (2010). *Investing in People: Financial Impact of Human Resource Initiatives*. Upper Saddle River, NJ: Pearson Education, Inc.

Cascio, W. F., & Boudreau, J. W. (2012). *Short Introduction to Strategic Human Resource Management*. Cambridge: Cambridge University Press.

Chang, P. L., & Chen, W. L. (2002). The effect of human resource management practices on firm performance: empirical evidence from high-tech firms in Taiwan. *International Journal of Management*, 19(4): 622–31.

Child, J. (1972). Organizational structure, environment and performance: the role of strategic choice. *Sociology*, 6(1): 1–22.

Child, J. (2000). Theorizing about organizations cross-nationally. *Advances in International Comparative Management*, 13: 27–75.

Cohen-Charash, Y., & Spector, P. E. (2001). The role of justice in organizations: A meta-analysis. *Organizational Behavior and Human Decision Processes*, 86(2), 278–321.

Coleman, J. (1990). *Foundations of Social Theory*. Cambridge, MA: Harvard University Press.

Colomy, P. (1998). Neofunctionalism and neoinstitutionalism: human agency and interest in institutional change. *Sociological Forum*, 13(2): 265–300.

Colquitt, J. A., Conlon, D. E., Wesson, M. J., Porter, C. O., & Ng, K. Y. (2001). Justice at the millennium: a meta-analytic review of 25 years of organizational justice research. *Journal of Applied Psychology*, 86(3): 425.

Combs, J. G., Liu, Y., Hall, A., & Ketchen, D. J. Jr (2006). How much do high-performance work practices matter? A meta-analysis of their effects on organizational performance. *Personnel Psychology*, 59(3): 501–28.

Cook, T. D., & Campbell, D. T. (1979). *Quasi-Experimentation: Design and Analysis Issues for Field Settings*. Chicago: Rand McNally.

Cooke, W. N. (2007). Integrating human resource and technological capabilities: the influence of global business strategies on workplace strategy choices. *Industrial Relations*, 46(2): 241–70.

Cordery, J., & Parker, S. K. (2007). Work organization. In P. Boxall, J. Purcell, & P. Wright (eds.), *Oxford Handbook of Human Resource Management*: 187–209. Oxford: Oxford University Press.

Currie, W. L. (2009). From professional dominance to market mechanisms: deinstitutionalization in the organizational field of health care. In R. Hirschheim, A. Heinzl, & J. Dibbern (eds.), *Information Systems Outsourcing: Enduring Themes, Global Challenges, and Process Opportunities*, 3rd edn: 563–89. Berlin: Springer.

Dacin, M. T. (1997). Isomorphism in context: the power and prescription of institutional norms. *Academy of Management Journal*, 40(1): 46–81.

Dacin, M. T., Goodstein, J., & Scott, W. R. (2002). Institutional theory and institutional change: introduction to the special research forum. *Academy of Management Journal*, 45(1): 45–56.

Daniels, C. (2002). Creating lasting value through people. Master's thesis, Rotterdam School of Management.

Davis, G., Dor, P., King, W., & Torkzadeh, R. (2006). IT offshoring: history, prospects, and challenges. *Journal of the Association for Information Services*, 7(11): 770–7.

DDI (Development Dimensions International). (2011). *Global Leadership Forecast 2011: Time for a Leadership Revolution*. Development Dimensions International, Inc. Available at: http://www.ddiworld.com/ddi/media/trend-research/globalleadershipforecast2011_globalreport_ddi.pdf(accessed 3 May 2017).

De Jong, P. R., & Mosca, I. (2006). *Changes and Challenges of the New Health Care Reform in the Netherlands: What should the Dutch be Aware of?* TILEC Discussion Paper No. DP2006-026. Available at: https://www.researchgate.net/publication/4867725_Changes_and_Challenges_of_the_New_Health_Care_Reform_in_the_Netherlands_What_Should_the_Dutch_be_Aware_of (accessed 3 May 2017).

De Wit, B., & Meyer, R. (1998). *Strategy: Process, Content, Context: An International Perspective*. London: Thompson.

De Wit, B., & Meyer, R. (2004). *Strategy: Process, Content, Context: An International Perspective*, 3rd edn. Cengage Learning.

De Wit, B., & Meyer, R. (2010). *Strategy: Process, Content, Context: An International Perspective*, 4th edn. Cengage Learning.

Deephouse, D. L. (1999). To be different, or to be the same? It's a question (and theory) of strategic balance. *Strategic Management Journal*, 20(2): 147–66.

Delery, J. E. (1998). Issues of fit in strategic human resource management: implications for research. *Human Resource Management Review*, 8(3): 289–309.

Delery, J. E., & Doty, D. H. (1996). Modes of theorizing in strategic human resource management: tests of universalistic, contingency, and configurational performance predictions. *Academy of Management Journal*, 39(4): 802–35.

Delery, J. E., & Shaw, J. D. (2001). The strategic management of people in work organizations: review, synthesis, and extension. Paper presented at the Academy of Management Meeting, August, Washington, DC.

Den Hartog, D., Boselie, P., & Paauwe, J. (2004). Performance management: a model and research agenda. *Applied Psychology: An International Review*, 53(4): 556–69.

DiMaggio, P. J., & Powell, W. W. (1983). The iron cage revisited: institutional isomorphism and collective rationality in organizational fields. *American Sociological Review*, 48(2): 147–60.

Doellgast, V. (2008). Collective bargaining and high-involvement management in comparative perspective: evidence from US and German call centers. *Journal of Industrial Relations*, 47(2): 284–319.

Dunlop, J. T. (1958). *Industrial Relations Systems*. Boston, MA: Harvard Business School.

Dyer, L. (1984). Studying human resource strategy: an approach and an agenda. *Industrial Relations*, 23(2): 156–69.

Dyer, L., & Reeves, T. (1995). Human resource strategies and firm performance: what do we know and where do we need to go? *International Journal of Human Resource Management*, 6: 657–67.

Dyer, L., & Shafer, R. (1999). Creating organizational agility: Implications for strategic human resource management. *Research in Personnel and Human Resource Management*, 4: 145–174.

Edwards, M. R., & Edwards, K. (2016). *Predictive HR Analytics: Mastering the HR Metric*. London: Kogan Page.

Edwards, T., & Ferner, A. (2002). The renewed American challenge: a review of employment practice in US multinationals. *Industrial Relations Journal*, 33(2): 94–111.

Edwards, T., & Kuruvilla, S. (2005). International HRM: national business systems, organizational politics and the international division of labour in MNCs. *International Journal of Human Resource Management*, 16(1): 1–21.

Edwards, T., Almond, P., Clark, I., Colling, T., & Ferner, A. (2005). 'diffusion in US multinationals: barriers from the American business system. *Journal of Management Studies*, 42(6): 1261–86.

Eisenberger, R., Huntington, R., Hutchinson, S., & Sowa, D. (1986). Perceived organizational support. *Journal of Applied Psychology*, 71(3): 500–7.

Ellram, L. M., Tate, W. L., & Billington, C. (2007). Services supply management: the next frontier for improved organizational performance. *California Management Review*, 49(4): 44–66.

Ellram, L. M., Tate, W. L., & Billington, C. (2008). Offshore outsourcing of professional services: a transaction cost economics perspective. *Journal of Operations Management*, 26(2): 148–63.

Enthoven, A. C., & Van de Ven, W. P. M. M. (2007). Going Dutch: managed-competition health insurance in the Netherlands. *New England Journal of Medicine*, 357: 2421–3.

Ernst & Young. (2001). *Measures that Matter: An Outside-In Perspective on Shareholder Value Recognition*. London: Ernst & Young.

Evans, P., Pucik, V., & Barsoux, J. (2002). *The Global Challenge: Frameworks for International Human Resource Management*. New York: McGraw-Hill.

Farndale, E. (2010). What is really driving differences and similarities in HRM across national boundaries in Europe? *European Journal of International Management*, 4(4): 362–81.

Farndale, E., & Kelliher, C. (2013). Implementing performance appraisal: exploring the employee experience. *Human Resource Management*, 52(6): 879–97.

Farndale, E., & Paauwe, J. (2007). Uncovering competitive and institutional drivers of HRM practices in multinational corporations. *Human Resource Management Journal*, 17(4): 355–75.

Farndale, E., Brewster, C., & Poutsma, E. (2008). Coordinated vs. liberal market HRM: the impact of institutionalization on multinational firms. *International Journal of Human Resource Management*, 19(11): 2004–23.

Farndale, E., Hope Hailey, V., & Kelliher, C. (2011). High commitment performance management: the roles of justice and trust. *Personnel Review*, 40(1): 5–23.

Farndale, E., Paauwe, J., & Boselie, P. (2010). An exploratory study of governance in the intra-firm human resources supply chain. *Human Resource Management*, 49(5): 849–68.

Farndale, E., Paauwe, J., & Boselie, P. (2011). Corporate crisis: professional identity (r)evolution? Paper presented at the Academy of Management Meeting, San Antonio, TX, 12–16 August.

Farndale, E., Paauwe, J., & Hoeksma, L. (2009). In-sourcing HR: shared service centres in the Netherlands. *International Journal of Human Resource Management*, 20(3): 544–61.

Farndale, E., Paauwe, J., Morris, S. S., Stahl, G. K., Stiles, P., Trevor, J., & Wright, P. M. (2010). Context-bound configurations of corporate HR functions in multinational corporations around the globe. *Human Resource Management*, 49(1): 45–66.

Farrell, D. (2006). Smarter offshoring. *Harvard Business Review*, 84(6): 84–92.

Ferner, A. (1997). Country of origin effects and HRM in multinational companies. *Human Resource Management Journal*, 7(1): 19–37.

Ferner, A., Almond, P., & Colling, T. (2005). Institutional theory and the cross-national transfer of employment policy: the case of 'workforce diversity' in US multinationals. *Journal of International Business Studies*, 36: 304–21.

Ferner, A., Almond, P., Colling, T., & Edwards, T. (2005). Policies on union representation in US multinationals in the UK: between micro-politics and macro-institutions. *British Journal of Industrial Relations*, 43(4): 703–28.

Fitz-Enz, J. (1980). Quantifying the human resources function. *Personnel*, 57(3): 41–52.

Fitz-Enz, J. (1990). *Human Value Management*. San Francisco: Jossey-Bass.

Fjeldstad, O. D., & Ketels, C. H. M. (2006). Competitive advantage and the value network configurations. *Journal of Long Range Planning*, 39(2): 109–31.

Flamholtz, E. G. (1985). *Human Resource Accounting*. San Francisco: Jossey-Bass.

Fleetwood, S., & Hesketh, A. (2010). *Explaining the Performance of Human Resource Management*. Cambridge: Cambridge University Press.

Flood, P. C., Gannon, M. J., & Paauwe, J. (1996). *Managing without Traditional Methods: International Innovations in Human Resource Management*. Wokingham: Addison-Wesley.

Fombrun, C. J., Tichy, N. M., & Devanna, M. A. (1984). *Strategic Human Resource Management*. New York: John Wiley & Sons.

Francis, H., & Keegan, A. (2006). The changing face of HRM: in search of balance. *Human Resource Management Journal*, 16(3): 231–49.

Fredrickson, B. L. (2001). The role of positive emotions in positive psychology: the broaden-and-build theory of positive emotions. *American Psychology*, 56: 218–26.

Friedland, R., & Alford, R. R. (1991). Bringing society back in: symbols, practices, and institutional contradictions. In W. W. Powell and P. J. DiMaggio (eds.), *The New Institutionalism in Organizational Analysis*. Chicago: University of Chicago Press.

Futuyma, D. J., & Slatkin, M. (1983). *Coevolution*. Sunderland, MA: Sinauer.

Garman, A. N., Leach, D. C., & Spector, N. (2006). Worldviews in collision: conflict and collaboration across professional lines. *Journal of Organizational Behavior*, 27: 829–49.

Geels, F. W. (2014). Reconceptualising the co-evolution of firms-in-industries and their environments: developing an inter-disciplinary triple embeddedness framework. *Research Policy*, 43(2): 261–77.

Geiger, S., & Prothero, A. (2007). Rhetoric versus reality: exploring consumer empowerment in a maternity setting. *Consumption Markets & Culture*, 10: 375–400.

Gençtürk, E. F., & Aulakh, P. S. (2007). Norms-and control-based governance of international manufacturer-distributor relational exchanges. *Journal of Marketing*, 15(1): 92–124.

Gerhart, B. (2004). Research on human resources and effectiveness: selected methodological challenges. Working Paper presented at the International Seminar on HRM: What's Next? Erasmus University Rotterdam, June.

Gerstner, C. R., & Day, D. V. (1997). Meta-analytic review of leader–member exchange theory: correlates and construct issues. *Journal of Applied Psychology*, 82(6): 827.

Giardini, A., & Kabst, R. (2008). Effects of work–family human resource practices: a longitudinal perspective. *International Journal of Human Resource Management*, 19(11): 2079–94.

Gittell, J. (2000). Organizing work to support relational coordination. *International Journal of Human Resource Management*, 11(3): 517–39.

Gittell, J. (2011). *Relational Coordination: Guidelines for Theory, Measurement and Analysis*. Waltham, MA: Brandeis University.

Gittell, J., Seidner, R. B., & Wimbush, J. (2010). A relational model of how high performance work systems work. *Organization Science*, 21(2): 490–506.

Godard, J. (2001). Beyond the high performance paradigm? An analysis of variation in Canadian managerial perceptions of reform programme effectiveness. *British Journal of Industrial Relations*, 39(1): 25–52.

Golden, B. R., Dukerich, J. M., & Fabian, F. H. (2000). The interpretation and resolution of resource allocation issues in professional organizations: a critical examination of the professional–manager dichotomy. *Journal of Management Studies*, 37: 1157–88.

Golden, K. A., & Ramanujam, V. (1985). Between a dream and a nightmare: on the integration of the human resource management and strategic business planning processes. *Human Resource Management*, 24(4): 429–52.

Gooderham, P. N., & Nordhaug, O. (2003). *International Management: Cross-Boundary Challenges*. Oxford: Blackwell Publishing.

Gooderham, P. N., & Nordhaug, O. (2011). One European model of HRM? Cranet empirical contributions. *Human Resource Management Review*, 21(1): 27–36.

Gooderham, P. N., Nordhaug, O., & Ringdal, K. (1999). Institutional and rational determinants of organizational practices: human resource management in European firms. *Administrative Science Quarterly*, 44(3): 507–31.

Gorjup, M. T., Valverde, M., & Ryan, G. (2009). In search of job quality in call centres. *Personnel Review*, 38(3): 253–69.

Gowler, D., & Legge, K. (1986). Personnel and paradigms: four perspectives on the future. *Industrial Relations Journal*, 17(3): 225–35.

Grant, A. M., Christianson, M. K., & Price, R. H. (2007). Happiness, health, or relationships? Managerial practices and employee well-being tradeoffs. *Academy of Management Perspectives*, 21(3): 51–63.

Grant, R. M. (2015). *Contemporary Strategy Analysis*. 9th edn. (text only). Chichester: John Wiley & Sons.

Gratton, L. (2000). *Living Strategy, Putting People at the Heart of Corporate Purpose*. Harlow / London: Financial Times / Prentice Hall.

Gratton, L., Hope-Hailey, V., Stiles, P., & Truss, C. (1999). Linking individual performance to business strategy: the people process model. *Human Resource Management*, 38(1): 17–31.

Greenwood, R., & Hinings, C. R. (1996). Understanding radical organizational change: bringing together the old and the new institutionalism. *Academy of Management Review*, 21(4): 1022–54.

Greenwood, R., Díaz, A. M., Li, S. X., & Lorente, J. C. (2010). The multiplicity of institutional logics and the heterogeneity of organizational responses. *Organization Science*, 21(2): 521–39.

Grol, R. (2006). *Quality Development in Health Care in the Netherlands*. Radboud University Nijmegen Medical Centre: Centre for Quality of Care Research.

Guest, D. E. (1987). Human resource management and industrial relations. *Journal of Management Studies*, 24(5): 503–21.

Guest, D. E. (1991). Personnel management: the end of orthodoxy? *British Journal of Industrial Relations*, 29(2): 149–75.

Guest, D. E. (1997). Human resource management and performance: a review and research agenda. *International Journal of Human Resource Management*, 8(3): 263–76.

Guest, D. E. (1999). Human resource management: the worker's verdict. *Human Resource Management Journal*, 9(3): 5–25.

Guest, D. E. (2011). Human resource management and performance: still searching for some answers. *Human Resource Management Journal*, 21(1): 3–13.

Guest, D. E. (2017). Human resource management and employee well-being: towards a new analytic framework. *Human Resource Management Journal*, 27(1): 21–38.

Guest D. E., & King, Z. (2004). Power, innovation and problem-solving: the personnel managers' three steps to heaven? *Journal of Management Studies*, 41(3): 401–23.

Guest, D. E., Michie, J., Conway, N., & Sheenan, M. (2003). Human resource management and corporate performance in the UK. *British Journal of Industrial Relations*, 41: 291–314.

Guthrie, J. P. (2001). High-involvement work practices, turnover, and productivity: evidence from New-Zealand. *Academy of Management Journal*, 44: 180–90.

Ham, C., & Brommels, M. (1994). Health care reform in the Netherlands, Sweden, and the United Kingdom. *Health Affairs*, 13: 106–19.

Hannan, M. T., & Freeman, J. (1977). The population ecology of organizations. *American Journal of Sociology*, 82: 929–64.

Harzing, A. W., & Sorge, A. (2003). The relative impact of country of origin and universal contingencies on internationalization strategies and corporate control in multinational enterprises: worldwide and European perspectives. *Organization Studies*, 24(2): 187–214.

Heider, F. (1958). *The Psychology of Interpersonal Relations*. New York: Wiley.

Hendry, C., & Pettigrew, A. (1986). The practice of strategic human resource management. *Personnel Review*, 15(5): 3–8.

Hendry, C., & Pettigrew, A. (1990). HRM: An agenda for the 1990s. *International Journal of Human Resource Management*, 1(1): 17–25.

Hesketh, A. (2006). *Outsourcing the HR Function: Possibilities and Pitfalls*. London: Corporate Research Forum.

Hesketh, A., & Fleetwood, S. (2006). Beyond measuring the human resources management-organizational performance link: applying critical realist meta-theory. *Organization*, 13(5): 677–99.

Hickson, D. J. (1993). *Management in Western Europe: Society, Culture and Organization in Twelve Nations*. Berlin: De Gruyter.

Hingst, R. (2006). Perceptions of working life in call centres. *Journal of Management Practice*, 7(1): 1–9.

Hoek, H. (1999). The art of governance of Dutch hospitals. *World Hospitals and Health Services: The Official Journal of the International Hospital Federation*, 35(3): 5–7.

Hofstede, G. (1980). Motivation, leadership, and organization: do American theories apply abroad? *Organizational Dynamics*, 9(1): 42–63.

Holman, D. J. (2003). Call centres. In D. J. Holman, T. D. Wall, C. W. Clegg, P. Sparrow, & A. Howard (eds.), *The New Workplace: A Guide to the Human Impact of Modern Working Practices*. Chichester: Wiley.

Holman, D. J., Batt, R., & Holtgrewe, U. (2007). The global call center report: international perspectives on management and employment. Research report. Available at: http://www.ilr.cornell.edu/globalcallcenter/ (accessed 22 May 2011).

Hoque, K. (1999). Human resource management and performance in the UK hotel industry. *British Journal of Industrial Relations*, 37(3): 419–43.

Huang, T. C. (1997). The effect of participative management on organizational performance: the case of Taiwan. *International Journal of Human Resource Management*, 8(5): 677–89.

Huselid, M. A. (1995). The impact of human resource management practices on turnover, productivity, and corporate financial performance. *Academy of Management Journal*, 38(3): 635–72.

Huselid, M. A., & Becker, B. E. (2000). Comment on 'Measurement error in research on human resources and firm performance: How much error is there and how does it influence effect size estimates?' by Gerhart, Wright, McMahan, and Snell. *Personnel Psychology*, 53(4): 835–54.

Huselid, M. A., Beatty, R. W., & Becker, B. E. (2005). 'A players' or 'A positions'? *Harvard Business Review*, 83(12): 110–17.

Ichniowski, C., & Shaw, K. (1999). The effects of human resource management systems on economic performance: an international comparison of US and Japanese plants. *Management Science*, 45(5): 704–21.

Jackson, S. E., & Schuler, R. S. (1995). Understanding human resource management in the context of organizations and their environments. In M. R. Rosenzweig & L. W. Porter (eds.), *Annual Review of Psychology*, vol. 46: 237–64. Palo Alto, CA: Annual Reviews.

Jackson, S. E., Schuler, R. S., & Jiang, K. (2014). An aspirational framework for strategic human resource management. *Academy of Management Annals*, 8(1): 1–56.

Jaffee, D. (2001). *Organization Theory: Tension and Change*. New York: McGraw-Hill.

Janssen, M., & Joha, A. (2006). Motives for establishing shared service centers in public administrations. *International Journal of Information Management*, 26(2): 102–15.

Jayaram, J., Droge, C., & Vickery, S. K. (1999). The impact of human resource management practices on manufacturing performance. *Journal of Operations Management*, 18(1): 1–20.

Jensen, J. M., Patel, P. C., & Messersmith, J. G. (2013). High-performance work systems and job control consequences for anxiety, role overload, and turnover intentions. *Journal of Management*, 39(6): 1699–1724.

Jensen, M. C., & Meckling, W. H. (1976). Theory of the firm: managerial behavior, agency costs and ownership structure. *Journal of Financial Economics*, 3(4): 305–60.

Jiang, B. (2009). The effects of inter-organizational governance on supplier's compliance with SCC: an empirical examination of compliant and non-compliant suppliers. *Journal of Operations Management*, 27(4): 267–80.

Jiang, K., Lepak, D. P., Hu, J., & Baer, J. C. (2012). How does human resource management influence organizational outcomes? A meta-analytic investigation of mediating mechanisms. *Academy of Management Journal*, 55(6): 1264–94.

Johnson, G., Scholes, K., & Whittington, R. (2009). *Fundamentals of Strategy*. Harlow: Pearson Education.

Johnson, R. E., Selenta, C., & Lord, R. G. (2006). When organizational justice and the self-concept meet: consequences for the organization and its members. *Organizational Behavior & Human Decision Processes*, 99: 175–201.

Kalleberg, A. L., Marsden, P. V., Reynolds, J., & Knoke, D. (2006). Beyond profit? Sectoral differences in high-performance work practices. *Work and Occupations*, 33(3): 271–302.

Kamoche, K. (1994). A critique and proposed reformulations of strategic human resource management. *Human Resource Management Journal*, 4(4): 29–43.

Kamoche, K. (1996). Strategic human resource management within a resource-capability view of the firm. *Journal of Management Studies*, 33(2): 213–33.

Kanfer, R. (1994). Work motivation: new directions in theory and research. In C. L. Cooper & I. T. Robertson (eds.), *Key Reviews in Managerial Psychology*: 158–88. New York: Wiley.

Kano, N. (1995). Upsizing the organization by attractive quality creation. In G. K. Kanji (ed.), *Total Quality Management: Proceedings of the First World Congress*: 60–72. Dordrecht: Springer.

Kaplan, R. S., & Norton, D. P. (1992). The balanced scorecard: measures that drive performance. *Harvard Business Review*, January/February: 71–9.

Kato, T., & Morishima, M. (2002). The productivity effects of participatory employment practices: evidence from new Japanese panel data. *Industrial Relations*, 41(4): 487–520.

Kaufman, B. E. (2012). Strategic human resource management research in the United States: a failing grade after 30 years? *Academy of Management Perspectives*, 26(2): 12–36.

Kaufman, B. E. (2014). History of the British industrial relations field reconsidered: getting from the Webbs to the new employment relations paradigm. *British Journal of Industrial Relations*, 52(1): 1–31.

Kaufman, B. E. (2015). Evolution of strategic HRM as seen through two founding books: a 30th anniversary perspective on development of the field. *Human Resource Management*, 54(3): 389–407.

Keegan, A., & Boselie, P. (2006). The lack of impact of dissensus inspired analysis on developments in the field of human resource management. *Journal of Management Studies*, 43(7): 1491–511.

Keenoy, T. (1997). HRMism and the languages of re-presentation. *Journal of Management Studies*, 34(5): 825–41.

Kets de Vries, M. F. R. (1990). The organizational fool: balancing a leader's hubris. *Human Relations*, 43(8): 751–70.

Kiechel, W. (2010). *The Lords of Strategy: The Secret Intellectual History of the New Corporate World*. Boston, MA: Harvard Business Press.

Kitchener, M. (2002). Mobilizing the logic of managerialism in professional fields: the case of academic health centre mergers. *Organization Studies*, 23(3): 391–420.

Klein, K. J., & Kozlowski, S. W. J. (2000). *Multilevel Theory, Research, and Methods in Organizations*. San Francisco, CA: Jossey-Bass.

Kleiner, A. (2008). *The Age of Heretics: A History of the Radical Thinkers Who Reinvented Corporate Management*, 2nd edn. San Francisco, CA: Jossey-Bass.

Koch, M. J., & McGrath, R. G. (1996). Improving labor productivity: human resource management policies do matter. *Strategic Management Journal*, 17: 335–54.

Kochan, T. A., Katz, H. C., & McKersie, R. B. (1986). *The Transformation of American Industrial Relations*. New York: Basic Books.

Kochan, T. A., McKersie, R. B., & Cappelli, P. (1984). Strategic choice and industrial relations theory. *Industrial Relations: A Journal of Economy and Society*, 23(1): 16–39.

Kooij, D. T. A. M., Tims, M., & Kanfer, R. (2015). Successful aging at work: the role of job crafting. In P. M. Bal, D. T. A. M. Kooij, & D. M. Rousseau (eds.), *Aging Workers and the Employee–Employer Relationship*: 145–61. New York: Springer.

Kooij, D. T. A. M., Jansen, P. G. W., Dikkers, J. S. E., & De Lange, A. H. (2010). The influence of age on the associations between HR practices and both affective commitment and job satisfaction: a meta-analysis. *Journal of Organizational Behavior*, 31(8): 1111–36.

Kooij, D. T. A. M., Jansen, P. G. W., Dikkers, J. S. E., & De Lange, A. H. (2014). Managing aging workers: a mixed methods study on bundles of HR practices for aging workers. *International Journal of Human Resource Management*, 25(15): 2192–212.

Kostova, T., & Roth, K. (2002). Adoption of an organizational practice by subsidiaries of multinational corporations: institutional and relational effects. *Academy of Management Journal*, 45(1): 215–33.

Kraatz, M. S., & Moore, J. H. (2002). Executive migration and institutional change. *Academy of Management Journal*, 45: 120–43.

Kristof-Brown, A. L., Zimmerman, R. D., & Johnson, E. C. (2005). Consequences of individuals' fit at work: a meta-analysis of person-job, person-organization, person-group, and person-supervisor fit. *Personnel Psychology*, 58(2): 281–342.

Kroon, B., & Paauwe, J. (2014). Structuration of precarious employment in economically constrained firms: the case of Dutch agriculture. *Human Resource Management Journal*, 24(1): 19–37.

Kroon, B., Freese, C., & Schalk, R. (2015). A strategic HRM perspective on i-deals. In M. Bal & D. M. Rousseau (eds.), *Idiosyncratic Deals between Employees and Organizations: Conceptual Issues, Applications and the Role of Co-Workers*: 73–91. Abingdon: Routledge.

Kydd, C. T., & Oppenheim, L. (1990). Using human resource management to enhance competitiveness: lessons from four excellent companies. *Human Resource Management*, 29(2): 145–66.

Laing, A., & Hogg, G. (2002). Political exhortation, patient expectation and professional execution: perspectives on the consumerization of health care. *British Journal of Management*, 13: 173–88.

Lammers, C. J. (1990). Sociology of organizations around the globe: similarities and differences between American, British, French, German and Dutch brands. *Organization Studies*, 11(2): 179–205.

Lammers, C. J., Mijs, A. A., & Van Noort, W. J., (2000). *Organisaties vergelijkenderwijs: ontwikkeling en relevantie van het sociologisch denken over organisaties*. Utrecht: Het Spectrum.

Larsen, H. H., & Brewster, C. (2003). Line management responsibility for HRM: what is happening in Europe? *Employee Relations*, 25(3): 228–44.

Lawler, E. E. (2005). Creating high performance organizations. *Asia Pacific Journal of Human Resources*, 43(1): 10–17.

Lawler, E. E., Levenson, A., & Boudreau, J. W. (2004). HR metrics and analytics: use and impact. *Human Resource Planning*, 27(4): 27–35.

Lawrence, P. R., & Lorsch, J. W. (1967). *Organization and Environment: Managing Differentiation and Integration*. Boston, MA: Division of Research, Graduate School of Business Administration.

Lefebvre, E. R. L. (2001). HR Leadership program lecture presented as part of HR Effectiveness Module, Rotterdam School of Management.

Lega, F., & DePietro, C. (2005). Converging patterns in hospital organization: beyond the professional bureaucracy. *Health Policy*, 74(3): 261–81.

Legge, K. (1978). *Power, Innovation and Problem-Solving in Personnel Management*. London: McGraw-Hill.

Legge, K. (1995). *Human Resource Management: Rhetorics and Realities*. Basingstoke and London: Palgrave Macmillan.

Legge, K. (2005). *Human Resource Management: Rhetorics and Realities: Anniversary Edition*. London: Palgrave Macmillan.

Lengnick-Hall, C. A., & Lengnick-Hall, M. L. (1988). Strategic human resources management: a review of the literature and a proposed typology. *Academy of Management Review*, 13(3): 454–70.

Lepak, D. P., & Snell, S. A. (1999). The human resource architecture: toward a theory of human capital allocation and development. *Academy of Management Review*, 24(1): 31–48.

Lepak, D. P., Bartol, K. M., & Erhardt, N. L. (2005). A contingency framework for the delivery of HR practices. *Human Resource Management Review*, 15: 139–59.

Lewin, A., & Peeters, C. (2006). Offshoring work: business hype or the onset of fundamental transformation. *Journal of Long Range Planning*, 39(3): 221–39.

Lewin, A. Y., & Volberda, H. W. (1999). Prolegomena on coevolution: a framework for research on strategy and new organisational forms. *Organization Science*, 10(5): 519–34.

Lewin, A. Y., Long, C. P., & Caroll, T. N. (1999). The coevolution of new organizational forms. *Organization Science*, 10(5): 535–50.

Lindblom, C. E. (1959). The science of 'muddling through'. *Public Administration Review*, 19(2): 79–88.

Locher, D. A. (2002). *Collective Behavior*. Upper Saddle River, NJ: Prentice Hall.

Looise, J. K., & Paauwe, J. (2001). HR research in the Netherlands: imitation and innovation. *International Journal of Human Resource Management*, 12(7): 1203–17.

Lowe, J., Delbridge, R., & Oliver, N. (1997). High-performance manufacturing: evidence from the automotive components industry. *Organization Studies*, 18(5): 783–98.

Lubatkin, M., Lane, P. J., Collin, S., & Very, P. (2007). An embeddedness framing of governance and opportunism: towards a cross-nationally accommodating theory of agency. *Journal of Organizational Behavior*, 28(1): 43–58.

Maarse, H., Mur-Veeman, I., & Spreeuwenberg, C. (1997). The reform of hospital care in the Netherlands. *Medical Care*, 35(10): OS26–OS39.

McCurry, L., & McIvor, R. (2002). Agile manufacturing: 21st century strategy for manufacturing on the periphery? *Irish Journal of Management*, 23(2): 75–93.

MacDuffie, J. P. (1995). Human resource bundles and manufacturing performance: organizational logic and flexible production systems in the world auto industry. *Industrial & Labor Relations Review*, 48(2): 197–221.

MacMillan, H., & Tampoe, M. (2000). *Strategic Management: Process, Content, and Implementation*. New York: Oxford University Press.

Mainardi, C., & Kleiner, A. (2010). The right to win. *Strategy + Business*: https://www.strategy-business.com/article/10407?gko=19c25 (accessed 13 June 2017).

Malone, T. W., & Crowston, K. (1994). The interdisciplinary study of coordination. *ACM Computing Surveys (CSUR)*, 26(1): 87–119.

March, J. G., & Simon, H. A. (1958). *Organizations*. Oxford: Wiley.

Marchington, M., & Grugulis, I. (2000). 'Best practice' human resource management: perfect opportunity or dangerous illusion? *International Journal of Human Resource Management*, 11(6): 1104–24.

Mayo, A. (2001). *The Human Value of the Enterprise: Valuing PEOPLE as Assets: Monitoring, Measuring, Managing*. London: Nicholas Brealey.

Meerveld, N. A. (2001). Strategievorming in de Nieuwe Economie naar een Conceptueel Raamwerk. MSc thesis, Erasmus University, Rotterdam.

Messersmith, J. G., Patel, P. C., Lepak, D. P., & Gould-Williams, J. (2011). Unlocking the black box: exploring the link between high-performance work systems and performance. *Journal of Applied Psychology*, 96(6): 1105–18.

Metters, R., & Verma, R. (2008). History of offshoring knowledge services. *Journal of Operations Management*, 26(2): 141–7.

Meyer, J. W., & Rowan, B. (1977). Institutionalized organizations: formal structure as myth and ceremony. *American Journal of Sociology*, 83: 340–63.

Meyers, M. C., Van Woerkom, M., & Bakker, A. B. (2013). The added value of the positive: a literature review of positive psychology interventions in organizations. *European Journal of Work and Organizational Psychology*, 22(5): 618–32.

Miles, R. E., & Snow, C. C. (1978). *Organizational Strategy, Structure, and Process.* New York: McGraw-Hill.

Miles, R. E., & Snow, C. C. (1984). Fit, failure and the hall of fame. *California Management Review,* 26: 10–28.

Miller, D., & Friesen, P. (1980). Archetypes of organizational transition. *Administrative Science Quarterly,* 25(2): 268–99.

Mintzberg, H. (1979). *The Structuring of Organizations.* Englewood Cliffs, NJ: Prentice Hall.

Mintzberg, H. (1987). The strategy concept I: five Ps for strategy. *California Management Review,* 30(1): 11–24.

Mintzberg, H. (1998). Covert leadership: notes on managing professionals. *Harvard Business Review,* 76: 140–8.

Mintzberg, H., Ahlstrand, B., & Lampel, J. (2009). *Strategy Safari: A Guided Tour through the Wilds of Strategic Management,* 2nd edn. New York: Simon & Schuster.

Mirvis, P. H. (1997). Human resource management: leaders, laggards, and followers. *Academy of Management Executive,* 11(2): 43–56.

Mondore, S., Douthitt, S., & Carson, M. (2011). Maximizing the impact and effectiveness of HR analytics to drive business outcomes. *People and Strategy,* 34(2): 20–7.

Monks, K. (1992). Models of personnel management: a means of understanding the diversity of personnel practices? *Human Resource Management Journal,* 3(2): 29–41.

Montemayor, E. F. (1996). Congruence between pay policy and competitive strategy in high-performing firms. *Journal of Management,* 22(6): 889–908.

Morris, S., & Calamai, R. (2009). Dynamic HR: Global applications from IBM. *Human Resource Management,* 48(4): 641–8.

Morris, S., Snell, S., & Wright, P. (2006). A resource-based view of international human resources: toward a framework of integrative and creative capabilities. In G. K. Stahl & I. Björkman (eds.), *Handbook of Research in International Human Resource Management:* 433–48. Cheltenham: Edward Elgar Publishing.

Morris, S., Wright, P. M., Trevor, J., Stiles, P., Stahl, G. K., Snell, S. A., Paauwe, J., & Farndale, E. (2009). Global challenges to replicating HR: the role of people, processes, and systems. *Human Resource Management,* 48(6): 973–95.

Murmann, J. P. (2013). The coevolution of industries and important features of their environments. *Organization Science,* 24(1): 58–78.

Murray, K. (1991). A test of service marketing theory: consumer information acquisition activities. *Journal of Marketing,* 55: 10–25.

Murthy, N., Challagalla, G., Vincent, L., & Shervani, T. (2008). The impact of simulation training on call center agent performance: a field-based investigation. *Journal of Management Science,* 54(2): 384–99.

Nembhard, I. M., & Edmondson, A. C. (2006). Making it safe: the effects of leader inclusiveness and professional status on psychological safety and improvement efforts in health care teams. *Journal of Organizational Behavior,* 27: 941–66.

Nijs, W. F. De (1996). Arbeidsverhoudingen en personeelsmanagement. In A. G. Nagelkerke & W. F. de Nijs (eds.), *Regels rond Arbeid:* 185–205. Leiden: Stenfert Kroese.

Nijssen, M., & Paauwe, J. (2012). HRM in turbulent times: how to achieve organizational agility. *International Journal of Human Resource Management,* 23(16): 3315–35.

Nishii, L., & Wright, P. (2008). Variability within organizations: implications for strategic human resources management. In D. B. Smith (ed.), *The People Make the Place:* 225–48. Mahwah, NJ: Erlbaum.

Nishii, L. H., Lepak, D. P., & Schneider, B. (2008). Employee attributions of the 'why' of HR practices: their effects on employee attitudes and behaviors, and customer satisfaction. *Personnel Psychology*, 61(3): 503–45.

Niven, M. M. (1967). *Personnel Management 1913–63*. London: Institute of Personnel Management.

Noe, R. A., Hollenbeck, J. R., Gerhart, B., & Wright, P. M. (2000). *Human Resource Management: Gaining a Competitive Advantage*. New York: McGraw-Hill.

Ocasio, W. (1997). Toward an attention-based view of the firm. *Strategic Management Journal*, 18(S1): 187–206.

Oliver, C. (1991). Strategic responses to institutional processes. *Academy of Management Review*, 16(1): 145–79.

Oliver, C. (1992). The antecedents of deinstitutionalization. *Organization Studies*, 13(4): 563–88.

Oliver, C. (1997). Sustainable competitive advantage: combining institutional and resource-based views. *Strategic Management Journal*, 18(9): 697–713.

Osterman, P. (1994). How common is workplace transformation and who adopts it? *Industrial and Labor Relations Review*, 47: 173–88.

Paauwe, J. (1989). *Sociaal ondernemingsbeleid: tussen dwang en ambities*. Alphen aan den Rijn: Samsom Bedrijfsinformatie.

Paauwe, J. (1991). Limitations to freedom: is there a choice for human resource management? *British Journal of Management*, 2(2): 1–17.

Paauwe, J. (1994). *Organiseren: Een Grensoverschrijdende Passie*. Alphen aan den Rijn: Samson Bedrijfsinformatie.

Paauwe, J. (1998). HRM and performance: the linkage between resources and institutional context. RIBES Working Paper, Erasmus University, Rotterdam.

Paauwe, J. (2004). *HRM and Performance: Achieving Long-Term Viability*. Oxford: Oxford University Press.

Paauwe, J. (2009). HRM and performance: achievements, methodological issues and prospects. *Journal of Management Studies*, 46(1): 129–42.

Paauwe, J., & Blok, T. (2015). Unravelling the different black boxes: in search of theories that explain the black boxes between HRM and Performance. In R. Valle-Cabrera & A. López- Cabrales (eds.), *New Clues for Analysing the HRM Black Box*: 5–36. Newcastle upon Tyne: Cambridge Scholars Publishing.

Paauwe, J., & Boselie, P. (2003). Challenging 'strategic HRM' and the relevance of the institutional setting. *Human Resource Management Journal*, 13(3): 56–70.

Paauwe, J., & Boselie, P. (2005a). 'Best practices…in spite of performance': just a matter of imitation? *International Journal of Human Resource Management*, 16(6): 987–1003.

Paauwe, J., & Boselie, P. (2005b). HRM and performance: what next? *Human Resource Management Journal*, 15(4): 68–83.

Paauwe, J., & Farndale, E. (2008). De Nederlandse HR-Functie voor het voetlicht. Een vergelijking tussen Nederlandse en Amerikaanse/Britse HR-rollen. [The Dutch HR function under the spotlight. A comparison of Dutch and American/British HR roles.]. *Maandblad voor Accountancy en Bedrijfseconomie*, 82 (7–8): 345–56

Paauwe, J., & Richardson, R. (1997). Introduction to special issue on HRM and performance. *International Journal of Human Resource Management*, 8(3): 257–62.

Paauwe, J., & Richardson, R. (2001). HRM and performance: confronting theory and reality. *International Journal of Human Resource Management*, 12(7): 1085–91.

Paauwe, J., Guest, D. E., & Wright, P. M. (2013). *HRM and Performance: Achievements and Challenges*. Chichester: John Wiley & Sons Ltd.

Paauwe, J., Boon, C., Boselie, P., & Den Hartog, D. (2013). Reconceptualizing fit in strategic human resource management: 'Lost in translation?'. In J. Paauwe, D. E. Guest, & P. M. Wright (eds.), *HRM and Performance: Achievements and Challenges*: 61–79. Chichester: John Wiley & Sons Ltd.

Pache, A. C., & Santos, F. (2010). When worlds collide: the internal dynamics of organizational responses to conflicting institutional demands. *Academy of Management Review*, 35(3): 455–76.

Paine, L. S. (2003). *Value shift*. New York: McGraw Hill.

Palmisano, S., Hemp, P., & Stewart, T. A. (2004). Leading change when business is good: the HBR interview—Samuel J. Palmisano. *Harvard Business Review*, 82(12): 60–71.

Park, H. J., Gardner, T. M., & Wright, P. M. (2004). HR practices or HR capabilities: which matters? Insights from the Asia Pacific region. *Asia Pacific Journal of Human Resources*, 42(3): 260–73.

Park, H. J., Mitsuhashi, H., Fey, C. F., & Björkman, I. (2003). The effect of human resource management practices on Japanese subsidiary performance: a partial mediating model. *International Journal of Human Resource Management*, 14(8): 1391–406.

Peccei, R. (2004). Human resource management and the search for the happy workplace. Inaugural Address, Erasmus Research Institute of Management, Rotterdam, 15 January.

Peccei, R., Van De Voorde, K., & Van Veldhoven, M. (2013). HRM, well-being and performance: a theoretical and empirical review. In J. Paauwe, D. E. Guest, & P. Wright (eds.), *HRM and Performance: Achievements and Challenges*. Chichester: Wiley.

Peppard, J., & Rylander, A. (2001). Using an intellectual capital perspective to design and implement a growth strategy: the case of APiON. *European Management Journal*, 19: 510–25.

Perlmutter, H. V. (1969). The tortuous evolution of the multinational corporation. *Columbia Journal of World Business*, 4(1): 9–18.

Perlmutter, H. V., & Heenan, D. A. (1974). How multinational should your top managers be? *Harvard Business Review*, 52(6): 121–32.

Pfeffer, J. (1994). *Competitive Advantage through People*. Boston, MA: Harvard Business School Press.

Pfeffer, J. (1995). Producing sustainable competitive advantage through the effective management of people. *Academy of Management Executive*, 9(1): 55–69.

Pfeffer, J. (1997). Pitfalls on the road to measurement: the dangerous liaison of human resources with ideas of accounting and finance. *Human Resource Management*, 36: 357–65.

Pfeffer, J. (1998). *The Human Equation: Building Profits by Putting People First*. Boston, MA: Harvard Business School Press.

Pfeffer, J., & Salancik, G. (1978). *The External Control of Organizations: A Resource-Dependence Perspective*. New York: Harper & Row.

Phillips, J. J., Stone, R. D., & Phillips, P. P. (2001). *The Human Resources Scorecard: Measuring the Return on Investment*. Woburn, MA: Butterworth Heinemann.

Poole, M. J. F. (1986). *Industrial Relations: Origins and Patterns of National Diversity*. London: Routledge.

Poole, M. J. F. (1990). Human resource management in an international perspective. *International Journal of Human Resource Management*, 1(1): 1–15.

Porter, M. E. (1980). *Competitive Strategy: Techniques for Analyzing Industries and Competitors*. New York: Free Press.

Porter, M. E. (1985). *Competitive Advantage: Creating and Sustaining Superior Performance*. New York: Free Press.

Pot, F., & Paauwe, J. (2004). Continuing divergence of HRM practices: US and European-based company-level HRM practices. In J. Paauwe, *Human Resource Management and Performance: Achieving Long-term Viability*: 155–78. Oxford: Oxford University Press.

Powell, W. W. (1998). Institutional theory. In C. L. Cooper and C. Argyris (eds.), *Encyclopaedia of Management*. Oxford: Blackwell.

Powell, W. W., & DiMaggio, P. J. (eds.) (1991). *The New Institutionalism in Organizational Analysis*. Chicago: University of Chicago Press.

Prahalad, C. K., & Hamel, G. (1990). The core competence of the corporation. *Harvard Business Review*, 68(3): 79–91.

Purcell, J. (1999). Best practice and best fit: chimera or cul-de-sac? *Human Resource Management Journal*, 9(3): 26–41.

Purcell, J., & Ahlstrand, B. (1994). *Human Resource Management in the Multi-Divisional Company*. Oxford: Oxford University Press.

Purcell, J., & Hutchinson, S. (2007). Front-line managers as agents in the HRM–performance causal chain: theory, analysis and evidence. *Human Resource Management Journal*, 17(1): 3–20.

Quinn, J. B. (1980). Managing strategic change. *Sloan Management Review*, 21(4): 3–20.

Ramsay, H., Scholarios, D., & Harley, B. (2000). Employees and high-performance work systems: testing inside the black box. *British Journal of Labour Relations*, 38(4): 501–31.

Randstad. (2015). Tech and touch: annual report 2015. Available at: https://www.ir.randstad.com/~/media/Files/R/Randstad-IR/annual-reports/annual_report_randstad_2015.pdf (accessed 8 May 2017).

Rao, M. (2004). Key issues for global it sourcing: country and individual factors. *Information Systems Management*, 21(3): 16–21.

Reay, T., & Hinings, C. R. (2009). Managing the rivalry of competing institutional logics. *Organization Studies*, 30(6): 629–52.

Reilly, P., & Williams, T. (2003). *How to Get the Best Value from HR: The Shared Service Option*. Aldershot: Gower.

Renwick, D. (2003). Line manager involvement in HRM: an inside view. *Employee Relations*, 25(3): 262–80.

Roughgarden, J. (1983). Competition and theory in community ecology. *American Naturalist*, 122(5): 583–601.

Rousseau, D. M. (1989). Psychological and implied contracts in organizations. *Employee Responsibilities and Rights Journal*, 2(2): 121–39.

Rousseau, D. M. (1995). *Psychological Contracts in Organizations: Understanding Written and Unwritten Agreements*. Thousand Oaks, CA: Sage Publications.

Rousseau, D. M. (2005). *I-deals: Idiosyncratic Deals Workers Bargain for Themselves*. New York: M. E. Sharpe.

Ruef, M., & Scott, W. R. (1998). A multidimensional model of organizational legitimacy: hospital survival in changing institutional environments. *Administrative Science Quarterly*, 43(4): 877–904.

Ruël, H. J. M., Bondarouk, T., & Looise, J. C. (2004). *E-HRM: Innovation or Irritation? An Exploration of Web-Based Human Resource Management in Large Companies*. Utrecht: Lemma Publishers.

Scarpello, V., & Theeke, H. E. (1989). Human resource accounting: a measured critique. *Journal of Accounting Literature*, 8: 265–80.

Schilstra, K. (1998). Industrial relations and human resource management. Tinbergen Institute Research Series, no. 185. Amsterdam: Thela Thesis.

Schilstra, K., Dietz, G., & Paauwe, J. (2004). Contrasting metal and IT sectors: internal versus external regulation of flexibility. In J. Paauwe, *HRM and Performance: Achieving Long-Term Viability*. Oxford: Oxford University Press.

Schneider, B. (1990). The climate for service: an application of the climate construct. *Organizational Climate and Culture*, 1: 383–412.

Schneider, B., Ehrhart, M. G., & Macey, W. H. (2013). Organizational climate and culture. *Annual Review of Psychology*, 64: 361–88.

Schoemaker, P. J. (1992). How to link strategic vision to core capabilities. *Sloan Management Review*, 34(1): 67.

Scholten, G., & Van Der Grinten, T. E. D. (2002). Integrating medical specialists and hospitals: the growing relevance of collective organisation of medical specialists for Dutch hospital governance. *Health Policy*, 62: 131–9.

Schuler, R. S. (1990). Repositioning the human resource function: transformation or demise? *Academy of Management Executive*, 4(3): 49–59.

Schuler, R. S. (2013). Opportunities abound in HRM and innovation. *Journal of Chinese Human Resource Management*, 4(2): 121–7.

Schuler, R. S., & Jackson, S. E. (1987). Linking competitive strategies with human resource management practices. *Academy of Management Executive*, 1(3): 207–19.

Schuler, R. S., & Jackson, S. E. (2001). HR roles, competences, partnerships and structure. In M. Warner & M. Poole (eds.), *International Encyclopaedia of Business and Management*. London: ITP.

Schuler, R. S., & Jackson, S. E. (2014). Human resource management and organizational effectiveness: yesterday and today. *Journal of Organizational Effectiveness: People and Performance*, 1(1): 33–55.

Schuler, R. S., & Rogovsky, N. (1998). Understanding compensation practice variations across firms: the impact of national culture. *Journal of International Business Studies*, 29(1): 159–77.

Schulman, D. S., Lusk, J. S., Dunleavy, J. R., & Harmer, M. J. (1999). *Shared Services: Adding Value to the Business Units*. New York: John Wiley & Sons.

Schultz, E. B., Bennett, N., & Ketchen Jr, D. J. (2015). An examination of the relationship between strategy and human resource management practices among small businesses. *Journal of Small Business Strategy*, 8(1): 35–48.

Schumpeter, J. A. (1934). *The Theory of Economic Development: An Inquiry into Profits, Capital, Credit, Interest, and the Business Cycle*, vol. 55. Piscataway, NJ: Transaction Publishers.

Schut, F. T. (1995). Health care reform in the Netherlands: balancing corporatism, etatism, and market mechanisms. *Journal of Health Politics, Policy and Law*, 20: 615–52.

Scott, W. R. (1992). *Organisations: Rational, Natural and Open Systems*. Englewood Cliffs, NJ: Prentice Hall.

Scott, W. R. (1994). Institutions and organizations: toward a theoretical synthesis. In W. R Scott & J. W. Meyer (eds.), *Institutional Environments and Organizations: Structural Complexity and Individualism*: 55–80. Thousand Oaks, CA: Sage.

Scott, W. R. (1995). *Institutions and Organizations*. Thousand Oaks, CA: Sage.

Scott, W. R. (2008). *Institutions and Organizations*. Thousand Oaks, CA: Sage Publications.

Scott, W. R., & Meyer, J. W. (1994). *Institutional Environments and Organizations: Structural Complexity and Individualism*. Thousand Oaks, CA: Sage.

Scott, W. R., Ruef, M., Mendel, M., & Caronna, G. (2000). *Institutional Change and Healthcare Organizations: From Professional Dominance to Managed Care*. Chicago: University of Chicago Press.

Selznick, P. (1957). *Leadership in Administration: A Sociological Perspective*. New York: Harper & Row.

Senge, P. M. (1990). *The Art and Practice of the Learning Organization*. New York: Doubleday.

Shaw, J. D., Gupta, N., & Delery, J. E. (2001). Congruence between technology and compensation systems: implications for strategy implementation. *Strategic Management Journal*, 22(4): 379–86.

Shaw, J. D., Delery, J. E., Jenkins, G. D., & Gupta, N. (1998). An organization-level analysis of voluntary and involuntary turnover. *Academy of Management Journal*, 41(5): 511–25.

Sherer, P. D., & Lee, K. (2002). Institutional change in large law firms: a resource dependency and institutional perspective. *Academy of Management Journal*, 45: 102–19.

Shipton, J., & McAuley, J. (1994). Issues of power and marginality in personnel. *Human Resource Management Journal*, 4(1): 1–13.

Simon, H. A. (1947). *Administrative Behavior: A Study of Decision-Making in Administrative Organizations*. New York: Macmillan.

Simon, H. A. (1957). *Administrative Behavior: A Study of Decision-Making in Administrative Organizations*, 2nd edn. New York: Macmillan.

Snell, S. A., & Dean, J. W. (1992). Integrated manufacturing and human resource management: a human capital perspective. *Academy of Management Journal*, 35(3): 467–504.

Sparrow, P., & Braun, W. (2008). HR sourcing and shoring: strategies, drivers, success factors and implications for HR. In C. Brewster, M. Dickmann, & P. Sparrow (eds.), *International HRM: Contemporary Issues in Europe*: 39–66. London: Routledge.

Sparrow, P., & Hiltrop, J. M. (1997). Redefining the field of European human resource management: a battle between national mindsets and forces of business transition? *Human Resource Management*, 36(2): 201–19.

Sparrow, P., Schuler, R. S., & Jackson, S. E. (1994). Convergence or divergence: human resource practices and policies for competitive advantage worldwide. *International Journal of Human Resource Management*, 5(2): 267–99.

Sparrow, P., Scullion, H., & Farndale, E. (2010). Global talent management: new roles for the corporate HR function? In D. G. Collings & H. Scullion (eds.), *Global Talent Management*: 39–55. Abingdon: Routledge.

Spence, M. (1973). Job market signaling. *Quarterly Journal of Economics*, 87(3): 355–74.

Srivastava, J., & Lurie, N. (2001). A consumer perspective on price-matching refund policies: effect on price perceptions and search behavior. *Journal of Consumer Research*, 28(2): 296–307.

Stiles, P., Trevor, J., Farndale, E. Morris, S. S., Paauwe, J., Stahl, G. K., & Wright, P. M. (2015). Changing routine: reframing performance management within a multinational. *Journal of Management Studies*, 52(1): 63–88.

Stopford, J. M., & Baden-Fuller, C. W. (1994). Creating corporate entrepreneurship. *Strategic Management Journal*, 15(7): 521–36.

Storey, J. (1989). *New Perspectives on Human Resource Management*. London: Routledge.

Storey, J. (1992). *Developments in the Management of Human Resources: An Analytical Review*. Oxford: Wiley-Blackwell.

Storey, J. (1995). *Human Resource Management: A Critical Text*. London: Routledge.

Storey, J., & Sisson, K. (1993). *Managing Human Resources and Industrial Relations*. Buckingham: Open University Press.

Subramony, M. (2009). A meta-analytic investigation of the relationship between HRM bundles and firm performance. *Human Resource Management*, 48(5): 745–68.

Sveiby, K. E. (1997). *The New Organizational Wealth*. San Francisco: Berrett-Koehler.

Taylor, P., & Bain, P. (1999). An assembly line in the head: the call centre labour process. *Industrial Relations Journal*, 30(2): 101–17.

Taylor, P., & Bain, P. (2008). United by a common language? Trade union responses in the UK and India to call centre offshoring. *Antipode*, 40(1): 131–54.

Teece, D. J., Pisano, G., & Shuen, A. A. (1997). Dynamic capabilities and strategic management. *Strategic Management Journal*, 18(7): 504–34.

Thornton, P. H., & Ocasio, W. (2008). Institutional logics. In R. Greenwood, C. Oliver, K. Sahlin-Andersson and R. Suddaby (eds.), *Handbook of Organizational Institutionalism*. Thousand Oaks, CA: Sage.

Thornton, P. H., Ocasio, W., & Lounsbury, M. (2012). *The Institutional Logics Perspective: A New Approach to Culture, Structure, and Process*. Oxford: Oxford University Press.

Toh, S. M., Morgeson, F. P., & Campion, M. A. (2008). Human resource configurations: investigating fit with the organizational context. *Journal of Applied Psychology*, 93(4): 864.

Townley, B. (2002). The role of competing rationalities in institutional change. *Academy of Management Journal*, 45: 163–79.

Trampusch, C. (2006). Industrial relations and welfare states: the different dynamics of retrenchment in Germany and the Netherlands. *Journal of European Social Policy*, 16(2): 121–33.

Trist, E. (1977). A concept of organizational ecology. *Australian Journal of Management*, 2(2): 161–75.

Trompenaars, F., & Coebergh, P.-H. (2014). Model 51: the contextually-based human resource theory. In F. Trompenaars & P.-H. Coebergh, *100+ Management Models: How to Understand and Apply the World's Most Powerful Business Tools*: 311–13. Oxford: Infinite Ideas Limited.

Tsui, A. S., & Gomez-Mejia, L. R. (1988). 'human resource effectiveness. In L. Dyer and G. Holder (eds.), *Human Resource Management Evolving Roles and Responsibilities*. Washington, DC: Bureau of National Affairs.

Tsui, A. S., Pearce, J. L., Porter, L. W., & Tripoli, A. M. (1997). Alternative approaches to the employee-organization relationship: does investment in employees pay off? *Academy of Management*, 40(5): 1089–21.

Tybout, J. (2000). Manufacturing firms in developing countries: how well do they do, and why? *Journal of Economic Literature*, 38(1): 11–44.

Tyson, S., & Fell, A. (1986). *Evaluating the Personnel Function*. London: Hutchinson.

Ulrich, D. (1995). Shared services: from vogue to value. *Human Resource Planning*, 18(3): 12–33.

Ulrich, D. (1997). *Human Resource Champions: The Next Agenda for Adding Value and Delivering Results*. Boston, MA: Harvard Business School Press.

Ulrich, D. (1998). A new mandate for human resources. *Harvard Business Review*, 76(1): 124–34.

Ulrich, D., & Brockbank, W. (2005). *The HR Value Proposition*. Boston, MA: Harvard Business School Press.

Ulrich, D., Younger, J., Brockbank, W., & Ulrich, M. (2012). *HR from the Outside In: Six Competencies for the Future of Human Resources*. New York: McGraw Hill.

Ulrich, D., Brockbank, W., Johnson, D., Sandholtz, K., & Younger, J. (2008). *HR Competencies: Mastery at the Intersection of People and Business*. Alexandria, VA: SHRM.

Vachon, S. (2007). Green supply chain practices and the selection of environmental technologies. *International Journal of Production Research*, 45(18–19): 4357–79.

Van de Voorde, K., Paauwe, J., & Van Veldhoven, M. (2010). Predicting business unit performance using employee surveys: monitoring HRM-related changes. *Human Resource Management Journal*, 20(1): 44–63.

Van de Voorde, K., Paauwe, J., & Van Veldhoven, M. (2012). Employee well-being and the HRM-organizational performance relationship: a review of quantitative studies. *International Journal of Management Reviews*, 14(4): 391–407.

Van den Broek, J., Boselie, P., & Paauwe, J. (2013). Multiple institutional logics in health care: productive ward: 'releasing time to care', *Public Management Review*, 16(1): 1–20.

Van Gestel, N., & Nyberg, D. (2009). Translating national policy changes into local HRM practices. *Personnel Review*, 38(5): 544–59.

Van Veldhoven, M. J. P. M. (2005). Financial performance and the long-term link with HR practices, work climate and job stress. *Human Resource Management Journal*, 15: 30–53.

Van Veldhoven, M. J. P. M. (2012). *About Tubs and Tents: Work Behavior as the Foundation of Strategic Human Resource Management.* Tilburg: Prismaprint.

Van Vianen, A. E. M. (2000). Person-organization fit: the match between newcomers' and recruiters' preferences for organizational culture. *Personnel Psychology,* 53(1): 113–49.

Veld, M. (2012). *HRM, Strategic Climate and Employee Outcomes in Hospitals.* Enschede: Ipskamp Drukkers.

Veld, M., Paauwe, J., & Boselie, P. (2010). HRM and strategic climates in hospitals: does the message come across at the ward level? *Human Resource Management Journal,* 20(4): 339–56.

Venkatesan, R. (1992). Strategic sourcing: to make or not to make. *Harvard Business Review,* 70(6): 98–107.

Verburg, R. M., Den Hartog, D. N., & Koopman, P. L. (2007). Configurations of human resource management practices: a theoretical model and empirical test of internal fit. *International Journal of Human Resource Management,* 18(2): 184–208.

Verdú, A., Maestre, A., Lopez, P., Gil, V., Martin-Hidalgo, A., & Castano, J. A. (2009). Clinical pathways as a healthcare tool: design, implementation and assessment of a clinical pathway for lower-extremity deep venous thrombosis. *Quality and Safety in Health Care,* 18(4): 314–20.

Vloeberghs, D. (1997). *Handboek human resource management: Managementcompetencies voor de 21ste eeuw.* Leuven: Uitgeverij Acco.

Volberda, H. W. (1998). Building the flexible firm: how to remain competitive. *Corporate Reputation Review,* 2(1): 94–6.

Volberda, H. W. (2004). Crisis in strategy: fragmentation, integration or synthesis. *European Management Review,* 1(1): 35–42.

Volberda, H. W., & Elfring, T. (2001). *Rethinking Strategy.* London: Sage.

Wah, L. S., Ismail, M. N., & Ibrahim, A. R. (2004). Strategic balance and performance: a study of Malaysian Banks. *Asia Pacific Management Review,* 9(3): 557–83.

Walker, K. F. (1969). Strategic factors in industrial relations systems: a programme of international comparative industry studies. *International Institute for Labour Studies Bulletin,* 6 (June): 187–209.

Wall, T. D., & Wood, S. J. (2005). The romance of human resource management and business performance, and the case for big science. *Human Relations,* 58(4): 429–62.

Walton, R. A. (1985). From control to commitment in the workplace. *Harvard Business Review,* 63(2): 77–84.

Ward Lilley, B. (1991). Be ready to be unpopular. *Personnel Management Plus,* April: 2.

Watson, T. J. (1977). *The Personnel Managers: A Study in the Sociology of Work and Employment.* London: Routledge & Kegan Paul.

Watson, T. J. (2004). HRM and critical social science analysis. *Journal of Management Studies,* 41(3): 447–67.

Weber, M. (1946). *From Max Weber: Essays in Sociology.* Oxford: Oxford University Press.

Weick, K. (2009). Organization: Environment. In R. Westwood & S. Clegg (eds.), *Debating Organization: Point-Counterpoint in Organization Studies*: 184–94. Oxford: Wiley-Blackwell.

Whitehead, J. (2005). Insourcing, outsourcing? How about self-sourcing? *HRO Today,* December. Available at: http://www.hrotoday.com/contributors/insourcing-outsourcing-how-about-self-sourcing/ (accessed 7 May 2017).

Whitener, E. M. (2001). Do 'high commitment' human resource practices affect employee commitment? *Journal of Management,* 27: 515–35.

Whitley, R. (1992). *European Business Systems: Firms and Markets in their National Contexts.* London: Sage Publications.

Whittington, R. (2001). *What is Strategy: And Does It Matter?* London: Cengage Learning EMEA.

Wood, S. (1999). Human resource management and performance. *International Journal of Management Reviews*, 1(4): 367–413.

Wright, P. M., & Boswell, W. R. (2002). Desegregating HRM: a review and synthesis of micro and macro human resource management research. *Journal of Management*, 28(3): 247–76.

Wright, P. M., & Gardner, T. M. (2001). Theoretical and empirical challenges in studying the HR practices: firm performance relationship. Working paper 00-04, Center for Advanced Human Resource Studies, Cornell University, USA.

Wright, P. M., & Gardner, T. M. (2003). The human resource–firm performance relationship: methodological and theoretical challenges. In D. Holman, T. D. Wall, P. Clegg, P. Sparrow, & A. Howard (eds.), *The New Workplace: A Guide to the Human Impact of Modern Working Practices*: 311–30. London: John Wiley & Sons.

Wright, P. M., & Haggerty, J. J. (2005). Missing variables in theories of strategic human resource management: time, cause and individuals. *Management Review*, 16: 164–73.

Wright, P. M., & McMahan, G. C. (1992). Theoretical perspectives for strategic human resource management. *Journal of Management*, 18(2): 295–320.

Wright, P. M., & Nishii, L. H. (2007). *Strategic HRM and Organizational Behavior: Integrating Multiple Levels of Analysis*. CAHRS Working Paper #07-03. Ithaca, NY: Cornell University, School of Industrial and Labor Relations, Center for Advanced Human Resource Studies. Available at: http://digitalcommons.ilr.cornell.edu/cahrswp/468 (accessed 9 May 2017).

Wright, P. M., & Nishii, L. H. (2013). Strategic HRM and organizational behavior: integrating multiple levels of analysis. In J. Paauwe, D. Guest, & P. M. Wright (eds.), *HRM and Performance: Achievements and Challenges*: 97–110. New York: Wiley.

Wright, P. M., & Snell, S. A. (1998). Toward a unifying framework for exploring fit and flexibility in strategic human resource management. *Academy of Management Review*, 23(4): 756–72.

Wright, P. M., Dunford, B. B., & Snell, S. A. (2001). Human resources and the resource based view of the firm. *Journal of Management*, 27(6): 701–21.

Wright, P. M., Gardner, T. M., & Moynihan, L. M. (2003). The impact of HR practices on the performance of business units. *Human Resource Management Journal*, 13(3): 21–36.

Wright, P. M., McMahan, G. C., & McWilliams, A. (1994). Human resources and sustained competitive advantage: a resource-based perspective. *International Journal of Human Resource Management*, 5(2): 301–26.

Wright, P. M., Gardner, T., Moynihan, L., & Allen, M. (2005). The HR–performance relationship: examining causal direction. *Personnel Psychology*, 58: 409–46.

Wright, P. M., Boudreau, J. W., Pace D. A., Sartain, E. L., McKinnon, P., & Antoine, R. L. (2011). *The Chief HR Officer: Defining the New Role of Human Resource Leaders*. New York: John Wiley & Sons, Inc.

Wrzesniewski, A., & Dutton, J. E. (2001). Crafting a job: revisioning employees as active crafters of their work. *Academy of Management Review*, 26(2): 179–201.

Yeung, A. K., & Berman, B. (1997). Adding value through human resources: reorienting human resource measurement to drive business performance. *Human Resource Management*, 36: 321–35.

Youndt, M. A., Snell, S. A., Dean Jr, J. W., & Lepak, D. P. (1996). Human resource management, manufacturing strategy, and firm performance. *Academy of Management Journal*, 39: 836–65.

Zedeck, S., & Cascio, W. F. (1984). Psychological issues in personnel decisions. *Annual Review of Psychology*, 35: 461–518.

Zilber, T. (2002). Institutionalization as an interplay between actions, meanings, and actors: the case of a rape crisis center in Israel. *Academy of Management Journal*, 45: 234–54.

Zucker, L. (1977). The role of institutionalization in cultural persistence. *American Sociological Review*, 42: 726–43.

■ INDEX